"Starting with her own daughter, Jodi lends her powerful voice to those whose own voices are marginalized in society. This book shouts empowerment to people who have real challenges and differing abilities. Jodi's book, *Chutzpah, Wisdom and Wine*, is filled with poignant, touching and unpleasant examples from her own life dealing with the challenges of disabilities. Jodi's shows us what being an activist really means with her dedication to change the world for her daughter."

Isaac Zabloki, Director of The Israel Film Center and ReelAbilities Film Festival: New York.

"Jodi Samuels is a great student of business and social entrepreneurship showing tremendous flexibility and adaptability in challenging situations and in many countries. *Chutzpah, Wisdom and Wine* is a testament to her successes — and failures. Jodi brings her powerful personality to these pages showing us how to work hard and play hard."

Dan Schawbel, *New York Times* bestselling author of *Back to Human*.

"I laughed, I cried, I cheered, and couldn't put it down until the very last word. Reading Jodi Samuels, book both validated my own personal journey, and inspired me to reach even higher. A must for every woman seeking clarity and courage."

Lori Palatnik, Author, international speaker, and founding director of Momentum.

"Jodi Samuels' book is the powerful story of a mother who decided to turn the 'destiny' forced upon her into the 'destiny' of her choice. Jodi shows us by her example that one can change the narrative when it comes to special needs and that love and acceptance are decisions that take hard work but are worth the effort. *Chutzpah, Wisdom and Wine* is a blueprint for a parent of a child with special needs seeking the best path for they child. The Feuerstein Method's approach to inclu-sion is given a personal and moving overview in these pages."

Rabbi Rafael Feuerstein, Chairman of the Feuerstein Institute, author of *Beyond Smarter* and *A Think-Aloud Talk-Aloud Approach to Building Language*.

"This remarkable autobiography reflects the classic definition of 'chutzpah' through the audacity, courage and ardor of Jodi Samuels. From her childhood in apartheid South Africa, to her journeys and experiences with people and places around the globe, this engaging story is both inspiring and humbling. *Chutzpah, Wisdom and Wine* reveals the transformational principle that giving back is the best expression of gratitude. I highly recommend this book to anyone willing to reexamine their priorities and to anyone who wants to learn how 'chutzpah' can help you make the hard choices to live a life of generosity."

Bishop Robert Stearns, Executive Director, Eagles' Wings NY, author of *Keepers of the Flame*, international speaker.

"Jodi Samuels shows us how it is possible to weave Jewish values and Torah wisdom into everyday situations in our businesses, organizations and relationships. In this powerful and humorous book, Jodi is refreshingly honest about her own struggles and challenges and inspires us by example to look to heaven for solutions."

Rabbi David Aaron, Author of *Endless Light* and *The G-d Powered Life*.

"*Chutzpah, Wisdom, and Wine* is a thought-provoking memoir written by an author who lives Judaism in the most active and positive way possible. This book shares with the reader profound insights about her experiences of the world in a fun, relatable way."

Michael Bassin, Author of *I am not a Spy*.

"Having worked closely with Jodi for over a decade as chairman of JICNY, I'm so excited for *you* to read her story. I've already had the privilege to observe, and sometimes ride, in real time, much of this rollercoaster of a book. That's why I recommend that you read it the way I tried to experience it in real time; twice. Once for the stories that will tug at your heartstrings and inspire your spirit. And once for the invaluable personal lessons you can glean from these true tales if you work to apply them to your own difficult struggles and joyous opportunities."

Jeff Stier, Former Chairman at JICNY, senior fellow at Taxpayers Protection Alliance.

"If anyone understands the challenges of busy mom-entrepreneurs it is Jodi Samuels. *Chutzpah, Wisdom and Wine* is a recipe for women who are balancing family and career while also not giving up on our passions. We can glean much from Jodi's example of Jewish outreach as a super hostess of hundreds of events and Shabbat dinners a year. Jodi's experiences are both inspiring and hilarious as she carved her own path and niche in the world on her long route to Israel."

Jamie Geller, Israeli-American food writer, celebrity chef, television producer and businesswoman.

"Jodi Samuels has written a book that is highly inspirational and engaging—a true-life account that weaves bold honesty with unrelenting courage."

David J. Lieberman, Ph.D., Noted Psychotherapist, internationally acclaimed speaker and *New York Times* bestselling author.

"Holding no punches, *Chutzpah, Wisdom and Wine* is a fresh reminder of the relevance of one's heritage in today's demanding world. Jodi takes us on her journey from downtown New York to Jerusalem, with a behind-the-curtain look as to how Jewish values shape her everyday life as mother, wife, community leader and immigrant. Expect to laugh a lot along the way."

David Kramer, Author of *State of The Heart* and social entrepreneur.

"Jodi invites you on her personal, introspective journey which is inspiring, uplifting, often humorous and touches the heart deeply. The constant message of her unwavering faith is prevalent on every page, a type of faith we all could use.

Jodi challenges social stigmas enabling the reader to truly see the unique soul of a child with special needs. They themselves are raising their daughter to defy all odds, surpass boundaries, truly enhancing their growing community and family at large.

Jodi and her family remind us that superheroes do, in fact, live among us."

Brig. Gen. Bentzi Gruber, Board member of Special in Uniform and founder of Ethics in the Field, bringing together people with special needs and Israeli soldiers.

"Jodi's writing is fast paced and full of energy. Her fascinating journey from her childhood in South Africa, across the globe and finally to Israel is a page turner. Her positivity and determination is infectious and the love of a mother through adversity heartwarming."

Fleur Hassan-Nahoum, Deputy Mayor of Jerusalem.

"An absolutely wonderful read that everyone and anyone can relate to filled with passion and compassion. Jodi Samuels so beautifully and courageously shares her journey providing nuggets of deep and meaningful insights while taking you through the ups, downs and in betweens that life throws her way. You're bound to feel inspired, empowered, validated and hopeful."

Orly Wahba, Author of *Kindness Boomerang* and founder of Life Vest Inside.

"In real life, when Jodi speaks, people listen. And in her book, she shares the same passion, compassion, humility, and credibility about her journey and story. Reading *Chutzpah, Wisdom and Wine: The Journey of an Unstoppable Woman* feels like you're learning from an expert in life who can just as easily be your best friend."

Deborah Grayson Riegel, Keynote speaker, author and leadership consultant.

CHUTZPAH, WISDOM AND WINE

The Journey of an Unstoppable Woman

Jodi Samuels

EMEK VALLEY PRESS

The events in this book have been set down to the best of the author's memory. Some names and determining characteristics of people and institutions have been omitted, de-identified or modified to protect privacy and anonymity. The conversations in the book come from the author's recollections. They are not written to represent word-for-word transcripts but rather retold in a way that evokes the same emotions and meaning as what was said. The essence of the dialogue is in all cases accurate. The intent of the author is to raise issues for contemplation and debate and not to hurt or offend anyone.

Cover design: Shanie Cooper

ISBN paperback: 978-965-599-264-9

American Edition

Published by Emek Valley Press
www.jodisvoice.com
info@jodisvoice.com

Dedicated to Chava Fachler, of blessed memory, the
"Mother of all Mothers"

PREFACE

Grieving and emotionally fragile, I boarded a plane from Israel to meet up with the Jewish Heritage tour to Morocco that I was leading in the winter of 2019. My spiritual mother, Chava Fachler, had just passed away, leaving a hole in my soul and tears in my eyes. I was devastated that I couldn't stay for the shivah.

Right after Chava's funeral in Jerusalem, I headed to Casablanca, wiped my tears and put on my leadership face.

I met my group, a mixed bunch of twenty-four secular and religious Jews from several countries on a trip organized by Jewish International Connection New York (JICNY), the not-for-profit organization I had founded some twenty years earlier. A few days later we arrived in Marrakesh to have a Shabbat dinner with a local Jewish family that regularly hosted groups such as ours. The guests included my group, thirty Hasidic men on their own tour and a smattering of other tourists.

At meals such as this, we like to share words of inspiration and say a few toasts, or *lechayims*. I used the opportunity to honor Chava's life. She and her husband, Eli, had taken me in when I was a wayward teenager traipsing around the world. I merely needed a place to stay in London, but what I got was so much more. I knew very little about Judaism as a young girl, but after I met Chava and saw her living example of Jewish values, I wanted nothing more than to be like her. Thanks to the Fachlers, I began to carve out my own bumpy path toward a serious commitment to Orthodox Judaism. This eventually culminated in my organization, JICNY. My time with the Fachlers was a turning point in my life, and we maintained a deep connection for the rest of their lives.

As I offered this *lechayim*, many of the Hasidic men were staring at me, their mouths agape, and I assumed that they were taken aback that a woman was speaking in a mixed setting. Or perhaps, I thought, they had trouble reconciling my spiritual message with my uncovered hair and less-than-strict attire.

Yet, afterwards, many of them told me that it was one of the most inspirational talks they had ever heard. They saw past my outward appearance and heard my passion for Jewish outreach and how that inspired my journey. I was floored and humbled. We all departed that night with full hearts.

As we continued our tour that week, my JICNY participants pressed me about my motivation to work so tirelessly for Jewish outreach. Many people have asked me over the years why I pour myself into hosting events, tours, Shabbat dinners, Torah classes and more, adding up to about three hundred events a year, without taking any salary or remuneration. I joke that if I weren't doing this, I would be out saving dolphins or advocating for another cause. It's just my nature. I cannot bear to live without purpose.

A good friend of mine actually confronted me once: "I know why you do all this: You just love when people say *lechayims* to you. You love being the hero," he said.

I've often questioned my own motives. Am I working for glory and recognition? The truth is, if that is what I wanted, I could just make a donation in exchange for a plaque on a wall – without having had to do any of the work. The way it stands now, I'm usually the one setting up and cleaning up after my own events, taking registrations and responding to every email.

I thought for a moment and responded honestly.

"I do this because, in my own way, I want to change the world."

I know I cannot change the whole world, but I will not rest if I have not made a difference somehow. If I can move the needle just a little bit, in my own way, in my own world, then I have contributed. I need to feel that I'm contributing.

As I spoke of my spiritual journey on that bus in Morocco, I could not help but sprinkle in the everyday realities that make me uniquely Jodi – my egregious blunders, princess foibles (I have never changed a diaper) and overwhelming public embarrassments as well. Yes, I build companies, travel the world and staunchly advocate for my daughter with Down syndrome, but the truth is I manage all that with an ongoing, abject fear of audiences, and I am a candidate for world's most scatterbrained person.

We spent hours on that bus in Morocco keeled over with laughter as I recounted my "tales." One participant suggested I pull all these vignettes into a book, and the whole bus unanimously agreed.

I did not think so at the time, but it did get me reflecting on my life. A few months later, I started to write my story, the real story of my journey, with the good and the bad all mixed together. Just like that diverse Shabbat table, my personal encounters, challenges and relationships have transcended religion and ethnicity. I wanted to tell those stories.

I also realized that this book is about more than just me. We as Jews are connected to five thousand years of history, an unbroken heritage. This explains why I continue to work as I do, why we still keep centuries-old traditions and wisdom today and apply these in our modern world. And why we must never stop.

CHAPTER 1

Gam zu letovah – **This too is for the good.**

Nachum Ish Gamzu
Babylonian Talmud, Taanit 21a

I was recovering in my hospital room in Manhattan a few days after giving birth to our third child, and my biggest concern was how to keep our newborn warm in the taxi on the way home during that typically gray and bitter New York winter. Gavin and I had already sent photos of our new baby girl to friends and family informing them that mother and baby were doing well. Congratulatory flowers and balloons provided a colorful contrast to the gray skies beyond our window. We were generally feeling on top of the world as couples normally do after having a new baby.

Until the pediatrician walked in on the third day.

"Mrs. Samuels, did you do genetic testing?" he asked as he strode into the room.

Despite having just had my third C-section, I sat bolt upright. Every nerve in my body was on edge. It was the question that would change my life.

Several months prior, I had experienced a definitive moment during my pregnancy when I felt something was wrong. The feeling defied logic. The results of all my prenatal tests were fine. The baby was healthy. And yet, I cried during one of my checkups as a feeling of dread overcame me. The doctor, shocked because I was normally so stoic, asked why I was crying. I had no answer.

All through the pregnancy I would pray for the baby, but oddly, even my prayers took a new direction than they had for my prior two children, Meron and Temira. Instead of praying for the baby's health, my petitions turned to myself instead. "Please, God, give me the strength to deal with what comes my way," I would implore. Jewish sages say that an extra measure of intuition, *binah*, was given to women, but I kept these odd feelings to myself as I went along the pregnancy.

From the outside, it may have looked like we had the "perfect" life. After we were married, Gavin and I lived and worked in exotic (and sometimes outback) places thanks to his job as a doctor. And despite being South Africans, we found ourselves as American citizens, having won coveted green cards. We started our latest adventure on the Upper West Side, and we were enjoying New York City life to the fullest. We had good jobs, lived in Manhattan and traveled extensively. After our first two children came along, I could see why the singles we counseled would say, "When I get married, I want a life just like the Samuels."

By this point, Gavin and I had become well known in our Modern Orthodox community in New York City. We also had an open-door policy at home. The door to our apartment was always unlocked and was literally open most of the time. Our guests ranged from wealthy and connected Wall Street businesspeople to recovering drug addicts and homeless people. Before we were married, Gavin and I discovered we shared two passions: having a home full of guests and an obsession with adventurous travel. Our love of hosting was part of an ongoing passion to galvanize and connect Jewish people to their local community, wherever that may be. In New York, I started an organization – Jewish International Connection New York (JICNY) – that puts these beliefs into action. But even in our personal lives, wherever we lived, we had an open house and a revolving door of guests, invited or not, but always welcome in our home.

Living in Manhattan was the pinnacle of the dream. I had always been obsessed with success, and now I had come to the place where achievement was sought after and rewarded. My dream was to make it to the cover of *Fortune* magazine as a successful businessperson. If I could make it in New York…well, you know the song.

After we moved to New York in 2000, we settled quite nicely into Manhattan life. Gavin had a fantastic job, and I was now a mom, businesswoman, entrepreneur and full-time volunteer at JICNY. Our two children were attending a great Jewish day school in the city. As a family, we hosted Shabbat dinners and mentored young professionals, while through JICNY, we sponsored Torah classes, networking sessions and seminars for singles and couples. We were pillars in our community as we built our New York lives over those eight years. We were busy – and that's how I wanted it.

I had suffered two miscarriages after Temira's birth, so when I was finally pregnant with our third child, I knew I should be grateful – and I was. But I also could not shake this sense of foreboding that followed me into appointments with the obstetrician and during ultrasounds. I recall how this apprehension crept to the forefront when my father, who lived in South Africa, called and asked, "How's the baby?"

I hesitated. A bit too long.

"Is something wrong?" he asked.

"No, not technically," I responded. And then I reassured him all the checkups were fine as I tried to explain away my pointless hesitation.

Then the doctor walked in on that third day and asked the dreaded question that changed my life.

Had we done genetic testing? Gavin and I were very aware of the various dangers lurking in the genes of Ashkenazi Jews. Gaucher disease, cystic fibrosis and Tay-Sachs are some of the most common diseases passed on among our people. Before we got engaged, Gavin told me he was a carrier of the Tay-Sachs gene, and so was my father, meaning there was a 50 percent chance I was a carrier as well. Tay-Sachs is a mutation on the fifteenth chromosome that manifests with degeneration of the neurons in the brain and spinal cord resulting in death before age five. If I were a carrier of this disease too, our children would each have a 25 percent risk of being born with a sealed and terrible fate.

I got tested for Tay-Sachs and ran the gamut of Ashkenazi genetic screening as well. Then Gavin and I spent the next two weeks wondering whether we would get married. Thankfully, the results came back negative, and we did get married, unafraid of replicating any of these diseases in our future children.

During my pregnancies Gavin and I opted to forgo amniocentesis. We would not terminate the pregnancy anyway. But with this third baby, my doctor pressured me to do the amnio because, at thirty-four, I was almost a "mature age mom." In any case, we had done both the non-invasive triple screen test and the nuchal fold ultrasound. I had "passed" with flying colors. In fact, my risk score based on these tests was the same low odds as that of a twenty-one-year-old mother to be – a one in five thousand chance of a significant abnormality.

"With a score like this, I'm okay if you don't proceed with the amnio," my gynecologist conceded.

Then Caila was born, and when we held her, all my fears were laid to rest. She was healthy, and she looked like any other baby. She even had the distinctive slightly curved pinky finger common in Gavin's family: "the Grasko finger" they called it, after his mother's family name. Both Gavin's mother and grandfather have this trait, and already at birth Caila proved herself part of the family with a matching pinky to her grandmother and great-grandfather.

But while the curved finger was a family trait, it was also a sign of something else: Down syndrome.

The pediatrician had our attention with his question.

"Of course we did genetic testing," I answered. "Well…some genetic testing."

The doctor had noticed Caila's low muscle tone and the curved finger – clinodactyly – both signs of trisomy 21, or Down syndrome.

My gynecologist, who was with us in the hospital room, wondered aloud: "What are the chances that she is the one in five thousand with a chromosomal abnormality?"

"Exactly one in five thousand," Gavin responded dryly.

And it was true. Our princess was born with an extra copy of chromosome 21 and had Down syndrome.

After about thirty minutes with the doctors, I excused myself and made my way to the bathroom, the only place in the hospital I could be alone with my thoughts.

I had been broadsided by this news.

Why us? Why me?

I was not expecting news like this and I was quite angry at first that God would choose *us* to raise a child with intellectual disabilities. I never questioned whether he made a mistake, but I wanted to know why he would send us this precious soul while we were busy carrying out *His* work. My mind was racing with all of the uncertainty that comes with this diagnosis and how we were going to handle it.

I had always been an overachiever, but the stereotype in my mind of Down syndrome was of slower, if any, achievement. I knew there would be time-consuming therapies. I wrestled with how this would affect our lifestyle. Would we have to slow down or stop altogether? I also worried how my other children would be affected by this diagnosis. Would this ruin their chances of getting married due to prejudice, or because they would they be burdened to look after their sister in the future?

Looking in the mirror, I confronted myself. My mind, as it normally does in times of stress, sought to rationalize the shocking revelation. I chased the questions racing through my soul and answered them with intellectual honesty.

Why us? God chose us.

Why did He choose us? We have an open-door policy. If we accept everyone, we also have to accept our own daughter.

But I wanted to change the world and now I won't have time! I will change the world, just another aspect I never thought of before.

If I could not accept my own child, then my whole life was a lie. I resolved, then and there, this would be my approach. I walked out and informed Gavin. He was already on the same page.

Gavin always had a habit of saying: "We don't ask *why*, we ask *how*."

How were we going to deal with this shock and this news? First of all, we decided that from that very moment we would control the message: *Don't feel sorry for us. Don't label our daughter. Don't Google "Down syndrome" because what you might read on the internet can be scary! We do not know her potential yet, and we will love her no matter what. Caila is our princess.* That was the message.

As we checked out of the hospital and the security guard snipped the identification bracelets from our wrists, Gavin looked at me and said, "They may as well have branded the word 'Activist' on our foreheads because that is what we have just become."

We knew, as we headed into the world, that our future would be one of tireless advocacy, struggles for acceptance and crusading for our child's rights on a daily basis, whether in schools, government or social settings.

CHAPTER 2

One who does *teshuvah* (returns to an observant Jewish life) is considered as if he went to Jerusalem, rebuilt the Temple, erected the altar, and offered all the sacrifices ordained by the Torah....

Leviticus Rabbah 7:2

Though I had reconciled with the question, *"Why us?"* and though I accepted this change of life plans of having a child with disabilities, a heaviness still loomed in the back of my soul that I could not quite define or resolve. I was terrified of the unknown.

Six weeks after Caila was born, we were on a trip during Passover, hiking the hills of West Virginia. As we hiked, Caila strapped to me, I was deep in thought, fretting about everything. It was times like this when I found the space to be alone with my concerns, and they were rolling through my mind. Would we be able to both work full time? Would Caila develop thyroid issues? Would she ever speak? I knew and already worried that we would give her more attention than our other children, and I wondered whether our extended families would ever come to terms with her diagnosis and accept her. This was constantly going on in the back of my mind.

Out of the blue, Gavin joked about something and we both burst out laughing. This moment jerked me from my morass of worry. It was then I realized, I was going to release this heaviness, eventually, and I was going to sort out all these issues.

I'm grateful that I was unaware of Caila's diagnosis during the pregnancy (even though my intuition was screaming at me that something wasn't right!) and for a few days after her birth. I had normal mother-baby bonding time without the label of Down syndrome attached to her. Caila was just my baby. I think that was what helped me move on so fast. I know it can take new parents weeks to months to adjust to their new reality of having a child with Down syndrome. I believe that I had the advantage of "ignorance is bliss" in those first few days.

And while anxiety threatened to cloud my soul, I have my own (perhaps warped) way of dealing with stress. I retreat from my feelings, take cover in my mind and start making to-do lists. A list gives me tasks, and if I am doing something to try to solve the problem, I feel better.

That's what I did after Caila was born. I made lists. I had to figure out her rights, her needs, early intervention, find a mentor for me and, of course, learn how to be an effective activist.

Becoming an activist was going to be interesting. I was a walking paradox. From earliest memory, I was painfully shy in public settings. But at home, and outside of the public eye, I was highly motivated, opinionated and often quite rebellious. Growing up in Johannesburg, I decided I was going to change the world somehow. I made no small plans. I thought big, I planned big and I took "no" as a challenge to make things happen – bigger, better and more successful. For fun I read *Fortune* magazine as a teenager. Many of the adjectives that describe me today – Type-A personality, entrepreneur, workaholic, activist – were traits that were already apparent in my early years, but through the filter of a rash teenager or a defiant and adventurous young adult.

You would not have to look far to understand where I got my ambition. My parents were extremely hard working and always on the go. My father worked late into the night for his business while my mother worked full time and attended graduate school. My childhood memory of our home is of my parents sitting at the dining room table every evening working on their own assignments late into the night.

I drew from their example. Our home had a charged and productive environment. But once I stepped outside, I morphed into a church mouse. At school I hated being called on. This shyness plagues me to this day – even in my own board meetings and Hebrew classes, I am anxious to utter a word and pick at the skin around my nails. People who only know me from a speech I've given at one of my events assume I am bold and confident, but what they do not know is that I had to down a few glasses of wine to even be able to get up on stage.

Nevertheless, I had a strong, get-it-done personality. I determined that I would control my own fate. I pursued my plans with drive and ambition. That's why it was shocking that a simple question – "Did you do genetic testing?" – could rattle me and then change my life to the extent that it did…. Down syndrome – this randomly occurring translocation of genetic material which thumbs its nose at genetic screening – was hard to swallow from that perspective. Some people are at a higher risk, but no one has zero risk of having a child with Down syndrome. At conception, an extra copy of the twenty-first chromosome is found in the cells, and that extra chromosome expresses itself in the various signs and symptoms associated with Down syndrome.

Though we quickly came to terms with our own daughter's diagnosis, the specter of Down syndrome conjured up scary images and bad memories in my family, some based on experience, but more so on ignorance. When the doctor told us about Caila's diagnosis, every image that flashed through my mind was negative. My own cousin, who is around my age and also has Down syndrome, lived in an institution from early on in her life. My cousins brought her home once a month and I only saw her a few times a year. With no means to communicate with her and little contact throughout the years, I was unsure how to relate to her. That was my first connection with Down syndrome.

The very news of my cousin's diagnosis when she was born wreaked havoc on extended family members who were reeling from the news. Later another cousin was diagnosed with a genetic disease – achondroplasia, a genetic disorder that results in dwarfism. At that point my grandparents decided there was no God and from that moment, they ceased to observe the few nominal Jewish customs they had kept.

I had another less-than-positive memory associated with the diagnosis. During the High Holidays our Johannesburg synagogue would welcome the Jewish residents of the nearby home for people with disabilities who were brought in to attend services on special occasions. I always shied away from that crowd, not knowing how to interact or respond to their eccentricities. So, my experience with special needs and disabilities was still fairly undeveloped at the time of Caila's birth.

A unique and homogeneous community of about seventy thousand, the South African Jews were a tight-knit community with a well-established Jewish infrastructure. We had *shuls*, schools, summer camps and yeshivas. Even if you were not "religious" you went to an Orthodox synagogue on holidays and identified as Jewish in a cultural sense. The Jo'burg Jews were also about as uniform in lifestyle and outlook as well as our predominantly Lithuanian origin: They all wanted to live in the same sought-after neighborhood, drive the same specific car, wear specific brands and take the same enviable vacations at the same destinations. Most Jewish South Africans aspired to become the stereotypical doctors, lawyers or accountants. You knew you made it when you looked, acted and had a job exactly like the Joneses or perhaps, in this case, the Goldbergs.

I was never the typical Jewish Jo'burg girl. My parents didn't have the means to attain the outward trappings of the proverbial Goldbergs so when I wanted to take a trip to Israel with my youth group, I was on my own. I had to get a job to pay for it myself. I worked at a supermarket for two years from five to seven in the evening from the time I was thirteen and financed the trip myself apart from about a hundred dollars which my grandparents gave me toward it. Working at the age of thirteen was unheard of (and illegal!). Most children in our community, especially girls, lived off their parents' income. I actually discovered I liked working, however, and I was especially drawn to starting my own business.

Religiously, I grew up on the secular side of the tracks. Our family did the perfunctory requirements such as going to synagogue on the High Holidays and making *kiddush* on Friday nights – before eating a seafood dinner in front of the TV or rushing through an abridged Passover Seder. On Jewish holidays, we were not allowed to go to school, but my parents let us go to the movies.

Despite this tepid religious observance, I had a strong Jewish identity. My mother was a teacher at the local Jewish day school. She was a secular studies teacher, and we lived in the heart of the Jewish "ghetto" in a suburb of Johannesburg called Glenhazel. On Saturday mornings it was not uncommon for my family to go out to our car just as all the religious kids were walking to synagogue. "Good Shabbos, Mrs. Newman," they would say to my mother as they passed our house. I called them "the Yarmy Army," "the God Squad" and "the Nerds." I would never be part of their crowd. The community stuck together as Jews, but within that bubble we parted along religious lines.

Toward the end of high school, I moved to a private school that attracted many students from the Orthodox Jewish day schools, and we all rode the bus together. This was my first "integration," if you will, with the religious crowd I was trying to avoid. We all became friendly and chatted on the way to school. On the bus one Friday, one of the "cute guys" who also happened to be religious asked me if he would see me at synagogue that night. Um, of course! That question was the teenage equivalent of being asked on a date! I went to synagogue that night because I was also secretly hoping for a *Good Shabbos* kiss goodbye – a dream come true for a sixteen-year-old girl. But this was inadvertently the beginning of my religious journey. It's amazing the ploys that God will use to lure someone back into the fold.

There was no kiss that night, but I did make many new friends. I was amazed by the sense of community they shared and how they embraced their religious rituals. These "religious" kids began inviting me for Shabbat meals at their homes. I remember being intrigued watching families sit together around the table talking about matters of Torah. Even younger siblings got involved sharing what they learned in school about the week's Torah portion. Being from a family that barely did weekday dinners together let alone Shabbat, I enjoyed the warmth, the singing, the sharing.

The whole experience awoke within me a thirst to be more serious about my religion. I even began volunteering for a program that sought to prevent assimilation and apathy toward Judaism. I would take school children with limited Jewish backgrounds on *Shabbatons* where we visited a "museum of the future" that portrayed Judaism as an ancient and extinct religion. The message was that if we fail to guard our heritage as Jews then, one day, our grandchildren would only see our religion in museums. Jewish life would cease to exist.

While this was a meaningful activity, it seemed a bit far-fetched in South Africa where we stuck together. Intermarriage was not an issue. This experience did, however, plant the seeds in my heart that would eventually become a life's mission to protect 5,000 years of unbroken Jewish history. The Greeks, the Romans and even Adolf Hitler could not kill Judaism. But in modern times ignorance and assimilation have been more effective.

As my involvement with Judaism grew, so did my interest in Israel. For my gap year, after high school, I wanted to study in Israel as is common for students in Jewish day schools. My parents were aghast at delaying university to live abroad for a year. Most students who went to Israel were religious Jews attending yeshivas in Jerusalem to study Torah. I reached a compromise with my parents to attend a pre-university program at Bar-Ilan University in Tel Aviv rather than a seminary. At least it would be educational and on track with university when I returned.

And that was the first of my big adventures abroad. I headed to Israel looking for adventure and answers. But it didn't take long until that became an adventure of epic proportions and war-time challenges. It was 1991, and just after I arrived in Israel, the First Gulf War broke out.

Within days everyone on the Bar-Ilan campus scattered, and anyone who hadn't fled walked around with a gas mask. Saddam Hussein was threatening to rain down Scud missiles on all of Israel. Most of my friends had gone to stay with family and friends around the country. A friend and I were left in the now deserted university. We were sure the campus rabbi would help two stranded overseas students who did not speak the language. We looked for him, but he too was gone!

We were alone and terrified. In hindsight, it is hard to believe that an organized program for overseas students had no idea that two of their enrollees were stranded on campus. Israel's Homefront Command issued gas masks, designated safe rooms and ordered everyone to hunker down. With every siren we assumed it was our last minute on earth. Since we had no discernible means of getting help in Israel, my friend appealed to her uncle in the UK who bought us plane tickets to London. We caught the last flight out, and as we landed in England Scud missiles began pummeling Israel.

My overseas adventure continued, but with a new address. My friend and I had fun for a couple of weeks in London, but soon I needed to move on and find my own accommodations. My parents wanted me to return home, but I was determined to enjoy my entire year away – despite having no money, nowhere to stay and not being in Israel. War be damned, this wasn't going to put a damper on my year out of South Africa. I would find a solution.

When my mother – never underestimate a mother's intervention even from afar – mentioned my predicament to the other teachers at her school, a colleague suggested that her in-laws, who split their time living between Israel and London, would be happy to host me. The next day I knocked on the door of people I had never met. With big smiles and open arms, a genteel couple appeared in the doorway and invited me in. I didn't realize at that time how much influence this couple was going have on my life.

From the second I stepped through their door, the Fachlers took me in and I found a home away from home. Right away, Chava Fachler asked if I was hungry. I politely declined – even though I was starving – and she insisted I eat anyway. That was the first of many meals we shared.

The Fachler household absolutely fascinated me. It was a revolving door of guests, both at their London and Jerusalem homes. In Israel, Chava would call local yeshivas and the neighborhood absorption center looking for anyone who might be lonely or hungry. The

Fachlers were blind to religious level, financial status or background. They loved every Jew and wanted to host any who needed a meal or a place to stay.

On a practical level, they helped me find a job as an *au pair* and they agreed to help me return to Israel after the war ended. On a spiritual level, the Fachlers' very way of life lit within me a flame for Jewish outreach. And at this point I started adopting a more Orthodox lifestyle just like them.

Chava Fachler, lovingly described as the "Mother of all Mothers," became my mentor. In addition to seven children of their own, she and her husband claimed countless "adopted children" – myself included – that they had influenced over the years. Chava would have such a profound impact on my Jewish journey and the life I live now. This gentle and welcoming soul survived the horrors of Nazi Germany by escaping to England. She was sent via the *Kindertransport*, the mobilization to rescue Jewish children from the Nazis in war-torn Europe during World War II. Yet, despite her traumatic experience – or perhaps because of it – she forged a life of service and giving.

Totally dependent on their kindness during my time in England, I would tell my hosts how embarrassed I was to be unable to reciprocate their help. The Fachlers always responded that the best way to say thank you is to pay it forward. Their example of hospitality was stamped on my heart. I was so deeply touched by their willingness to help me that I wanted to emulate their kindness for others as soon as I had the means to do so.

What I learned from Chava is that one person's impact on someone else's life can be the ripple that changes the world. I would take this lesson with me as I made my way back to Israel.

Tales of a Modern Jewish Woman

Jodi – gullible? Nah.

As Gavin got to know me, he soon figured out that one of my incurable qualities is my extreme gullibility.

He saw it play out when we were helping to lead a Shabbat weekend for children from non-observant Jewish families in South Africa. We were several leaders and about a hundred children staying in rustic bungalows in the countryside. (As it happens, decades later the rabbi who ran that organization became the leader of my JICNY trips to Poland.)

As we were convening for Friday prayers, somebody made an announcement that a gorilla escaped while being transported to a zoo and that it was loose nearby on the banks of the Vaal river. This sent up a nervous yelp from among the children – and me too. When the curtain rustled, I joined in with the terrified shrieks of the ten-year-old girls. It was just the wind though.

The leaders made a big deal about traveling in groups and staying with a leader at all times for safety. Some of the young girls asked me to accompany them to the bathroom, and others to sleep in their bedroom with them. I thought to myself, "No way! I'm more terrified than you!"

By the end of the evening, all of the leaders somehow knew this was a prank – except for me. And when it became apparent that I had no idea this was a joke, the leaders played on me more than the children.

After dinner, the children were all seated and ready for the next activity when suddenly a man dressed in a gorilla outfit burst into the room beating his chest and roaring. All of the children ran screaming from the room. But who was leading the pack of screaming, terrified kids? Me, their fearless leader.

I've never lived it down to this day.

Gavin played on my gullibility many times. Once he visited where I was working at my father's office. I had been opening the mail and saw that a pharmaceutical company had sent promotional samples of their product with candy instead of actual medication. They were M&Ms in a blister pack; without even a thought, I popped them into my mouth just as Gavin walked in.

"How many of these did you eat?" Gavin looked at the label and asked me with a serious face.

Panic started rising in my gut. Gavin "called" the poison information hotline before ushering me to the car to go to the ER. My thoughts were racing: Was I poisoned? Would I need a stomach pump? Would I die? My lips started going numb and tingling.

After about five minutes of driving – me in abject panic and my lips entirely numb at this point – Gavin burst out laughing.

I don't know how I fell for his sham, but it is a testament to true love that we are still together.

CHAPTER 3

**The best preacher is the heart; the best
teacher is time; the best book is
the world; the best friend is God.**

Anonymous

When Coalition air forces, led by the United States, attacked Iraq in January 1991, Iraq responded by attacking Israel. For about a month, thirty-eight Iraqi Scud missiles hit Israel, causing two deaths and damaging hundreds of homes. Right before any of that happened, I had fled. But not before seeing the Israel Defense Forces mobilize under the serious threat, distribute gas masks and prepare the bomb shelters. Israel was ready to defend its citizens. The nation remained under a state of emergency.

After five weeks, Coalition forces liberated Kuwait from Iraqi forces, and for the most part, the situation in Israel stabilized and normal life resumed. It was safe for me to return.

At that point, influenced by my time with the Fachlers, I decided I wanted something more serious from my year abroad when I returned to Israel. I ditched the party-all-night, sleep-all-day program at Bar-Ilan and transferred to Neve Yerushalayim, a place for beginners like me to learn about Judaism and study Torah. It was located in Har Nof, one of Jerusalem's Haredi (Ultra-Orthodox) neighborhoods. By then the Fachlers were also living in Israel. I would go to their home every week for Shabbat.

My parents, on the other hand, were appalled. Not only was I back in Israel, to which they were opposed in the first place, but now I was also on a religious track. Even though it was quite foreign to me, I found myself in the world of black hats, long skirts, "bullet-proof stockings" and all sorts of hair coverings.

However, a few months into my stay at the seminary, I committed the cardinal sin of having a male visitor to my room. My best friend's boyfriend was delivering some coveted and desperately needed South African chocolates to me, a care package from home. Until now, I cannot go a day without chocolate. And at the time my supply there in the seminary had reached critically low levels. Unfortunately, this mission of mercy was deemed "unacceptable." *No men in the women's dorms!* My explanation that he was only there to deliver chocolate was disregarded by the yeshiva management. The administrators politely suggested that I "find a more suitable seminary" and with that, again, I defiantly went packing. Despite my short time and abrupt ending with this seminary, somehow I kept in contact with friends I made there. One amazing and somewhat uncanny bond is that, of the twenty-four girls in our dorm from that time, four of us now have children with Down syndrome.

After I left, I was homeless and yeshiva-less, so I did what any scorned teenager would do – I let that rebellious streak that had marked my youth rear its head again. This time, instead of finding a more "suitable" seminary, I left Israel again. And I did so with flare. I took scissors to my long religious skirts and cut them super short, abandoning religion yet again. Then, off I went with my friend Susan for a month of partying and backpacking across Europe. I was just eighteen at the time.

Susan and I joined a group that was backpacking through Europe. The trip was kosher, Shabbat observant and budget-style. After a few days of travel, Susan and I agreed that the tour wasn't right for us and we wanted to venture out on our own. Our tour leader was appalled – we were traveling in rough areas including countries that had just emerged from behind the Iron Curtain. These places were neither tourist nor female friendly. Our leader knew this and was concerned about two young women wandering around with wads of cash and no clue where we were. This was pre-cell phones, pre-Internet, pre-GPS days. We barely had a clue how to get around. The tour guide had promised our parents that we would be on a protected tour with an experienced guide, but we made this man's life so miserable that he finally gave us a refund and sent us on our way.

Fifteen years later, I found myself sitting in a class in New York City. The man next to me looked familiar so we started playing "Jewish Geography." Suddenly it dawned on him, "You are Susan's friend!" He was that very same tour guide! With a sense of inescapable embarrassment, I pleaded an apology.

"My only defense is that I was young," I told him. Did I mention I was eighteen?

Our behavior had only deteriorated along the way during this adventure. Susan and I made our way south, eventually ending in Greece where we managed to spend three nights – unpaid – at Club Med in Corfu before getting caught. The day we were caught, security guards came to find us at the breakfast room. They removed all of our possessions down to and including our junk jewelry, hair clips and sunglasses in front of a packed dining room. We understood our free ride was over. But knowing she was going to have to pay in the end, Susan refused to leave until she had eaten seconds at the buffet. Yes, we made another scene.

Disclaimer: I was eighteen, in every sense of the number. Oh, the folly of youth.

Having reached so far south, it was time to jump across the Mediterranean and head back to Israel. When I got back, it was Friday afternoon. I had no money, no idea where to stay and, since it was almost Shabbat, I had few options left before sunset. I headed to a free youth hostel in Jerusalem's Old City. Lugging my heavy backpack and sporting a short skirt, I was flattered when a tall, dark and handsome soldier offered to help me with my bag. When you are a teenager from abroad and a mysterious man in uniform offers to carry your bags you think you have died and gone to heaven. I happily accepted his offer to help.

Coming from Jewish Johannesburg where all the Jews look and act the same, this Sabra soldier was intriguing. From his Sephardic looks to his Zionistic ideals, Moshe was the antithesis of everything I knew as normal for a Jew. After our chance encounter, we decided to meet again the next day. We ended up spending thirteen hours together talking about every possible topic. He was passionate about Judaism, about Israel and about changing the world. He was a Zionist of the radical variety – he wanted to live in a settlement after he finished the army to further put stakes in the ground of the Jewish state. He would be living out his beliefs quite literally, planting himself in a potential danger zone. I was mesmerized by his zeal.

Moshe convinced me to go back to seminary and resume my religious journey, which I did. As my pendulum again swung dramatically in the other direction, I abandoned my secular spree and grabbed on to the ideological and religious leanings held by Moshe.

Our relationship blossomed and within a few months we got engaged.

At this point my parents were convinced that I had lost my mind. Who was this foreigner, speaking another language, who was taking their daughter away and dragging her into religion? They were completely opposed to our union. I, on the other hand, was happier than ever as innocent idealism washed over me. Moshe and I intended to live in a caravan – a portable home – in a settlement near Hebron, one of the nation's most volatile flashpoints for violence between Jews and Arabs. I signed up for National Service, an alternative to serving in the Israel Defense Forces that some religious girls choose. Moshe's rabbi, Moshe Levinger from Hebron, blessed our union. Levinger was a polarizing figure who helped build settlements in the West Bank and Gaza after Israel gained territory in the Six-Day War and was involved in violent confrontations with Palestinians. He and his followers believed that the biblical heartland was promised to the Jewish people and it was their duty to keep it. I was along for the ride and did not really sit and reflect on any of this.

This all happened so fast and, as plans raced ahead, I began to doubt this frantic journey. It was all so new and foreign from my previous life that I wavered between thrill and panic. When I would share my fears and concerns with the eloquent and passionate soldier, he would assure me I was just scared, but that I was doing the right thing.

One evening a friend and I headed to Ben Yehuda Street for falafel and to hash out life's turn of events. Halfway through my pita as we sat on the busy pedestrian walkway, a young man approached me and asked if I spoke English. "*Ja*," I answered in perfect South African English. He spotted the accent right away. Turns out Gavin Samuels was also South African and was in Israel completing his medical elective for university. But never mind Gavin. I recalled meeting in Johannesburg another medical student also with the last name Samuels who happened to be tall, dark and handsome. Maybe Gavin knew him? It turned out, in this small world, that Owen Samuels was Gavin's brother. Well, that got my attention, and so I carried on chatting with this guy. Initially, I gave him a wrong phone number, but then, thinking of Owen, I corrected it. I figured if things didn't work out with Moshe, maybe Gavin could introduce me to his brother.

But being engaged and trying to keep it a secret while holding out the possibility of meeting Doctor-to-Be Owen Samuels through his brother proved to be complicated. For example, I would tell Gavin, I could only meet for a drink in the early evening because I had a Torah class at ten o'clock. He somehow believed this, when in actuality I was rushing back to meet Moshe after he finished his yeshiva class.

Charming and clearly tenacious, Gavin called every day. This became the routine for the next two weeks: I would meet Gavin early and scurry back by ten to meet Moshe.

This was Gavin's first time in Israel and, like all good Jews, observant or not, he had tucked a written petition into the cracks of the Western Wall when he arrived asking for God's help to find his wife (even though he was just twenty-two years old). He met me the next day. From the first time we met for coffee, Gavin knew I was the answer to his prayer. He likes to say, if you want good service you have to go to the head office. "The Boss" came through rather quickly this time.

Gavin, who had also not grown up in a religious environment, was moderately observant at the time. He started wearing a *kippah* while in high school mainly because he wanted to identify as a Jew, but that same year the principal forbade wearing religious head coverings. Gavin campaigned against this policy – and has worn a *kippah* ever since. His religious transformation was sealed while in medical school. As he studied the workings of the human body, Gavin began thinking there must be a God. He was heavily influenced by Akiva Tatz, a rabbi and physician who is world-renowned for his expertise in medical ethics and Jewish philosophy.

So here I was, eighteen years old and extremely confused. In one year I had experienced war, partied through Europe and the Iron Curtain, gone from a black-hat religious environment to short-skirt secular, then adopted a zealous Zionistic approach. I knew that I wanted my life to be guided by the Torah, yet I was still experimenting with which form of religious expression I preferred. I was also confused in my relationships. I was engaged to Moshe, a foreigner who was the most idealistic and passionate person I had ever met. Yet, I was seeing Gavin every day as well while hoping this would open the door to meet his brother.

My identity crisis further deepened as I prepared to return to South Africa. I was going to sort through my belongings then head back to Israel for National Service and marriage. Moshe took me to the airport. There, he romantically gave me a stack of love letters that I was to read every day. This was back in the days of expensive long-distance phone calls and before there was email. Then off I was on a nine-hour flight to a different continent, and a different world.

Several hours later I found myself sitting in my parents' living room, the maid serving us tea, such a sedate moment after a whirlwind year of adventure. Far from the dusty alleys of the Old City, my year of escape felt like a distant dream. Hilltop caravans, army service and a zealous soldier who was going to defend Israel's settlements to the death were so out of place in my "real life." I had been swept away by Moshe's idealism, particularly his passion for Israel, and of course his fondness for me. But I started to doubt whether I really wanted to marry him and live his life. I was not the kind of woman who would be happy as a mother of ten children living on a settlement with a rifle slung over my shoulder.

In the next couple of days, I decided to end the engagement. I felt guilty for the long-distance break up, but at the same time I was awash with relief. My year abroad had been a frenzied experiment in trying to find myself. I had dipped my toes into every extreme from the secular to the Haredi. It was only when I returned home did I realize that Moshe's passions were foreign to mine. I wanted to practice my religion in way I could be comfortable with and feel "at home."

Many years later I saw a documentary about the disengagement of Jewish residents living in Gaza in 2005. In it, a familiar man tore his army uniform in the tradition of Jewish mourning, buried it and said *kaddish*. That man could have been Moshe and beside him could have been me had I married him.

As fate would have it, Gavin returned to South Africa shortly afterward. Gavin did not fit my three requirements for a potential husband – he was shorter than me, he wore glasses and he was religious. But I found myself very comfortable with Gavin. We had similar backgrounds and upbringings as Johannesburg Jews. We had common goals and dreams. The day he got back to South Africa, he asked me out. Our first date was a romantic dinner that he cooked, followed by a chocolate fondue…and more chocolate. Clearly, he knew the way to my heart!

Five months later Gavin and I were engaged. His persistence and his character won over Moshe's idealism and the specter of Owen. Gavin was also a person who would be a tad more palatable for my parents, more so than the Middle Eastern Moshe. First of all, Gavin was South African, and he spoke English. Secondly, he was going to be a doctor, which was a large bonus in the eyes of any South African Jewish family.

I did not tell Gavin about my previous engagement, however, until later that year before Yom Kippur, when I decided it wise to confess the secrets of my "complicated" year before Judgment Day.

Tales of a Modern Jewish Woman

Meeting the in-laws

*Who isn't nervous to meet their potential in-laws for their first time? I
stood skittishly beside Gavin as he knocked on the door of his parents'
home. His mother answered the door with a flourish. Mascara streaked
down her face, Myrna was sobbing.*

"We're getting divorced," she threw herself into Gavin's arms.

*Gavin spent the next few hours listening to his mother pour out her
heart…while I sat on the side twiddling my thumbs. This was before the
days of smart phones, so I literally had nothing to do. I did not really
get to meet my future mother-in-law that day, but I sure did learn a lot
about her life. I left that day not having met Myrna.*

*The second attempt was not much better. We went to Gavin's family
for Passover. With our newfound religious observance far outpacing that of
any of our parents, Gavin wrapped the entire kitchen in aluminum foil so
as to make sure everything cooked would be kosher for Passover.*

His mother swept into her kitchen and gasped in horror.

*"I will not live in a spaceship," Myrna declared — and proceeded to
rip off all of the foil!*

*We delayed our "getting to know each other" session yet again. But I
was staying the weekend so we would have time, I hoped!*

*My father-in-law made a different impression. When I stayed there
one Shabbat he made breakfast and brought me a delicious meal before
I woke up. What a stunning gesture. I thanked him profusely. But when
I shut the door, I panicked. What on earth was I supposed to do? When
a Jew breaks Shabbat to make breakfast, the food is no longer kosher. I*

pretended to eat it, but really I flushed some of it down the toilet! Decades later I confessed to him what I had done and we had a good laugh.

The takeaway for me, non-kosher food aside, was that Gavin had a good role model if breakfast in bed was in the cards!

Both sets of parents were opposed to our union. I was only nineteen when we got engaged and neither of us had finished studying. On top of that, everyone close to us thought we had been kidnapped by a cult since we both returned from Israel as practicing Orthodox Jews.

So the first meeting of all the in-laws was brewing like a gathering storm…or a funeral. And to make that encounter even more somber, Gavin's parents – who were in the midst of their own divorce – agreed to come to this meeting together, and brought his eighty-year-old grandmother to this afternoon tea at my parents' home.

Now my father was a jokester who constantly tossed out one-liners, some more appropriate than others. He had never met nor seen Gavin's parents in his entire life, yet he chose a less appropriate one that day as he flung open the door and made a valiant effort to break the ice.

"Wow, Myrna, I almost didn't recognize you – you look so different with your clothes on!"

Dead silence followed. And then everyone tittered with nervous laughter.

Yes, my father, who had never seen Myrna (with or without clothes) just blundered into perhaps his worst all-time joke.

Welcome to my family!

Somehow we got married – and stayed married – despite our rocky start with the in-laws. And this is now a big joke among the families: "What not *to say when you meet the in-laws for the first time!"*

Our parents were united on one thing, however – that Gavin and I would abandon our newfound religious lifestyle, which was obviously just a phase, they thought. When my parents came to visit us in Australia after we were married, I asked them to pick up some alcohol from duty free at the airport since it was significantly cheaper than in the Australian stores. My father took this as a sign that he was right! We were having marital problems and that we had turned to alcohol to solve our woes, he assumed. He was even considering getting us an intervention! For years, our parents continued to wait for us to wake up one day and renounce our Orthodox lifestyle.

Chapter 4

Love your fellow man as you love yourself.

Leviticus 19:18

Break-ins. Gun shots. Home invasions. Being held up at gunpoint on a deserted street.

In certain situations, I am a very nervous person and I don't need a psychologist to figure out why.

When I said that Gavin and I had much in common, one shared goal was to leave South Africa. Though I have a deep connection to my beautiful homeland, I was scarred and traumatized by a litany of incidents that affected me personally.

The last incident that drove me out occurred when I was nineteen years old, driving through Johannesburg to pick up my dress for a family bar mitzvah. As I was driving, I had experienced a premonition of sorts, a voice in my head warning me that I was going to be held up at gunpoint. But louder than that came my mother's voice, also lurking in the back of my head. *"You're just being neurotic."*

Yes, probably.

I was on my way to a dress fitting. I had no reason to be nervous, so I shook off the feeling.

Then I noticed a bunch of men in a pickup truck that appeared to be following me. I continued to the seamstress's house when I noticed this same vehicle turn into the street behind me. I kept the car in drive.

Suddenly, as if choreographed, the men all sprang out of the pickup and surrounded my car. A gun was pressed to my head. The sage advice in crime-ridden South Africa is: *Remain quiet and calm and give them what they want.* That all went out the window in a split second. I screamed at the top of my lungs and gunned the gas pedal as hard as I could, not even noticing if I hit any of my assailants. I sped away and it wasn't long before I noticed they were following me! I wove in and out of streets heading for a busy commercial center. It was five minutes which felt like a lifetime. Eventually I lost them and I drove to the closest familiar place to where I found myself, my doctor's office. The staff at least knew me and I was in a public area. I screeched the car to a halt and ran up to the receptionist. Before she could finish asking, "How can I help you?" I passed out on the floor.

I suppose the doctor's office was as good a choice as could be made in such a situation. Since they had no idea what had happened to me, it was only after I came to that the bewildered staff understood that I had fainted. They gave me tranquilizers to calm me down and I called a friend to bring me home. When my parents, who had been away, got home and learned what happened, their first reaction was to ask, "Has anyone gone to get the car?"

This was South Africa. Crime was so "normal" that their main concern was the car, rather than their daughter's well-being.

We all normalized these outrageous acts. Once my brother was picking up pizza when two criminals burst into the restaurant and held up the workers and customers – and killed the owner in cold blood. After it was over, my brother did admit he was upset – because he had to go elsewhere to buy pizza after he had paid. Of course, this bravado didn't mean that he was heartless. He was just implementing the typical coping mechanism of most South Africans – distancing oneself mentally and emotionally from death and danger. Rather than face the reality that you too could have been killed, you convinced yourself that you were upset over something more trivial, such as pizza.

Homes in South Africa were secured with gates, alarms and electrified fences and many of the white people were armed. That did not stop thieves from breaking in on a regular basis. One Friday night, we had some friends over at our house. After everyone left I heard voices in the garden, and I went to tell my father.

"No, it's just your friends, go back to sleep," he said.

I did but was convinced I was either hearing voices or was paranoid. I slept fitfully. The next day we awoke to discover our house was ransacked and many items stolen. Another time my parents weren't home and I was getting back late to an empty house. When I arrived I noticed the gate was open and our dog was in the street. I immediately knew something was wrong. Yet again, our home had been cleaned out.

If I thought my trauma was bad, my cousin's family was once held up at gunpoint and all the members of the family – the children included – were tied up. My uncle had to make a heart-breaking choice. My cousin had been accosted outside the house by some men who asked him, with a gun in their hands, to open up the house. He pretended that he did not have a key and knocked on the window to get his father's attention to let him know that some "gentlemen" wanted to have a word with him. My uncle's dilemma was whether to keep them out in order to protect his wife and daughter from possibly being raped, or sacrifice his son by keeping the doors shut. He reluctantly let them in. They roughed up the family, tied them up and robbed the house. When they were wrapping up they debated whether they should kill the family. My uncle understood their language and he heard one of the men convince the other they should spare their lives.

"He's a *sangoma* (witch doctor) so if we kill them we will have bad luck," he said of my cousin, who is an achondroplastic dwarf. Some tribes are superstitious that dwarves have supernatural powers.

There were so many incidents. At age three, after the kindergarten carpool dropped me off, the nanny whisked me quietly from the vehicle and hid me in a closet warning me to be quiet. I could see through the keyhole the gardener chasing some burglars that were running through the house. I worried about my four-month-old brother asleep in his crib. Another time, on Christmas day, we returned to a group of about ten youth in our house who overpowered my parents. In those days everyone kept a can of Mace handy. My father grabbed his and chased the youths outside. Another time, I awoke to gunshots. My father was scaring off some home invaders that broke in while we slept.

Once my uncle left my cousin and I unattended in the car – in our driveway – for two minutes when a man snuck up to the car and *stole the shoes off our feet* in those few seconds. All of these stories and many more occurred before I was even five years old. These are some of my earliest memories.

Crime was so rampant that you would hear or experience stories like this all the time. I could not handle it, and from an early age I was biding my time till I could leave the country. Was I "just neurotic"? I wasn't prepared to find out.

I have an amazing ability to cope with stress. I can manage a huge work load, a child with special needs and anxiety without missing a beat. I cannot deal, however, with the stress and trauma I endured in South Africa stemming from crime. I wouldn't walk to my car alone, I refused to enter an empty house. A rabbi once told me that my response was normal and helped me cope by accepting reality. And I feel like my fear is justified: The number of murders in South Africa in 2018 – 21,000 – was comparable to the number of people killed in the Syrian Civil War that same year!

I am so affected by it, that to this day – more than twenty-five years removed from South Africa – I cannot be alone at night and I am very nervous as soon as I enter a shady neighborhood. Just a discussion on crime can make me have a nightmare. If Gavin is away on a business trip, I ask the children to sleep in my bed.

Despite my ongoing trauma from those days, I still have strong emotional connections to the country of my birth. I was saddened upon hearing of Nelson Mandela's death. He was a true statesman and leader, a complex person who was more than a terrorist, freedom fighter and president. If you did not live in South Africa, it's hard to appreciate just how on edge the country was at the time. It was his leadership as a peacemaker that allowed South Africa to make a nonviolent transition from apartheid to democracy.

Mandela's death evoked many emotions and lots of memories. I was reminded of Gavin's time working as a doctor at the Chris Hani Baragwanath Hospital in Soweto, the largest hospital in the Southern

Hemisphere. During his thirty-six hour shifts in the emergency room, he sometimes had to wear rubber boots because there was so much blood. The victims of the tribal in-fighting gathered in triage with stab and gunshot wounds or draped in sheets waiting to go to the mortuary. Gavin also worked in a clinic in Alexander Township, on the outskirts of Johannesburg. "Alex," as it was called, according to the apartheid government, was an illegal squatter settlement. Although more than a million people lived there, there was no local public hospital, so Gavin's medical school staffed a basic clinic with final-year medical students. The township was a war zone.

One night when Gavin was on duty, he delivered a baby that was born prematurely and weighed nine hundred grams. Clinics such as these had no pediatric ICU facilities and no ventilators, so Gavin had to try and find a ventilator at one of the hospitals in the greater Johannesburg area. A baby had to weigh one kilogram or more in order to be a candidate for a scarce ventilator in the public health system (this "policy" was interpreted much more liberally if the baby had white skin). At nine hundred grams, this baby – who was black – was just shy of the minimum, but he had a fighting chance if only he could get a ventilator. Gavin called all the surrounding hospitals and was refused access to a ventilator. Thinking that no one could refuse a baby if he came in person, Gavin got in an ambulance and had the driver drive to all the nearby hospitals and clinics, all the while hand ventilating the baby. Not one clinic or hospital allowed him to use the available ventilators – even though they had empty ones! One hospital superintendent even called the police and had Gavin and the baby escorted off the premises. The baby eventually died in Gavin's arms that night.

This was only one of three times I saw Gavin lose his temper. He swore he would never again work in a medical system that discriminated against babies based on their skin color. This occurred shortly before apartheid was dismantled.

This township, characterized by extreme poverty and hardship, was just a few kilometers away from where I grew up in a fancy, well-to-do Jewish neighborhood. Unless you were a doctor like Gavin, most white people never stepped foot into a place like Soweto. The only images we ever saw were from CNN, just like anyone else around the world.

When I was growing up, the government banned the media from publishing photos of Mandela. We were taught in school that African National Congress (ANC) members were terrorists. Black history was not taught and we were indoctrinated to fear black people. At school we frequently had drills on what to do if the ANC attacked. Images of Nelson Mandela flitted through my mind as a pirate with scars on his face and evil eyes. I had no idea what he actually looked like. The first photos of Mandela were only published the week of his release from prison. I was in my final year of high school. I was so shocked to see a gentle looking grandfather full of poise and dignity. The apartheid regime had manipulated all our minds.

The indoctrination of prejudice was ingrained in us from a very young age. It wasn't defined as prejudice, it was merely reality. One incident I still remember like it was yesterday was when I was five years old. At our kindergarten, every child contributed supplies, including soap. After washing my hands one day I noticed that the soap had the distinct smell that I associated with a brand of soap commonly used by black people. It reminded me of our gardener. Suddenly I started crying and refused to come out of the bathroom because I smelled like a black person. I had zero understanding of the intricacies of apartheid and no ability to process what I was feeling at five years old. I only knew this: In my world it was not good to smell like a black person. In apartheid South Africa, there was a hierarchy. And even as a young girl, without the vocabulary for this, I just knew it.

Another irony was the situation with domestic help. Through we lived under apartheid, we all had nannies who were black and they lived on our properties. Apartheid laws demanded though that the quarters for the domestic help be a set distance from the house with small, high windows. So the nannies lived on their white bosses' properties bringing up the white children while their own children were living in government designated homelands being looked after by their grandmothers. The nannies who were raising us barely saw their own children. My parents had the same lady working for them more than thirty years, and I still call her "Mama" to this day.

A few brave families defied the laws and allowed their nannies' children to live on the property with their mothers. Gavin's family did that and he shares many terrifying stories of midnight raids by police and living with the fear that the children would be caught. These little ones that lived with Gavin's family were so close to us that we had them in our bridal party. Since we were married before apartheid had officially ended, we definitely raised eyebrows at our wedding.

There were many incongruities concerning having a nanny. I laugh now at how our parents entrusted their children with the nanny for safekeeping, yet they locked up their jewels, the meat and even the cocoa pops so she wouldn't steal them.

While I've never overcome the traumas of break-ins, being held up at gunpoint and living in terror that I'd be the next victim, I have spent decades extricating the tentacles of the racism with which I was raised. I've always had a conscience and I always felt uncomfortable with having a nanny and treating her "well," but not equally. It would only make sense to me later as to why our lives were just plain hypocritical.

One of my earlier awakenings, when I was about fourteen, happened when a black woman approached my grandfather right outside their house. "Master, can I please have some water?" My grandfather brought her some and she complained her stomach was hurting bad. Suddenly she was having a baby – right there on the street. My grandmother immediately called for an ambulance and this is when I learned that even ambulances were segregated, and that it took a "black" ambulance longer to come than a "white" one. This one took so long, in fact, that my grandparents ended up delivering the baby! My grandmother even cut the umbilical cord. This woman was so grateful she named her baby after my grandfather.

That story impacted me deeply. It was then I realized that the blacks had limited access to health care and education. Before this, I never thought of the plight of the black person in South Africa. We weren't taught of their struggles.

In many ways, South Africa was an extremely authoritarian nation. From police to school principals, we cringed in fear of authority. The country only started allowing televisions in the mid-1970s and even then, programming was censored: two hours a day of propaganda. We lived completely sheltered lives.

An awakening I had was in Israel during my gap year. I was sitting at a Shabbat table with other expats and we spoke about our school uniforms. We were required to wear the school blazer no matter what the weather was. Imagine standing outside for a school assembly under the hot African sun with a blazer. Someone at the table – not South African – asked why we didn't just protest. I had just finished twelve years of schooling and it didn't even cross my mind to protest! There was no space for even disagreement with authority. Not in any area. Our parents didn't even complain. Students would get caned for disciplinary purposes, yet no parent protested this.

My apartheid awakening only began after I left the country and started being exposed to the world. I started reading books to understand apartheid. What an oppressive system. I remember that around this time I was traveling abroad and I saw a black man pushing his child in a stroller. I was in shock. We had always been fed the thinking that black men couldn't be good fathers. And then in London, I saw another black man in an expensive suit striding among the crowds to his high-powered job. Again, our narrative had taught us that surely blacks couldn't hold good jobs. These feelings now seem so naive and disgusting, but this was what we learned. No one ever explained to me they were victims of a system. Our history books never told their story.

It took years for me to truly eradicate the inbred racism and to become truly color blind. Intellectually and emotionally I knew it was wrong, but my reactions would continually show me the depths of my entrenched beliefs.

My generation was just at the cusp of this challenge to apartheid. It had always been challenged to some extent, but during my teen years there was a new freedom of expression that was rising up. The music of Johnny Clegg and his band Juluka was revolutionary. He and Sipho Mchunu formed the first black-and-white musical duo during South Africa's apartheid era. Concerts were raided by the police because blacks and whites were together in the same concert hall. With concerts such as these and university protests, it began to feel safer to think differently. In addition, anti-apartheid songs like Eddy Grant's "Gimme Hope Joanna" and Sixto Rodriguez's "Sugar Man" were banned from the radio, so everyone scurried to get copies of them. Those were the days of exploration. It was still illegal to oppose apartheid, but it was becoming okay to ask questions.

Gavin was once detained for participating in an anti-apartheid demonstration and another relative just fled because, as an activist, he knew he was about to be arrested.

When I started traveling and seeing the equality of races in other parts of the world, my mind started opening up to the truth. My Jewish education also helped. There is nothing remotely biblical about a system as evil as apartheid. What's more, Gavin's stories and his understanding of the bias through the eyes of a doctor helped me see the injustices even more deeply.

My children are being raised in societies that value equality. They don't see color. And with Caila already being "other" as well, her siblings – Meron, our oldest, and Temira, our middle child – are extremely sensitive to any hint of discrimination. Thankfully, we stamped out the appalling strains of apartheid and racism from our family in a just one generation.

Tales of a Modern Jewish Woman

It's a small world (of South African Jews)

When I studied at the Haredi yeshiva, Neve Yerushalayim, Johnny Clegg's sister was actually one of the counselors for my group. We happened to find out because all South Africans play our own version of "six degrees of separation." Anyway, clearly the counselor, now known as Chaya, had chosen a different path than her brother, the famed rocker.

She happily told me she was soon getting married. But in true Orthodox tradition, she would have separate dancing for the genders. Meanwhile, Johnny had Zulu dancing at his wedding. Either way, she told me, her father had truly thrown up his hands in surrender – the weddings ranged from one extreme to the polar opposite.

At my own wedding a few years later we also had separate dancing. My father was adamant he would not attend a wedding with separate dancing, even if it was his own daughter's.

Since I was only twenty, my parents had to sign consent papers for me to get married. You had to be twenty-one to officially get married in South Africa. My parents were convinced I was too young and that I had made rash decisions that year abroad. They said Gavin and I hadn't thought this through.

"I'm not signing this and I'm not coming to a wedding with separate dancing!" My father was obdurate and serious.

In the end, he did come to the wedding, albeit kicking and screaming. He signed the papers and even walked me down the aisle.

It took my parents nine years to accept that this new religious lifestyle of mine was here to stay. And the fact that Gavin and I still looked happy and somewhat normal helped. And of course their first grandchild helped push them over the edge in accepting our union.

As a white South African, I grew up in a land of milk and honey, but our world was precarious and, sometimes, dangerous. Now, many people live in gated communities with private security guards and police forces assigned to each neighborhood.

This is common to South Africans, but foreign to most other people – and now, even to my own children. During one of our trips to Johannesburg after we had been living in New York City, we were walking with my eight-year-old nephew on Shabbat when a private security vehicle sped past us. Meron asked what was going on. Matter-of-factly, my nephew responded, "Oh that's GAP (Glenhazel Area Police). There must have been a break-in."

He then asked Meron, "What's your private police force in New York called?"

"Private? We don't have that in New York," Meron replied, confused. The NYPD clearly was not his private security team.

My nephew was equally confused – and feared for our safety.

"So how can you go anywhere? How can you walk outside without a private security force?"

Here were cousins who were close in age, yet the realities in which they were being raised were more than the literal oceans apart.

Chapter 5

In Jewish history there are no coincidences.

Elie Wiesel

In my experience, South Africans can generally be divided into two camps: Those who stayed to focus on the opportunities and those of us who fled to escape the challenges. I was one of the escapees. Having that gun pressed to my head was like a farewell present, as I fled just a week later.

But it was in South Africa that my interest in Judaism and Jewish outreach began to take shape. That passion was sealed when I stayed with the Fachlers in London. On our very first date, I told Gavin that I want a home just like the Fachlers – an open home and a Shabbat table full of guests. I was so inspired by Chava Fachler. My youthful idealism and passion to change the world would begin to play out one Shabbat table at a time. Gavin resonated with that and this mutual passion has defined our marriage over the years.

Two other key ideals bonded us including our yearning to make aliyah and also to see the world in the process. I already had developed quite the travel bug by this point, which remains an insatiable desire to this day. Gavin and I married after just a few months of dating. After his medical studies he worked as a doctor for a short time until he was offered a job at a hospital in New Zealand. We jumped at the opportunity. Our plan was to work hard, save money, then make aliyah to Israel in two years. (Side note: This would later become known as the two-year twenty-three-year plan. But I digress.)

With student loans to pay from medical school, Gavin took this lucrative but challenging job as a doctor far away from South Africa. When we headed to New Zealand, I was in the middle of working toward my undergraduate degree. I continued my studies by correspondence, but these were the days when you mailed in your assignment by post or used a fax machine or a dial-up internet connection, which risked getting knocked offline halfway through transmission. It took forty-five excruciating minutes to send my final assignment and I spent the whole time sweating and praying it would go through. Thankfully, it did and I received a Bachelor of Arts in Sociology. I studied counseling for my post-graduate degree and I liked it – until I got to the practical where I had to counsel actual people with real problems. It was there I realized I might need a counselor myself. I'd be committed before doing this as career. It also dawned on me that this path of studies – counseling, psychology and sociology – were topics I had chosen as a way of rebelling against my parents' expectations that I become a lawyer. While I didn't want to become a lawyer, it became apparent to me that I wanted nothing to do with those other fields either. Instead, I discovered that I truly connected to business. That should have been obvious from my high school tutoring business and the handmade South African goods that I sold to family members overseas. So, I enrolled in another program and received a Bachelor of Commerce.

Living in the most remote parts of New Zealand and then later the Australian outback, however, I wasn't about to practice any of what I had learned. We were extremely isolated in some of our postings. In Invercargill, a tiny city near the southern tip of the South Island, we actually had to squeeze our own grapes for our Shabbat "wine." We met only two Jews in that entire city and they happened to be from the same town in Johannesburg as Gavin's father. My only option for a *mikveh* (ritual bath) as a newlywed of just a few months was the dangerous and *freezing* South Pacific Ocean where signs warned people against swimming.

We once drove nine hundred kilometers to Wellington – the nearest Jewish community – for Shabbat. It was an unforgettable weekend and we stayed in touch with a couple we met who now live in Israel.

After several months in New Zealand, we moved to Tasmania, an island off of Australia's southern coast that was largely undeveloped. There were only ten other Jews in our town and only two hundred on the entire island.

One day in Tasmania, a man wearing a *kippah* knocked on our door. My jaw probably dropped to the front stoop. I hadn't seen a religious Jew in six months. For all I knew this man could have been an axe murderer, but I was so excited to see another Jew that I immediately invited him in. David Walles looked us up thanks to the rabbi in Melbourne, who visited the island regularly. The rabbi told him the general area where we lived, but didn't have our exact address so the man scoured the neighborhood near the Chabad house until he found a home with a mezuzah on the door.

We had an amazing discussion of our beliefs and Jewish conti-nuity – a shared vision of ours. What a refreshing conversation after months in Jewish isolation. David stayed for dinner and told us about an organization he represented that sponsored trips to Israel for Jews living overseas. The program was designed to introduce foreign Jews to Israel while also providing unaffiliated Jews the opportunity to learn more about their faith in a comfortable environment.

When he realized we would soon be relocating to the Gold Coast, he posed an offer: If I could recruit fifteen Jews from that small uni-versity town to go to Israel with his program, he would give Gavin and I free plane tickets and accommodations for six weeks in Israel. I was certainly up to the challenge especially since it involved our mutual dreams: Israel and traveling, not to mention, *free!* As soon as we moved, and even while I was working on my MBA, I set to work. Without the help of advertising on social media as this was still pre-internet, somehow I managed to convince fifteen students to come on this trip merely through word of mouth and a couple of signs I hung up around the school.

I was in for quite a shock though. Once we got to Israel, I took note that everyone involved in this tour on the Israeli side wore black hats if they were men and long skirts if they were women. I didn't even *bring* a skirt. This just goes to show how little I knew about this organization for which I just recruited. It turns out Aish HaTorah, "The Fire of Torah," is an international Orthodox organization that focuses on Jewish education and encourages Jews to discover their heritage in Israel. Religious fashion faux pas aside, the rabbi involved realized my talent for recruiting and asked if I would establish branches for Aish HaTorah in Australia.

I turned down a job at a bank in Sydney and instead volunteered full time for Aish HaTorah while still in the Gold Coast. I traveled three weeks a month to various cities in Australia and New Zealand in order to recruit young Jewish people for experience trips to Israel. I would spend one week in Sydney, another in Melbourne and another in the Gold Coast. Then I would take a week to organize administrative details. I continued doing this after we moved to Sydney when Gavin took a job there in the pharmaceutical industry.

While we were still living in the Gold Coast, a beachside town on Australia's eastern seaboard, we found the Jewish community more sizable compared to Tasmania, but scarcely grounded in its identity. In fact, the Chabad rabbi told us he hadn't conducted one Jewish wedding there in nineteen years. (I later came to learn that someone who became a dear friend of mine did get married there during that time!)

Gavin's *kippah* was a conversation starter. People would tell him, "Oh my mom is Jewish too." Naturally, Gavin would respond, "So you are Jewish." To which the answer was usually a matter-of-fact, "No, my mother is, but I'm not." It was mind-boggling to us. Coming from our tight-knit Jewish community in Jo'burg, this was the first time we saw assimilation in action. Even if you were not religious, you still identified as Jewish! Suddenly what I used to teach those Jewish youth in South Africa about the dangers of assimilation wasn't a tale of the future. Here it was frighteningly real. Being a recent *baal teshuvah* – the term used to refer to a Jew who becomes religiously observant – I was rattled by this realization.

Right there in the Gold Coast was a lost generation – and an opportunity for outreach. Shortly after arriving, my idealistic self rose to the occasion. As I mentioned, these were the pre-internet days and so I did what was popular back then: That first week, I printed flyers and taped them to street poles inviting interested Jews to come to a Shabbat dinner at our apartment. In addition to the Jewish residents of the city, we knew that thousands of Israeli backpackers passed through the area each year so we left leaflets at the hostels inviting them to join us for Shabbat hospitality. We had no idea how many guests to expect or how much to cook.

That first night forty people came!

I didn't know then, but this was the beginning of our lifelong journey trying to engage young people in Jewish life. I was just twenty-one at the time and yet I clearly understood, this was my mission. After our own experience of returning to faith, Gavin and I shared a passion to reach out, connect Jews to each other and give them the opportunity to experience the beauty of our beliefs.

As we continued hosting, word spread about our dinners. Sometimes as many as fifty people would show up. We would just slide the furniture onto the balcony and sardine into our apartment.

One week at *shul* a secular couple from England who were back-packing through Australia attended services, and I invited them to our dinner. When they said they were sleeping in their car I suggested they stay at our place. They ended up being with us for two weeks. Even several months later we met up after we had moved to Sydney and they told me how that two-week stay with us was the most memorable part of their travels. When they got home, they started observing Shabbat and the husband eventually quit his job in finance and became a rabbi. Today they live in Israel.

Talk about successful outreach. Actually, quite a few rabbis from around the world will testify that their religious journey began as a secular Jew at one of our Shabbat tables. And what's really ironic is that many of them are now Ultra-Orthodox and could not even eat at our table these days as they adhere to stricter kosher laws than we do!

Right around this time we ran into visa issues in Australia so Gavin took a rotation at a state medical service called The Royal Flying Doctor Service in far north Queensland. Gavin was on call 24/7 and would be flown to remote villages for routine visits as well as emergency surgeries. In South Africa, medical students train in all of the specialties, so before he graduated, Gavin had to deliver a certain number of babies, work in the ER and trauma units plus learn various medical disciplines. This prepared him perfectly for this type of job. It also supplied him with some crazy and harrowing tales. Once Gavin, as the only doctor at a small rural hospital, was required to administer an anesthetic and then perform a surgery *he had never done before* while a nurse held up a textbook. A doctor from the base hospital provided instructions over the phone.

Gavin was many times the only link between the people in these isolated places and the cities. He delivered the mail, picked up and returned video rentals and stocked the local pharmacy on his visits.

In the meantime, on a whim we put our names into the green card lottery for American citizenship. America doles out 50,000 immigrant visas annually through the U.S. State Department's Immigration and Nationality Act. About twenty million people apply. It was a one-in-a-million chance we would get it. But one day Gavin came home with a thin, nondescript envelope that could have easily been mistaken for junk mail. In it, however, was some surprising news: We had won the lottery!

The dream to immigrate to Israel got put on hold and we decided we would go to America to validate our green cards and keep our options open. As divine timing would have it, while we were in New York we met up with a South African doctor who referred Gavin for a job at another pharmaceutical company. So, we took the leap and decided to move continents yet again. We planned to be in New York for two years, and then make aliyah to Israel. (Side note: We ended up being in New York sixteen years in total!)

Those six years in Australia had been amazing and I wasn't emotionally prepared to leave. I had found my calling there. From Shabbat dinner outreaches to recruiting for trips to Israel, I knew what drove me in life and I loved doing it. What would I do in New York? Thousands of established Jewish organizations already existed. My work was effective in Australia where the need for outreach was more obvious. In New York, my work would be like a drop in the ocean. I shared these thoughts with the *rosh yeshivah* of Aish HaTorah in Jerusalem, a grandfatherly and kind man.

"You think there's no work for you in New York?" He responded to my dilemma with a thunderous laugh. "Follow your husband, you'll find plenty of work there."

I didn't understand, nor did I believe I could make a difference in one of the world's most densely populated Jewish areas.

From our outback living in Australia, we were now about to call the sophisticated Upper West Side of Manhattan home. After being the only Jews in some remote areas, we were moving to a neighborhood with an abundance of synagogues, kosher food and thousands of fellow Jews. In New York City's metropolitan area, the Jewish population numbered more than 1.5 million, making it the largest Jewish community in the world outside of Israel.

And yet, as I would soon come to realize, Jewish identity in America was under assault. Despite the high population of Jews in New York, the community was in as much of a crisis as the apathetic Gold Coast. Even with millions of dollars poured into Jewish initiatives, assimilation and intermarriage were shockingly high in the city. And for each person attending the voluminous Jewish events, five more did not.

Unbeknownst to me, the need for Jewish outreach was just as dire – if not more so – in America. I would come to learn that we were losing our people, not just in the isolated outback, but across the broad expanse of the Diaspora. On many levels, this move was going to be a transition far beyond what I had expected.

Tales of a Modern Jewish Woman

Keeping the faith

My newfound religion was put to the test during those first few months of marriage. In order to perform a mikveh, *the ritual immersion that a woman does after every monthly cycle, I had no choice while living in New Zealand but to immerse myself in the frigid South Pacific Ocean.*

Not only was it ice water, but the area closest to us was so dangerous with violent waves and ragged rocks that "No Swimming!" signs were plastered along this stretch of coast. In fact, the rabbi gave us an exception – I was allowed to do the mikveh *during the day rather than after dark. Heading into this water after dark would be suicidal. While anyone could have seen me stark naked during the day, hardly a soul dared to stop along this portion of the coast.*

I recall one time, the wind was gusting relentlessly making this even more grueling. I arrived, naked except for an overcoat which I would have to drop on the shore as Gavin helped me navigate into the water. I quickly dipped and wanted to die, then rushed out to Gavin who was holding my coat ready. But we couldn't even get it on! The wind wrenched the sleeves from me every time I tried to get my arms in. I just draped it over me and we raced to the car.

However, by that point our tiny Honda Civic was stuck! The wind had blown the sand all around the tires. Digging out the car required both of us – even me with my wet hair and overcoat flapping in the wind, and still no clothes.

These were days my newfound faith was certainly put to the test!

CHAPTER 6

According to the effort is the reward.

Ben Hei Hei, Ethics of the Fathers 5:26

New York and I did not get off to a great start. After we arrived in June, I went alone on a pre-planned backpacking trip to South America since Gavin had to start his new job. When I returned after two months, I dropped my bags and tried to find a new doctor since I had picked up an infection overseas.

Two days later, Gavin returned found me sobbing in a heap of frustration in the middle of the hotel lobby where we were staying.

Yes, me. The strong, stoic, determined Jodi out to change the world. I brought my passion and fire to America.

But after two days in New York, I was undone.

I had a simple mission those first two days: Make a doctor's appointment. The receptionist started taking my information then asked for my zip code. Suddenly the realization loomed heavily on me: I had left an established life replete with friends, influence and stability and was starting from zero. I did not even know my zip code.

I suddenly felt woefully incompetent. And despite being up for this new adventure, I was wistful for what we left behind in Sydney. I knew from experience that making a new place feel like home could take awhile. Feeling settled is more than just having a job and a home. It is about knowing your way around without a map, bumping into someone you know at the supermarket, knowing which hairdresser to go to and not feeling invisible at refreshments after *shul*. I knew that eventually I would sort those out, but in the moment, I was utterly rattled by this new move.

I tried to focus on the positive. We moved to an English-speaking country with a large Jewish community with a mind-blowing number of choices and opportunities for Jews in the city. Aside from the Jewish state itself, where else in the world could I choose from a number of kosher restaurants? What city would suspend parking rules on Jewish holidays? Where else would local TV stations use stars of David during the weather forecast during Hanukkah? In many ways, it was easy to be a Jew here.

Gavin and I both jumped into our new lives, making inroads into the community, meeting people and establishing ourselves in America. My first several years in the city were a learning curve, quite different from my other transitions. When we arrived in New York, we were overwhelmed with the cost of, quite frankly, everything. In Australia, we could rent a small palace for the price of a studio in Manhattan. I was floored that people paid $400 a month for a parking spot (back then!) which was the cost of a one-bedroom apartment where we had lived in Australia. I remember how quickly my perspective changed when a few months after arriving, someone told us about a parking place for just $220 a month and I thought, "*Wow, what a bargain!*" I could also never believe when the weatherman called 45 degrees Fahrenheit a *mild* day. That was the coldest day of the year where we had lived!

Around the time we were new to the city, a friend took me to a restaurant on the Hudson River. She wanted to show me how beautiful it was sitting there by the water. I remember being revolted! After spending so much time in Sydney where the bay was always blue and sunny, the stark contrast of the brown, murky Hudson was almost nauseating. A few years later I caught myself highlighting the beautiful sunset over the Hudson to a new arrival to the city that I took out to dinner. It is amazing how my perspective adapted.

Manhattan had its quirks such as the non-discriminatory mounds of garbage and rats in upper- and lower-class neighborhoods. It was also equal opportunity when it came to space: *No one* had space. One funny Shabbat interaction summed it up when our neighbors, who live in a one-bedroom with three kids, mentioned they were thinking of moving into the closet. Anywhere else in the world this sounds like a joke, but another couple at the table seamlessly chimed in that they had already moved into their closet. Anything to stay in Manhattan.

I was thankful to be living in a building complex with lots of gardens and a playground and thirty seconds from Central Park – the best, most well-maintained garden that I never needed to groom. I also never had to shovel snow or change a lightbulb thanks to the building maintenance crew.

We got to know the harshness of the city too. Some years after we arrived, I was on crutches having broken my ankle and I watched helplessly as people darted for cabs ahead of me banking on the fact that they could outrun me to the taxi. When I needed to get down the subway station stairs on crutches, several passersby emphatically refused to help. On a Friday night when my son, Meron, was sick, I went to our building lobby to find a gentile that could help. Without even waiting to find out what I actually needed, one man interrupted my plea.

"I'm sorry, I just ordered this pizza, I don't want it to get cold," he responded as the elevator door closed in my face.

It also didn't help that we were alone. Whenever we ran into crises, people's first suggestion would be to call my family for help. Only problem was my entire family was a seventeen-hour flight away.

Despite this, I loved New York City, and I still do. I loved that when I started hosting my own Shabbat dinners, I could have guests from forty countries including aspiring actors, successful lobbyists, journalists, businesspeople, political activists and more.

I loved the diversity and richness of Jewish life in the city. I could wear jeans, not cover my hair and have as my closest mentor someone like Slovie Jungreis-Wolff, a parenting coach and writer, who is way more traditional Orthodox than I am. I loved the broad and unique spectrum of Jewish life in Manhattan. Singles from outside New York were overwhelmed by the choices of religious affiliation when we tried to set them up: *machmir* (strict), Modern Orthodox, Egalitarian, Orthodox, Conservodox, etc. Just as the cliché says the Inuits have fifty words for snow, Jews in New York use dozens of categories to describe themselves.

It was great to be Jewish in New York. We loved "Sukkah City" in Union Square Park where twelve unique sukkahs were on display. I also took advantage of the city's thriving cultural scene. I spent six nights a week out on the town, never tiring of the city and always amazed that I could live here forever and still not see everything. And I remain enthralled that we would go to the regular comedy club and order kosher wine.

Jewish life was so common that even our local beggar, Dianne, who lived on our street corner, knew when a three-day Jewish holiday and Shabbat combination was coming up and would ask Gavin for a three-dollar donation instead of one dollar he gave her each morning on the way to the subway. Only in New York.

It was not long before I found my place and my purpose in such a big city. You know those moments that can change the course of your life? In this instance it was meeting Kevin who came on our very first Aish HaTorah trip. After that trip he had become a regular guest at our Shabbat table in Australia. Now, Kevin too was living in New York City while studying at Columbia University. A month after we arrived in the city, he got in touch and asked if I would host the foreign Jewish MBA students from the university for a Rosh Hashanah meal. Despite the fact that I was new to New York myself, I said yes immediately and shortly afterwards had thirty- six people – from thirty countries – over for Rosh Hashanah. That dinner made me realize that there was indeed a strong need to make connections for Jews from overseas who were living in the city. If it weren't for that dinner, those students would have had nowhere to go.

Soon after that, I hosted a Shabbat dinner for South Africans, then another for people from other commonwealth nations, followed later by another dinner for various nationalities. At these events I realized just how hungry these foreign Jews were for more than just dinners. Only a few weeks in the city and I was back in the swing of hosting, just like in Australia.

Before all of that began, my father happened to be in town on business. I used the opportunity to whine to him endlessly about how I had uprooted my life Down Under and now had no relationships, no friends and no network. As we were on our way to get our first taste of a famous New York-style kosher burger, we stopped at a Jewish bookstore where my father, secretly, implored the courteous cashier to befriend his lonely daughter and take me under her wings. I would've been mortified if I knew he was doing this, but this kind woman heeded his request and invited me to dinner the following week.

She took me to a kosher restaurant in the city. We were eating when a man strode in and all heads turned.

"Do you know Steve Eisenberg?" the woman asked. "You have to meet him."

She waved Steve over. If you know Steve, you also know the famous question that he poses pretty much right away to everyone.

"What are you doing for Shabbat?" he asked me.

He immediately set us up with a family for the upcoming Friday. He happened to be there too. During dinner I told him how much we also loved hosting people in Australia at our regular Shabbat dinners.

He grilled us regarding our level of kosher (we met the bar) and then he asked how many people we would be willing to host. Expecting the usual "four to eight" his jaw dropped when I casually said twenty to thirty. Almost immediately he started sending people to us on Shabbats. Steve got rave reviews about our dinners, so he kept sending me more people.

It was amazing to find a kindred spirit in New York. We were both passionate about providing a community for people to truly engage in Jewish life. People have a natural need to affiliate and be a part of something bigger than themselves. Shabbat is the crowning moment of our week which allows us to provide that. We impart the Jewish values of family and the teachings of the Bible as we recount the weekly Torah portion. It is a continuation of 5,000 years of tradition, interweaving generations of Jewish people. At Shabbat dinners, we build long-term relationships and familial connections.

Steve also helped me with my dinners. Once I was highly anxious when I organized a Shabbat dinner for eighty foreigners at a New

York restaurant. I hadn't reached the minimum required reservations and yet I had to pay the deposit before the dinner on Friday. I reached for a bar of chocolate, which always helped during stressful times. When Steve called in the midst of this crisis, I burst into tears.

"Don't worry," he said. "I know lots of internationals. I'll help you do this dinner."

In no time we sold out! Up until this point, Steve and I had been operating our own separate events, yet we saw how we worked together synergistically. This natural collaboration was later to burgeon into greater things.

I also found my place in the working world. Our arrival in New York coincided with the dot-com bubble and I easily found a job associated with what I had spent the previous few years learning. Toward the end of that first year though, the industry went bust. All of us in the industry were monitoring a dubiously named website called, pardon the language, fuckedcompanies.com. People would check in every day to see if their company was on the rumor mill as being poised to crash. I remember the morning my company's name appeared, as it was expected to go bust at any moment. I had a sinking feeling. Quietly, but quickly, I dispatched my team of employees to the local convenience store to buy bags and start packing up. When a company closed, they gave you only ten minutes to clear out, so I wanted us to be ready. Sure enough, the bags came in handy as we got our pink slips that very day.

So just a few months after arriving, I was already out of a job. We were supposed to sign the papers for a mortgage on an apartment in the Upper West Side the following week. If I couldn't show proof of income, we wouldn't be approved for the mortgage. Gavin, being the practical one in our relationship, was in an absolute panic and was quite sure the deal would be lost. I was unfazed.

"Give me a day, I'll have a job," I reassured him. He was skeptical.

I went straight to the local Aish HaTorah center in New York where I knew they held a weekly class on Monday. I approached the rabbi after the meeting and told him how I volunteered with the organization when I lived in Australia. I then proceeded to outline a job description tailor-made for me at Aish HaTorah in New York. I would do outreach and galvanize the young Jewish professionals of the city for dinners and other events. The rabbi had heard of my work in Australia and was keen to hire me. By the next day I had concluded negotiations to join the team – my main stipulation being that I needed to receive a paystub by the end of the month, so I had proof to show the bank. In the meantime, we signed the papers for the mortgage and moved into our new home, a great apartment on the Upper West Side that I still cherish to this day.

I was really starting to feel at home in New York. We were caught up in the New York state of mind, where everyone aspires for success and excellence. In Australia, people had "tall poppy syndrome," a term which describes marked hostility toward overachievers. New Yorkers are completely unaware of this idiom since they are all *pursuing* achievement. The *New York Daily News* even did a piece on us as immigrants who have "made it" in New York. Immigrants in general are known to be tenacious and tough. I once saw a statistic that 58 percent of American small businesses are owned by immigrants because of the endurance and persistence that comes with migrating countries.

It was a dynamic place to live. Much of what has shaped me into who I am today as a mother, businesswoman, nonprofit manager and social activist was birthed during those early years in New York. I settled in well and I thrived in both my work and spiritual life.

I truly loved this city. Who would think that in a few years I would be in for the fight of my life here?

Tales of a Modern Jewish Woman

Same army, different units

When people walk into our Manhattan apartment their eyes are immediately drawn to what may be an extremely bewildering plaque on our wall. Encased in a gold frame is certificate of gratitude from the founder and head rabbi at Aish HaTorah in Jerusalem thanking Gavin and me for our work in establishing the organization's Australian branch.

People who don't know us well will glance from the plaque to us to try to reconcile the dissonant information. Aish HaTorah followers are well known in the Orthodox world for their black hats and strict adherence to Jewish law. Anyone who knows Jodi and Gavin Samuels knows we are Modern Orthodox, we wear colors, I don't cover my hair and I sometimes even wear jeans.

These details may not mean much to people unfamiliar with the inner working of the Orthodox Jewish world, but our dissonant outward reflections of Judaism makes this plaque quite surprising!

Rabbi Yisrael Noah Weinberg, of blessed memory, was different.

Once I spoke to him about my wearing jeans, which was so out of place in his world.

"Jodi, God doesn't judge his soldiers and neither do I," he replied. "Just like an army needs many different types of soldiers and reinforcements, everybody plays a role in God's kingdom. And you're playing yours."

Rabbi Weinberg saw past my jeans. He saw in me someone that could contribute even though I didn't fit into his world and, somehow, I wasn't fired (from my volunteer role).

Weinberg's mission was to bring Jews closer to God. So was mine.

Rabbi Weinberg was famous for using the analogy that "the cattle cars have left the station" when comparing the loss of the Jewish people through assimilation to the Holocaust. He was very committed to see every single Jew return to the heritage.

After Rabbi Weinberg passed away in 2009 I was asked to speak at his shloshim (the observance thirty days after one's death) at Aish HaTorah headquarters in New York. The crowd was milling with mostly men and nearly all of them black-hat rabbis. I was wearing a modest dress, but with bright colors and a V-neck, clearly not modest enough. People couldn't believe that "she" was one of the speakers.

I texted a friend who worked there before I was to go up on stage. "There's no way I can speak to all these rabbis! Please pour me a glass of wine," I wrote. I slipped out to "the bathroom" and downed the wine to calm my nerves.

But going up on stage to honor a man who had been so influential and real all those years was an honor. I recounted how I ended up coming on board at Aish HaTorah because I wanted a free trip to Israel, and that I arrived without a skirt. I recalled how Rabbi Weinberg, years later, encouraged Gavin and me to go to New York and that I would surely continue my mission there. I was the girl who took his advice to change the world. And my own Jewish outreach organization was born.

Even though I'm no longer working for Aish HaTorah, I remain inspired by Rabbi Weinberg's vision that we should not rest until we bring every Jew back to their roots.

My own journey shows the vast influence Rabbi Weinberg had on me and the ability he had to get others to maximize their own potential – no matter how they dressed.

May that be a lesson for us all.

CHAPTER 7

If you don't know what you're living for, you haven't yet lived.

Rabbi Noah Weinberg, of blessed memory

I have never been one who readily takes no for an answer.

I had just hosted my first dinner under the auspices of Aish HaTorah in New York. I was excited to host new arrivals to the city and I assumed the head rabbi would share my enthusiasm. Instead, he called me in to his office after the event. He didn't understand why people who came to a city from overseas would want to be hosted at an event separate from native New Yorkers.

I explained that foreigners, such as myself, had different challenges in connecting to the Jewish community here. They needed help engaging especially since they were far away from home and family. But I failed to convince the rabbi and, to my chagrin, he refused to fund future events like this at Aish HaTorah.

If anybody knows Jodi, "no" is never the final answer.

As I walked out of that meeting, fuming, I contacted a graphic designer and started working on a logo for a new organization. My mission had just become crystal clear. I would connect expat Jews living in New York to the existing Jewish community. By the end of the day, I registered my website and I founded Jewish International Connection New York.

When I had hosted foreign Jewish students for a holiday dinner a few months prior, I realized this was something they were craving. Plus, as a foreigner myself, I understood the complexities and challenges facing Jews new to town and looking for connections. Jewish life in America is unlike Judaism in other countries and many foreign Jews are left on the outskirts of Jewish communities in America.

A few weeks after arriving in New York City, the words of Rabbi Weinberg came back to me when he laughed at my concern that Jewish New York had no need for outreach. I quickly began to notice chinks in the armor of this voluminous community. I found that in America, Jews are free to be who they are in society. They are equals and are not ostracized due to their ethnicity and religion. The same isn't necessarily true in other countries with smaller Jewish populations. Those tight-knit communities come with unwritten rules of social engagement – your professional, social and religious life is funneled through your Jewish community. And usually access to Jewish life is filtered through the one-and-only Orthodox synagogue or Chabad house. Because of this, a Jew from overseas has a higher level of knowledge about Judaism than his or her American counterpart and, even if they aren't religious, may observe Shabbat and eat kosher. But that same person in New York City, suddenly disconnected from his or her religion and home, can be overwhelmed. Suddenly he or she is presented with hundreds of synagogue options and millions of Friday night options, none of which may include an invitation to Shabbat dinner.

When it comes to Shabbat and holidays, the expat Jews were often left without friends and family with whom to celebrate. Without this community to tap into, many of them will make whatever friends they can, Jewish or not, and potentially drift away from their faith. Many end up intermarrying.

Being an outsider myself I was sensitive to the need for Jewish connectivity. That became one of the driving forces behind my hospitality and why I had become known as "the dinner queen." And that is why I initially took this idea to Aish HaTorah New York.

As I was speaking to the rabbi there trying to convince him of this urgent need, I remembered something that Rabbi Weinberg told the New York Aish HaTorah staff the prior week on a visit to New York:

"People who want to change the world start their own organization." I was inspired by that statement and those words came back to me as I sat there pleading with the rabbi.

These dinners where I connected Jewish people were *my* mission. I wanted to expand this vision and he saw no point. And that's when I realized, I should do my own thing.

Several months later Steve Eisenberg also came on board with JICNY. Up until now, Steve and I had been working together synergistically, supporting each other's Shabbat dinners. JICNY was a natural extension of our hearts and the work we were already doing. Plus, Steve was already teaching Torah classes in our home every Monday. (By the way, in eighteen years he never missed a Monday night and we soon had to move the class to a larger venue.)

The organization took off a lot faster than I expected. Suddenly we were hosting communal Shabbat dinners. And this was just the beginning. Remember those Shabbat dinners in Australia where we moved the furniture onto the balcony? Those days were just a small indicator of what was to come – events that would host hundreds of people at a time and thousands each year.

The moral of the story? Don't tell me no. The rabbi's refusal to host internationals sealed my desire to make it happen on an even larger scale than the few unofficial dinners we had already hosted. From our humble beginnings and volunteer staff, JICNY grew to serve as a home away from home for Jews who came from abroad to live in New York. And that remains our mission.

I left Aish HaTorah, and Meron was born shortly after that in 2002. Five weeks later I got another job as head of operations at a business that sold beauty products. It was a modern-day sweatshop in the sense that we crammed a bunch of staff into a two-room apartment. And it was just what I needed. The "offices" were just around the block from our apartment and the nanny could bring Meron to me during the day to visit. Two of the partners there were both newly religious at the time, and so they understood my passion as I was starting up my not-for-profit.

This was before online registration and payments were possible. I was frequently fielding calls, taking down names and manually running credit card numbers of those RSVPing for my events. Basically, it took up a full work day at my regular job. It sure helped that the partners were *baalei teshuvah* and that I set up one of them with his wife. They essentially "donated" a few hours of my work time to JICNY. The connection was long lasting. Years later that same couple that I set up made aliyah and serves on my JIC board in Israel. They remain good friends and faithful volunteers.

I worked at this company up until a few hours before I gave birth to Temira in June 2004. Gavin was at the office with me, timing my contractions, while I continued tying up loose ends at the job and simultaneously organizing a JICNY event that was set for that Saturday. It was a Thursday evening when Gavin dragged me from the office to the hospital. Though my contractions were regular, I wasn't dilated so they sent me home that night and told me to return at seven o'clock for another checkup.

When I arrived at hospital the next morning, my blood pressure was dangerously elevated and the doctor slated me for immediate admission and a C-section. She didn't realize I had an event to plan though. I told her I first needed to run to Costco to finish shopping for Saturday's dinner.

This is when it helps to be married to a doctor. Gavin, ever the voice of reason, put his foot down. I was not leaving the hospital. I would have to manage from my Blackberry while more or less strapped to a hospital bed. The event went on as scheduled, without me, as I was preoccupied with other things. Temira was born later that day.

Clearly JICNY was my first baby. My vision was that it be a gateway into the Jewish experience for people that relocate to New York. "JICNY provides participants with the resources and opportunities they require to secure a soft landing in New York, develop personal relationships with likeminded Jewish professionals, and connect with Jewish observance at an optimal personal level," our website says.

From these humble beginnings in 2002, JICNY now reaches more than 10,000 people from more than forty countries. More than 125 couples met through our programs and got married – a statistic we are proud of and hope to expand.

We host more than three hundred events a year in New York and Israel, from weekly Torah classes to monthly "gala" Shabbat dinners, lectures, film nights, art and photography exhibitions, walking tours of Jewish neighborhoods and cooking classes to name a few. We have professional networking events and matchmaking services, social events, holiday parties, Israel advocacy programs and specialized tours including birthright for moms and heritage tours to Berlin, Poland, Morocco and other places. We also offer lectures in Spanish, French and Russian. I try to cover all the bases and yet I'm sure there are still many opportunities we miss.

Though JICNY skyrocketed in terms of members, attendees and events, the staff was, and still is, really just me and a part-time assistant – the only paid person in the organization – with a group of dedicated volunteers. For all of our events, I am the contact person. That means that I receive about five hundred emails a day from mundane questions like what the weather will be in Poland during our tour there to the bombshell email I got from the Jerusalem Municipality telling me that they are pulling their funding just three days before an event with six hundred people! I am constantly fielding a wide range of inquiries and problems to solve, in addition to juggling my work, my home and keeping my relationships with friends fresh and ongoing.

Yet I wouldn't give it up for anything. I am so passionate about this work that I suck up all the volunteer hours and the stress that comes along with it. And this way I can keep costs down. Many Jewish activities are expensive and so only those with means are able to participate in communal life to the fullest extent. Shabbat dinners, holiday parties, *shul* memberships and of course, Jewish Day schools can be prohibitive. Our programs are purposely affordable, and we usually have a long waiting list after we are sold out. Finances should never be a reason for any Jew to be excluded. While I don't have immediate answers to solving the exorbitant costs of Jewish day schools or conferences, I do what I can in my own sphere.

Jewish continuity begins with one-on-one connections. And it starts in the home, sharing a meal, being personable, even vulnerable. Long before JICNY, my personal life was consumed with the same activities on a smaller scale. While thousands pass through our events at JICNY, hundreds still pass through our home. One Friday night we hosted one of our international Shabbat dinners for JICNY – nearly a hundred people from twenty-seven countries. Then on Saturday we had twenty couples over for Shabbat lunch at our home. The last guests lingered until after *havdalah* because we were just having such a great time.

One doesn't have to look too far to find the best biblical example of hospitality. Sarah and Abraham welcomed strangers into their tent and cooked a meal for them. We see in Genesis, Abraham generously welcomed three travelers who we learn later are divine messengers – angels. We try to live by Abraham's example.

Gavin asked me one June when our next free Shabbat would be.

"October," I replied after consulting my calendar.

What can I say? We like to keep our lives busy and crowded. When we were moving from the hotel to our apartment in New York, after having landed a month prior, someone asked if a friend could stay with us for a few weeks while she got settled in New York. I agreed. A few days later we met someone else who said, "Oh, you know Julie."

"Nope, I never met a Julie in New York," I replied.

"Aren't you the couple who just arrived from Australia, originally from South Africa, and are moving into the 'Key West' building?"

"Yes, that's us."

"So you must know Julie! She is moving in with you!"

I then realized that I had not even asked for any details about our soon-to-be houseguest. We were going to welcome her no matter who she was, and we would get the details once she arrived.

During our time in New York, our home was nearly always occupied by guests, often more than one. We called it "Camp Samuels." We hosted travelers, new arrivals, the scared, the lost and the lonely. Many arrived as strangers, nearly all left as friends. Some visitors were challenging, but most added so much to our home.

This was all a dream come true from the time I stayed with the Fachlers in London and watched the endless traffic of guests – myself included – who they welcomed and hosted.

I've always been very conscious of my blessings and I feel like this is my deal with God: You blessed me, so this is my way of acknowledging and sharing these gifts. I also love the real-life lessons our lives are for our children who see Jewish hospitality in action. We can all spend so much money sending our kids to Jewish day schools, but when they see Torah values active in real life the lesson is more meaningful. It's not about what is *comfortable* to do, but what is *right*. My children are being raised with an outward focus. Plus having the constant flow of different people with various needs and cultures has made my kids sensitive, resilient and empathic. They learn to give, not just take. We maintain at least one spare room so we can share it. This is a powerful message for our children.

There is another side to having an open home: You never know who is going to walk through your doors. We've had recovering drug addicts and, as it turns out, convicted criminals sitting at our Shabbat table or staying at our home for a period of time. The second you open your door you make yourself vulnerable.

The building doorman was so used to our flood of guests that when he saw obviously Jewish people wander into the lobby, he sent them directly to our apartment before they even asked. Since we had never met a good percentage of our guests, it was natural we were seeing many people for the first time. Only later did we realize that perhaps they weren't all meant for us. Once, after a long dinner, a guest finally asked, "Are you the Pearlmans?" It seems that we inadvertently, but happily, hosted many people who were actually meant to go to our neighbors' apartment.

When we first moved in, the doorman didn't understand what was going on. He saw all of our food deliveries and frequent guests, and called me over. "Oh, I understand now," he said. "You are running a soup kitchen for the needy!"

As ambitious as I was in founding JICNY, I never expected it to take off so fast and grow exponentially in the first few months. Clearly there was a need that wasn't being filled. I was passionate about this at twenty-one and the flame didn't wane as I moved to New York. Something I learned from Chava Fachler always comes back to me: "Never underestimate the effect of one life."

As we forged on in the Big Apple, my career was taking off and JICNY was burgeoning. Both of these would soon get railroaded by the birth of Caila. Or I should say, perhaps all of my passions would get woven together in a way I could not have mapped out for myself.

Tales of a Modern Jewish Woman

The Orthodox Jews and the almost impossible wedding

Susie started out as my personal trainer in New York and quickly became one of my dearest friends. When she heard that I ran a networking group for Jewish entrepreneurs, an extension of JICNY, she asked if she could be a part of it. Susie was just building her business at the time, and of course we were more than happy to welcome her. So Susie, a Canadian Jamaican, became the first non-Jew in the group.

This was also an eye opening experience for Susie to learn about Judaism and Jewish life – all aspects. She once attended a Shabbat dinner at my friend's house and after she got home she scrambled to call me.

"I can't believe how the wife told her husband what to do all the time! 'Throw out the garbage,' 'Change the baby's diaper!' This would never happen in my community." She left me several messages. Susie hadn't yet learned that I shut off my phone for Shabbat.

But she couldn't believe the level of influence Jewish women had in their homes. And by the end of her time with the networking group Susie knew more about Jewish culture and Judaism than many Jews.

During this time Susie also got engaged and she asked me to be in the bridal party. I was delighted to host her engagement party, where we had mingling in one room her friends and family from Harlem and our Jewish business owners from the group. Susie's own speech was laden with many Jewish gems as she talked about meeting her mensch *and how Gavin and I gave her fiancé the "kosher stamp of approval."*

Her wedding was planned for a Saturday, but by this point Susie knew enough about Orthodox Jews to realize it was going to be problematic for me to (1) get to her wedding on Shabbat, and (2) step foot into a church!

I assured her I would find a way.

Susie and her spouse specifically chose a church in Harlem that we could get to on foot from our Upper West Side apartment along with the other Orthodox Jews who were invited. It was still two miles away, though, and what Susie could not control was the weather. It happened to be one of those leftover hot and humid summer days that linger into September, pushing 96 degrees Fahrenheit. Gavin's suit was completely soaked by the time we arrived, and as for me, the bridesmaid, well, when we walked in the man who let us into the church asked if I had just been swimming!

I took a wet wipe bath and I stood in front of a fan to dry my hair.

It is a rare site to see Orthodox Jews in a church, let alone on a Shabbat and not to mention, one of them being the only white person in a wedding party at a black Pentecostal church in Harlem. But there I stood on the altar – next to an Israeli flag of all things.

We crossed racial and religious boundaries that day to celebrate with a friend. It is an honor I will always cherish.

Chapter 8

The day you were born is the day God decided the world could not exist without you.

Rabbi Nachman of Breslov

After I gave birth to Caila, I decided to read the book *What to Expect When You Have a Child with Down Syndrome*. Big mistake.

Half way through the book I looked at Gavin and asked, "Did I give birth to a monster?"

Every potential health, cognitive and other challenge was listed and explained in relentless detail. It painted a bleak and hopeless picture for children with trisomy 21. I was still processing the shock of this news and so my emotions were raw. Basically, by the end of the book I felt like I had delivered an alien.

We were overwhelmed. Thoughts raced through our heads, from "Why us?" and "What will life be like?" to, simply, "Oh my God, please help!"

It wasn't that I was upset by Caila's diagnosis. On the contrary, within a few minutes of hearing the news, I concluded that God must have sent us this baby for a reason. After two miscarriages between Temira and Caila, I knew God had handpicked Caila for our family.

Gavin's words reassured me even more.

"Look how beautiful she is, I can see the light in her eyes," he observed. "She is going to be fine – take it one day at a time."

Her eyes were truly switched on – she was destined to blow us all away. We didn't know at the time of course, and it is impossible to know from the outset, if your child will be high or low functioning.

None of this meant, however, that life would be easy or that we would be reprieved of grieving lost expectations at the outset. I more so struggled with questions about her future and whether we were equipped to deal with her needs. Did we have the resources? Could we afford to give her the best care and therapies? I worried about how this would impact the lives of my other children. We were such a public family, so how would this affect our interaction with the community? I read books and articles that painted generic pictures of people with Down syndrome, with all of their challenges. All negative and patronizing.

I had so many emotions, thoughts and fears raging through me.

Our family and friends were devastated. In fact, they took it harder than we did. We ended up doing most of the comforting. "Oh, I am so sorry," we heard over and over again. The most common responses were tears – *theirs not ours*. Then we even had a person ask us outright – while Gavin was holding Caila – why we did not abort her! All sorts of emotions were swirling strong in those first few weeks.

But Caila's eyes were switched on. Based on that, Gavin said, "I promise you she will be high functioning." I held onto that.

Regardless of her expected level of abilities, I knew that unless we embraced this baby, the life we lived would be a lie. We had always opened our home to the lost, the lonely, the searching and the challenged. If we open our home to strangers, how much more so should we embrace our daughter. It was because of who we are that God sent us this beautiful soul.

We went from asking, "Why us?" to saying, "Of course us!"

This was the beginning of the road in my coming to terms with Caila having Down syndrome.

I am grateful for a bit of sound advice that I read and that resonated with me – she is a baby first and then she has a diagnosis. Caila was simply my baby. She was a daughter, a sister, a granddaughter.

Gavin and I decided from the outset, we would control the narrative. People should not feel sorry for us because we had a child with special needs. Friends who came to the hospital after her birth can testify, they walked into a perfectly calm environment that gave no hint of the bombshell diagnosis we would share. This life-changing diagnosis required me to reprioritize. I developed an incredible capacity to not sweat the small stuff. I can now maintain a calm, controlled perspective.

I wore Caila in a baby carrier purposely facing out toward the world. We cast aside any shame associated with the extra chromosome.

A few years later I was asked to speak on a panel for a group of rabbinic interns who were learning about special needs in the community and wanted a parent's perspective. Reflecting on what to say, I recalled the serious and pitying looks we received from the pediatrician, the OB/GYN and the geneticist on the day we got the diagnosis. They, and all the books, presented us with a never-ending list of the potential problems for the baby from major disease and heart issues to being flatfooted, short-sighted and having thin hair. Caila was healthy and had none of these problems, but if I adhered to those books, I'd be a hypochondriac on her behalf.

If only I knew in the beginning what I was to discover later – the joy and wonder of this girl would be so far from the pain and worries thrown at us in the first few days. It was that perspective that I would convey to that group of interns, one of hope and possibility – and not the despair of those first moments.

I also had to prove to myself that our lives would not be disrupted. Caila was born on a Sunday, and by Thursday I was released from the hospital. That weekend – against reason and my husband's protests – I insisted on carrying on with my original plan of hosting forty guests for Shabbat dinner and another thirty for lunch on Saturday at our apartment. My only concession was that I would have the meals catered.

So there I was, doubled over from the aftermath of a C-section and mulling this surprising diagnosis with dozens of people milling through my home. But hosting was my oxygen. I needed to do that in order to feel that my life would continue normally.

And it did.

I also banned my parents from coming to New York until they could pull themselves together and not cry the whole time. I wanted to show Meron and Temira that life was wonderful. I didn't want people crying around Caila and sending the message that their sister was a burden.

Gavin and I pushed ourselves through the cloud of expected hardships associated with chromosomal disorders and we publicly celebrated our little girl. I would like to share how we welcomed her that special day of Caila's *simchat bat* in 2008.

Gavin's speech

Yesterday, in shul, we read in the parashah *about the purification process that one goes through after suffering from* tzaraat *(a biblical disease with physical symptoms resembling leprosy) – the physical manifestation of a spiritual problem. The process is quite bewildering and involves cedar wood, crimson thread, two birds, spring water and hyssop.*

When reading this, one cannot help but wonder why? Why birds, why hyssop, why crimson thread? As it turns out, there are very good and beautiful reasons for all these elements of the process, and in this situation, asking why is a good and elucidating question.

Seven weeks ago, Hashem blessed our family with a beautiful, healthy baby girl. And Hashem chose to send her to us with special needs and challenges.

It is again natural to ask the question, why? But sometimes in Judaism, why is not the right question – there are better and more insightful questions to ask because we cannot know the answer to why in this situation.

So we move on and we ask other questions: What? What can we learn from this Little Princess? And how? How can we become better people through this special person?

I will speak about the Who.

The first "who" is Caila Sara, this beautiful, smiling, content angel who has enriched our lives so much already. Who is also Sara Leah, my dear Grandmother z"l after whom Caila Sara is named. Caila has her same blue-hazel eyes, and if you look very carefully you can see glimpses of my grandmother's soul in those eyes.

Another who is Jodi. Her fierce and deep emunah *and* bitachon *are rare and inspiring. Her capacity for love and giving to her family and* the community is amazing. Jodi juggles a full-time job with running the JICNY and being a special wife and mother by sleeping only three hours a night. But don't worry, on the planet she comes from this is considered normal!

The who is also Caila's adoring brother and sister, Meron and Temira. They smother her with the therapy she needs more than any other – unconditional love. Meron even cut his security blanket that he has had since birth and gave Caily half when she came back from the hospital.

And lastly, the who is all of you. As the saying goes, it takes a village to raise a child – how much more so a special child.

My speech at Caila's *simchat bat*

God gave us a gift with Caila Sara.

When many of you heard the news about Caila Sara our precious baby, that she was diagnosed with Down syndrome, you shed a tear. Many of you asked, "Why them?"

Of course us!

After a very hard C-section, no sleep and receiving the shocking news, I had the clarity of mind to say to Gavin, "Who else would Hashem chose?"

Many of you know about the Samuels home. We always have guests staying. Many of you started your NY sojourn in our home. We host those who are new, those who are scared, those who are growing, those who are exploring and those just in need of caring. Our home is the place for many simchot – britot, sheva berachot, *engagement parties and more. Our home is the place where people come for counseling, advice, to share and to just hang out.

I am quite sure that when God was looking for a place for this precious* neshamah *he thought, "What about the home with the open door policy?"*

After two miscarriages between Temira and Caila and prenatal testing that gave us a one in five thousand chance of a having a baby with Down syndrome, I feel truly handpicked for this mission.

Gavin and I were not sad when Caila was born. Caila will always know that her parents always saw her as a* berachah *in their life. Our only expectation is that Caila achieve 100 percent of her unique potential. Well, I am a Jewish mother, so 110 percent of her potential!*

Caila Sara – our baby and berachah *is already impacting the world:*

- *Many of you, when you heard about Caila Sara, were forced to reevaluate your knee-jerk reaction to children with special needs.*
- *My cousin, also named Gavin, wrote a heartfelt prayer in her honor. So many people have told me they have used these wise words in their time of need.*
- *Even the geneticist who did our counseling at Mount Sinai was brought to tears when we explained our view on having a baby with Down syndrome. She asked if she could share our view with other families.*
- *Caila is already making me, her mother, a better person. I am now more sensitive, less judgmental and I too have had to reconsider my own stereotypes.*

Caila is our exercise in hope.

Caila Sara is the berachah, *the blessing, for all our community.*

CHAPTER 9

A little sleep, a little slumber, a little folding of the hands to rest – and poverty will come on you like a thief and scarcity like an armed man.

Proverbs 6:10–11

"Imma, since Caily was born everything has been different."

Temira, my seven-year-old at the time, said this about three years after Caila's birth.

Gulp.

Here it was. The big confession of the sibling of a child with special needs. We had failed as parents. I had failed as a mother. Having a child with Down syndrome was destroying my family. I steeled myself against becoming completely undone in front of my middle child, took a breath and asked, simply, "Why?"

"That is when you started jdeal and Metroimma, and since then you have so many meetings and you are always busy."

I was expecting a deep and meaningful conversation about how having a sister with Down syndrome has impacted her life. Instead, worse, it was like a dagger straight to my heart! My daughter was right. My life had certainly gone into overdrive a few years before. By choice, of course. But still I wondered if I had gone off course with my priorities.

Temira's perspective caused me to reflect on the past years. Was I too focused on business? Should I scrutinize my priorities? Should I strike a better work–life balance?

When I was pregnant with Caila, I was phasing out of the accounting training company in which I had been a partner and founder with a friend from Australia. It was odd because, being Type-A and restless, I couldn't go a few minutes without working. But by some premonition, I started withdrawing from the company without the prospect of another job. It was more than just Caila's upcoming diagnosis which would take me by surprise, but the market was going to surprise us too. Right before Caila was born I sold my shares of the company. Caila was born in February 2008. And, as my own world was cascading around the diagnosis that would change our lives, the financial markets came crashing down as well.

It was good that I got out of the financial training business, but six months after Caila was born I was getting antsy. I needed to do something. It is well known in my native continent that an African woman goes back to work the day after having a baby. She gets up, straps on the baby and heads back to the fields. I am African through and through – "Let's get on with it," I always say.

My true love has always been entrepreneurship, creating businesses and jobs rather than merely working them. When I was a student on the Gold Coast, I went into business with a friend. We split the duties of a direct marketing company. I managed the staff and logistics while he was responsible for sales. In those days, direct marketing meant door to door. Some of the salespeople would go out and others would make phone calls. In those days, when you went door to door in Australia you'd get invited in for a beer. But the internet started changing the way people do business. Technology also killed telemarketing as people were able to block calls. Nevertheless, it was a good experience for me and made me realize that I immensely enjoyed start-ups and business development.

And now I was in the perfect environment – one of the world's most thriving and energetic commercial capitals – to launch my own businesses. From the time I was twelve and tutoring friends in exchange for chocolate, I was a budding entrepreneur and my life's goal was to make it to the cover of *Business Week* or *Fortune*. That was my vision of success. Now was my time, I thought.

All kinds of social media networking sites were popping up on the internet at the time and they were absolutely scintillating to my entrepreneurial soul. Mom connections and mommy blogs were a big demographic. So, I decided to launch something new, a platform for Jewish moms. "Metroimma" became a place for Jewish moms in New York City to network with each other while writing about the common issues we faced.

I often joked that Jewish moms make the perfect bloggers: They are educated, highly opinionated and, often, bored. Jewish moms are decision makers, gatekeepers and influencers. As bloggers, they amplify all of the above. On the web, these moms have reach beyond their own families and friends. A mom can be an agent for change, an advocate for causes, a cheerleader for brands and so much more.

Years later I would run a Jewish blog contest in New York that highlighted the sheer quantity of Jewish bloggers. In fact, Jewish moms were one of the biggest groups out there. I became one of them as I took up Caila's cause with both a Facebook page called Caily's World and on my Metroimma blog.

Around the same time, the concept of group deals became the rage. I read an article in 2010, about this concept of daily deals. I mentioned this to my business partner, Allen.

"Why don't we do a Jewish version?" I suggested.

Once we agreed, the race was on. The week leading up to our launch was fraught with stress of epic proportions. I knew competition was coming and I was adamant that we should be the first to market. Our plan was to launch jdeal in 2010 on the Monday before Thanksgiving. We started getting word out about the launch, we did a pre-sign-up campaign, and at eight o'clock on Monday, we were officially a business.

Many entrepreneurs have war stories about their start-ups, and ours was no different. On the Sunday night before the launch, Allen, his wife, Frances, and Gavin and I worked through the night. I had a major proposal for a grant for Metroimma that was also due on

Monday and I was working on that concurrently. Thankfully, everything was going well on Monday – until I got into a car accident that night. Then Allen called to say we did not have a deal to send out on Tuesday. Our one prospect fell through and we had not yet amassed a pipeline of deals. What a scramble! I called a friend who was a photographer at ten that night and told him (not asked), "Guess what? You are our deal for tomorrow!"

Then on Tuesday night, Allen was in a freak accident when a window fell from a building as he was walking by. A shard of glass severed nerves and tendons in his finger as he moved to shield his daughter from the cascade of shattering window.

To compound the stress of that first week, I had planned a trip to Morocco over Thanksgiving – and flights were non-refundable. I had no idea, back when I booked the trip, that the first week of our launch would be so rocky and ridden with anxiety.

But we did it. And, as if it were divine confirmation, the very day we launched jdeal, Google offered Groupon *$6 billion*! I had dreams of being the next dotcom billionaire.

That first week, our launch garnered media coverage in *Fortune, The New York Times, The Washington Post, New York Post*, NY1, *Crain's New York, Adweek*, the *New York Jewish Week* and *Business Insider*. And I did make it to Morocco where I conducted a phone interview with *The Wall Street Journal* while I *rode a camel* in the desert!

The story of jdeal was also picked up by a collection of well-known websites and blogs and our launch-party guests ranged from our sponsors and media representatives to an esteemed collection of bloggers who were tweeting from the minute they stepped through the door.

We became the go-to place for a deal on anything Jewish. New Jewish musicals opening on Broadway, subscriptions to a Jewish newspaper, tickets to kosher wine events, vouchers to buy the wine, Jewish cruises, hotels, charities, kosher restaurants, summer camps, Jewish cooking classes, Judaica, Jewish author book launches. We even had you covered with travel to Israel with discounted tour packages or cell phone rentals. The list of possibilities was endless.

We learned to time our charity pitches with the Jewish holidays of Purim, Passover and Rosh Hashanah. If our subscribers already had their credit cards in our system, they could purchase or donate with one click. Many times we'd offer to match donations.

It was both chaotic and exhilarating. Allen and I bootstrapped our venture with zero outside funding. We started with a few hundred opt-in names and quickly shot up to 40,000. Many daily-deal sites had entered the Jewish market, but we were the largest and boldest.

With all the stress leading up to the launch it took a while for me to realize we had actually succeeded. There had been little sleep and a ton of stress. I had framed success my whole life in business terms and here I was climbing to what I hoped would be the pinnacle of success.

It was a crazy time and I was breathing work every second of the day. At one point, a complete stranger stopped me in the street.

"Excuse me, lady, I have been walking behind you for five minutes and you have not lifted your eyes from the phone even when crossing the street," he told me. "I think you have a problem!"

If a stranger feels compelled to stop you on the street, you probably do have a problem.

I admit: Since the phone (a Blackberry at the time) was helping my productivity levels, I was on it all the time. "A feeling of productivity ennobles a person, connecting him to a sense of higher calling," according to *Pirkei Avot* (Ethics of the Fathers). Hence, the phone kept me closer to my higher calling! Why wouldn't I be glued to it? This time of my life marked the beginning of my phone addiction.

I also took to sleeping less, even for me. To assuage my Jewish mother guilt I put work aside from the time the kids got home from school until they went to bed, but that meant I would work well into the night. And since I refused to compromise on my social life either – going out with friends or on dates with Gavin is how I maintain relationships and unwind from the stress of my day – sleep was the first logical thing to go. For decades now, I've only slept for about four hours a night.

I pedantically one day sat down and figured it out like a math equation. Let's assume each night I sleep three hours less than the average person getting eight hours of sleep a night. Four hours a night equals approximately 1,000 hours a year. Let's assume the average person is productive forty hours a week. If you take my extra 1,000 hours a year and divide it by a forty-hour work week, you get twenty- five. So by sleeping less, I gain the equivalent of an extra twenty-five work weeks – almost six extra months a year.

I realize this sounds crazy and extremely unhealthy, but I did not want to give up on any other part of my day – and to me, sleep was the most boring and unproductive part anyway. I do not encourage *others* to give up on sleep, this was just my zany solution for "wanting it all."

As an entrepreneur, you ride a rollercoaster: One day you imagine making millions, the next day you wonder how you will pay your bills. It is like competing in a triathlon every month. But despite the challenges, I would not want it any other way. I love the thrill, the challenge and the risk. When I had previously worked at start-ups I realized this was something I could do on my own. I thrive in the chaotic and fast-moving environments that start-ups such as jdeal and Metroimma provide. I am at my best when I am building and creating.

While jdeal and Metroimma were flourishing, we launched buyisraelweek.com, an initiative that created real opportunity to support Israel. Through this site, we purposely helped Israeli-based clients who were trying to reach the American market. We were also countering the BDS movement (Boycott, Divestment and Sanctions) and making a statement at the same time.

The daily-deal market was not destined to last forever though. It had become glutted and we had become one of many. Also, the companies on whose behalf we offered coupons realized they could bypass the middleman and offer coupons directly to their clients. While jdeal had amassed an email list of nearly a hundred thousand subscribers, the direct marketing ecosystem was changing and the market would eventually consolidate to just one or two sites. We were starting to see the writing on the wall.

Allen's family and ours were on vacation together when, at the exact same time, both our phones pinged. It was an email to both of us from a potential buyer asking if we wanted to sell. Later that day, a second email came in, again, at the same time, asking the same thing. We knew we were at a crossroads. We either had to invest more and adapt the business model, or sell. Even Metroimma, initially set up as a networking site for moms, was becoming obsolete. We ran events and contests and brought together some 9,000 moms across the city during its heyday. But after a while Facebook and other sites eliminated the need for a third-party business.

Along with our jdeal database, we ran a strong marketing consulting business. Nevertheless, we saw the writing on the wall. We took those simultaneous emails as a sign from heaven and entered into negotiations to sell off the business. After several months we arrived at an acceptable deal and sold off some of the assets. I kept the marketing consulting side of the business and Allen went back to promoting other emerging technologies which he had done before this venture.

The crazy ride was over for now. But already, I had bigger things looming on my horizon.

Tales of a Modern Jewish Woman

Wake up call!

Those were the days I believed were going to be the pinnacle of my entrepreneurial career. I was extremely busy and flying high, riding the business waves and advancing my nonprofit. But sometimes busyness and planning just got the best of me in other areas.

That year on the day of Rosh Hashanah eve I had just returned from a business trip on an overnight flight and immediately set to work preparing for the dinner I was hosting that night. Dozens of guests were coming to celebrate with us, and since I had been away, there was much work to do.

In the midst of this, Caila – normally a calm baby – was screaming her head off and I couldn't figure out why.

She was a few months old and had been very easygoing up until that point. But that day she decided to become our worst nightmare. Her persistent howling only added to the pre-holiday stress. We checked her for everything. Did she have a fever? Need a diaper change? Everything appeared to be okay and she was just interrupting our preparations.

Until it dawned on me.

"Did you feed the baby?" I asked Gavin.

"No, did you?"

Caila had been starving for hours, but we had assumed – or hoped – that the other person had fed her.

This incident was a wake-up call to readjust my priorities.

CHAPTER 10

If I am not for me, who is for me; and if I am (only) for myself, what am I. And if not now, when?

Hillel, Ethics of the Fathers 1:14

"I am sorry, Mr. and Mrs. Samuels, but we do not have the resources to accept your daughter at our school."

Gavin and I sat across from the principal at a top Jewish day school in one of the five wealthiest zip codes in the United States.

Resources? We were talking about a school with three teachers for sixteen students in each class. Caila, who was due to enter a program for two-year-olds, would be coming with a master's degree special education teacher as a shadow and therapists paid for by New York City's Commission on Special Pre-School Education. The city was also responsible to train the teachers on how to include a child with special needs.

Gavin and I sat there dumbfounded. I was on the verge of losing my cool. Not only was this school financially equipped to take in Caila, we offered to pay any extra cost related to her education. In addition, the school was already educating our two other children. It did not make sense that a leading Jewish day school would refuse the daughter of community members. Was it simply based on her diagnosis of Down syndrome?

After Caila was born, while still in the hospital, we had decided that we were going to control the message. We sent updates to our mailing list about what a blessing our new baby was to us. When I went out with Caila in her baby carrier, I purposely had her facing out. It was my way of showing the world I was okay with her diagnosis. We celebrated her birth with a *simchat bat*, as we would for any other child. We have the same expectations of all our children – they are expected to reach 100 percent of their potential. That went for Caila too. This has always been our approach.

When Caila was six months old we had the opportunity to meet Prof. Reuven Feuerstein (of blessed memory) in Jerusalem. The esteemed professor was ninety at the time and had become famous for his revolutionary philosophy about the plasticity of cognitive functioning. His theories became the basis of a world-renowned teaching method and an institute where therapists, trained in the "Mediated Learning Experience," work with the cognitive flexibility of a child and build on his or her abilities to learn and progress – this is otherwise known as the Feuerstein method.

As a clinical, developmental and cognitive psychologist, Prof. Feuerstein believed that we cannot know human potential, regardless of whether a person comes from an underprivileged background or is diagnosed with a specific disability. Cognition is not fixed, it is modifiable, he taught. Feuerstein began his work with children with Down syndrome, but eventually extended this concept to stroke victims and people with dementia, cerebral palsy and autism among other conditions.

This humble genius met us with Caila at his office in Rehavia, Jerusalem, where he founded The International Center for Enhanced Learning Potential.

"You can expect exactly what you expect from your other children – tertiary education and grandchildren," he told us. "You will have to work very hard and so will Caila, but she has the potential. Promise me two things – that you will never put this child in a special education school and that you will invite me to her *chupah*."

Feuerstein believed that inclusion in regular education was a cornerstone of a child's development. Being surrounded by neuro-typical behavior would enhance Caila's potential and would eventually lead to her wedding someday. He expected that with hard work, she could lead a normative life.

As we held our six-month-old baby our hearts were flooded with hope. We got a copy of Feuerstein's book. The title was enough for me: *You Love Me!! Don't Accept Me as I Am.* In other words, Caila's cognitive ability was not predetermined or limited and it was incumbent upon us to maintain an environment that would keep her challenged and in a constant state of development. We would set high goals and push her to achieve her highest potential – as we do for our other children.

From there we visited another center for children with special needs in Jerusalem. The focus there was on "easing the burden" of the parents and siblings of a child with disabilities. The founder shared with us that it was difficult fundraising since no one really saw the hope or potential for the children with disabilities. But at least by easing the family burden, the *siblings* of the children with special needs could be successful. We got the impression that they had already given up on the child with special needs himself so the focus was on helping the other family members to cope. It was so dissonant from the message we got from Feuerstein.

Our philosophy was defined that day: Feuerstein spoke our language. For us, inclusion was a given.

Gavin and I had already programmed the Feuerstein philosophy into our minds. So, as Caila grew and was ready to attend a nursery program for two-year-olds, our next logical step was to approach the school our older children attended. We sent our children to a Modern Orthodox Jewish day school because of the shared values our family had with the school: Judaism, Zionism, Torah. We had explored all Jewish school options in the city and concluded that this school most closely matched our *dati leumi* (religious Zionist) values. It was Modern Orthodox like us and close to home. Should Caila not have access to the same Jewish education as our other children?

Our first outreach to the school regarding Caila went unanswered. They ignored repeated requests for a meeting. This already raised our suspicions. When they finally scheduled a meeting, we were met with an icy reception by the school's principal, who is a rabbi, and the head of the early learning program.

"You called this meeting, so what is it you want?" the rabbi began.

They sat back with their arms crossed.

"What we want is what we would want for any other two-year-old child. Your stated objectives are to give the children social and communication skills. That's what we want for Caila," Gavin responded.

We noted that we have two other children in the school and that Caila was high functioning. We pleaded our case that it was incumbent on us to find an inclusive setting for our daughter in a community that also shared our values – as we had for our other children. We would be paying full tuition and the city would provide an aide and other resources.

If we put Caila in a public school, she would not receive a Jewish education and we would not be able to attend Saturday events since we observe Shabbat. The lack of shared values would already impede her ability to thrive socially. Caila would always face challenges, but being at this school would ease those on a social and religious level. Maybe if you live in the middle of the country, these are points on which you will have to compromise. But we were living in the most highly populated Jewish city in the nation (and world, outside of Israel), thus, educating Caila in a Jewish setting should have been an easy objective. This is what we wanted for our daughter, we argued.

"Our school is not in that business," they told us, at the end of all that, shrugging off our request.

What business is that? I thought the school was in the business of Torah education. We as Jews have an obligation to give every Jewish child a Torah education. And what about the Special Needs Fund of the school to which everyone contributed – what was the purpose of that if not to include Caila?

"There is no room for shadows in the classrooms," they said. However, we knew there were shadows with students in other classrooms.

"The school cannot afford to have a Down syndrome child in the school."

What is there to afford? The New York City Board of Education would send an aide and we pledged to cover any extra costs including hiring an integration consultant.

"If Caila is let into the school, she will have to come with two shadows and this will take up the space of three toddlers costing the school thousands of dollars in tuition." Let's do the math. A child with Down syndrome comes with only *one* shadow.

"Well, those children scratch and bite," they also proffered as a reason. *Those* children? This was outrageous for its stereotypical and *inaccurate* statement about children with Down syndrome.

The excuses kept coming. We had responses for each one. Finally, we asked for at least an assessment as every other prospective toddler is afforded. We were refused that as well.

As we left, I explained to the rabbi that it was incumbent on us as parents to not accept this as the final answer.

A short time after that meeting, the rabbi called me to say he had done some research.

"I've spoken to the powers that be and the answer is still no," he said. "We consulted with hundreds of professionals and they unanimously agree that our school is not the right environment for your daughter."

"Hundreds, Rabbi? Really? There are *hundreds* of professionals who would provide an opinion without even meeting, let alone assessing, Caila?"

He faltered. I pressed on.

"Give me their names. Okay, give me the name of one. I'd like to know one professional who sight unseen would say the school is not suitable."

"We just don't have the space."

"But you have other kids with shadows in other classes."

Finally, I decided to cut to the heart of the matter.

"Are you saying you don't have room for shadows or are you saying you don't have room for a child with Down syndrome?"

"We just don't have room." Then, "It's also a liability issue."

"How? She's coming with a shadow and she will be a full paying student."

"The answer is still no."

Clearly the reason could be summed up by one extra chromosome. But this conversation was going nowhere.

"I will take this further," I told him. "I need to speak to people who make decisions."

"You can speak to whoever you need to. The answer will still be no."

We asked for and got a meeting with the co-presidents of the board, whose daughters, ironically, were assigned to Caila as a *chesed* (kindness) project, meaning they came over and played with her on Friday afternoons. Going into the meeting we already knew the response was going to be negative: We were given only a fifteen-minute slot. The co-presidents were both from wealthy families who had donated to JICNY and had hosted my Shabbat guests. One of them was a lawyer. He opened the meeting on a sharp note.

"Nothing you say can or will change our minds. We've made a decision and it is final."

"We are not here to ask to do what is easy, but to do what is right," Gavin responded.

Gavin reiterated that we would be paying full tuition and would be responsible for any extra costs that the city did not cover.

"We don't understand how you can lock her out of a program for two-year-old children," Gavin persisted.

The answer remained no. We had hit a brick wall and we understood there was no amount of persuading we could do. Gavin left them with this thought: "When God gives you a special needs child that's His choice. How you choose to treat this child is yours."

"Doing what is right, not what is convenient": This became our mantra as we continued to push the issue.

But this outright rejection shook me to the core. Being someone who was not raised religious but had my own experience of finding God at an older age, I began to question my faith. I dedicated my life to Torah principles because I gravitated to the message of love and equality inherent in its teachings. I truly believed that inclusion in education was simply a natural extension of biblical principles.

Our own Shabbat table exemplified inclusion. People from all countries and walks of life. People with challenges, both emotional and physical. Secular Jews, Ultra-Orthodox Jews and everything in between plus non-Jews as well! We had an open table and an open home. This is what defined us. The question of including someone with Down syndrome never fazed us.

And now people I held up as leaders, who had been faithful Jews way longer than I had, were outright rejecting my daughter and deeming her as beneath them, sight unseen. Gavin reminded me to judge Judaism by the Torah and not by Jews, who are also human and are prone to errors in judgment. But I was rattled. I spent weeks anguishing over this and I felt disillusioned since these were the people to whom I had entrusted my other children for their Jewish education.

For the next five months this battle dragged on. During that time, the school staff refused to meet with Caila for an assessment as they give to every toddler who applies. Finally, they stopped even giving reasons saying that we would not accept them anyway. We had countered every excuse that they gave with research and rabbinical arguments in favor of inclusion. They were clearly running out of ammunition, and excuses.

And if you know me, I don't take no for an answer.

By this point, I had already strategized a campaign to get Caila's case in front of the public eye while educating and persuading about the benefits of inclusion and equality. But I reined it in while Gavin and I weighed our options.

Before going public, Gavin and I wanted to consult a few rabbis to make sure we were on the right path regarding inclusion and whether we were doing the right thing by taking our situation public. We wanted to know what the Torah says about inclusion of children with special needs and we asked if sharing our experiences publicly would create a *chilul HaShem* (desecration of God's name).

Every single rabbi we spoke with – both in America and in Israel – except for one said that Caila absolutely should be entitled to a full Jewish education at a regular school. One said the school's position was "unconscionable." Some even called the school on our behalf. They also assured us that not only could we make this issue public, but that we *should,* not only for our daughter but for others in the special needs community. This was not just about us.

On Shavuot we read about how all of Israel stood together at Mount Sinai "like one man with one heart." No one was excluded. There was no special section for those with disabilities at Mount Sinai. Can we not learn from our forefathers' example?

With the blessing of many rabbis and a tide of anger carrying us, we were about to embark on dark times as we waged a campaign on behalf of our daughter. Telling me no is generally a bad idea. They did not realize what I meant when I said they would hear from us again. And little did *we* know just how vicious – even dangerous – things would get.

CHAPTER 11

Our lives begin to end the day we become silent about things that matter.

Martin Luther King, Jr.

"I am going to bring your organization to its knees. I'll make you pay for this." A member of the school's board of directors leveled this threat in response to our now very public inclusion battle for Caila's acceptance.

While I cannot prove whether by direct result of this threat, or mere coincidence, over the next few months, several strange challenges arose for the JICNY. I received a shocking letter from New York State informing us that JICNY owed $110,000 for workers compensation payments plus penalties and interest. But we didn't have any employees for the period in question. I was a full-time volunteer and we had no staff.

Proving this, as it turns out is not easy to do. How do you prove that an organization does *not* have an employee? It took a full year, many hours on the phone to New York State and some astronomical legal fees until the amount claimed was determined to be "a clerical error."

Just as we were solving that crisis, about a year later, one of our regular donors to JICNY was trying to make an online contribution when he received a notice that the organization was no longer registered as a 501(c)(3) not-for-profit organization. We called the IRS to resolve the issue and we were shocked to discover that we were indeed deregistered! When we asked why, we were told that as far as they could tell a request to terminate the 501(c)(3) status had been received from the organization. Certainly no one from our board, which included Gavin and I, had made such a request.

Naturally, it took the agency several months to determine that these forms did not even exist and that JICNY was fully compliant with all regulatory requirements of a not-for-profit organization. After dozens of unsuccessful calls to correct this problem, one particularly helpful IRS supervisor spent three hours with Gavin on the phone checking every possible reason for the situation. Again, after much tedious, expensive and time-consuming checking, it was determined to be a clerical error. This took nine months and, in that time, we were unable to take donations.

I could not prove that this man had made good on his threat, and maybe it was just a confluence of coincidental bad luck, but the timing was quite suspicious. In addition to the two coincidental "clerical errors," many wealthy families began pulling their funding from JICNY and left us financially struggling. We also received several anonymous *death threats* in the mail!

People would stop me in the supermarket and ask, "Are you Jodi Samuels?" This always ended in one of two ways. Either I was accused of wanting to drain resources from the school or I was lauded for my stance on inclusion. Even rabbis that tried to intervene on our behalf were warned that funding for their synagogues would dry up if they continued to lobby on our behalf.

Immediately following that unsuccessful meeting with the co-presidents of the school, we retained Richard Bernstein, a well-known disability lawyer who happens to be blind (Bernstein is now a Michigan Supreme Court Justice). We informed the school that our legal counsel wanted to understand why our daughter was being locked out without even being given an assessment.

Apparently, the name Bernstein caused ripples of trepidation at the school. While waiting for the school bus one morning with our children, a wife of one of the board members told me we were wasting our time: A former school executive had started a legal fund to make sure Caila "never stepped over the threshold of the school!"

Then Gavin got a call from a past president of the school, who had pushed us to send our other kids there years prior, encouraging us to "let it go" because this was creating a big headache for the school. The conversation started out friendly, but when Gavin insisted that mainstreaming Caila was the right thing, this man threatened to use his influence to destroy JICNY if we did not drop it.

Others had encouraged us to speak directly to an influential member of the board, someone with whom we attended synagogue. He attended services with Gavin at same *minyan* every morning and so Gavin caught up with him after services one day and explained our situation.

"Why don't you just put her in the Chabad nursery?" he asked.

"Chabad is not a long-term solution – it only has a pre-school program and at age five, we will still have to find her a school," Gavin replied.

"What's it to you? Perhaps in another three years *Mashiach* will come and you'll have nothing to worry about."

An absurd thought and clearly meant to brush us off. Gavin challenged him.

"What would you do in our situation?"

"I'd send her to a non-Jewish school. Look, you can bring her to the school for Hanukkah – we will let her light a candle or two. Bring her for Purim we will give her half a *hamantashan*."

He then turned and walked off. The audacity of someone in leadership speaking about your child as though she were are a dog coming to the school for *half* a biscuit, and us grateful for the favor!

Mama grizzly Jodi was unleashed after this episode. Around this time, we went very public with our issue. I wrote a letter to the rabbi who headed the school. I sent it to him, all the parents at the school, my own JICNY mailing list and I posted it online. I wanted to make sure that for the upcoming Shabbat, inclusion would be the topic of conversation at every dinner table in town. It created quite a stir. Many people had no idea what we were going through and were shocked at the situation.

After receiving such an overwhelming response, mostly positive, I saw an opportunity to create a more visible platform for inclusion. I started Caily's World, a Facebook page that advocates and brings awareness to special needs. One of our articles, "Caily's Story,"[1] was posted on Aish HaTorah and went viral. I also started hosting community forums to talk about inclusion. At our very first meeting, we had 160 participants plus local media coverage.

During this time, I also received a call from the office of the Archdiocese of New York. They had read the media reports about our battle with a Jewish school and they called to offer Caila *automatic acceptance* at any of their parochial schools if we wanted. That ought to shame the Jewish community that the Catholic Church not only caught wind of our problems but also offered to be the solution! Inclusion – both of special needs *and* a different religion.

As we were creating waves, we got an appalling email from one of the school's board members demanding that we desist. "You chose to bring this problem into the world. Don't make your problem our problem," she wrote.

"No, God chose to bring this person into the world, not me. Again…how you choose to treat this child is your choice," I sent off my reply.

As I mentioned, I did not know in advance that Caila was going to be diagnosed with Down syndrome, nor would I ever have expected that an official representing an Orthodox school suggest that I should have aborted my child! You can see why I was beginning to question my own religion.

All during this very public battle, I decided to keep my two older children in the school. We refused to succumb to intimidation, and we did not want the school to think that they could do this to other families – simply get rid of the problem. I was not going to let them get away with it. For the rest of the year I held strong.

Eventually our eldest child, Meron, who was nine at the time, started asking questions about the situation. Without saying anything

---

1. https://www.aish.com/jw/s/91699184.html

negative about the school or the principal, we simply explained they did not have the same expectations as we did for Caila. We mentioned New York Governor David Paterson as an example of someone with a disability who became successful because he was given the opportunity. The former governor, who is legally blind due to an infection he contracted as a baby, had parents like us. The family actually moved to another school district in New York so their son could learn in mainstream classes. He became the first disabled student in a Hempstead public school and graduated in 1971. We told Meron we were hoping that the school would allow Caila an opportunity such as this.

But our sensitive child found it difficult to fathom that Caila was still being blocked. At one point he admitted, "Imma, every time I see the principal, I want to talk to him about the Caila situation, but there are always people around and I am embarrassed." That was my wake-up call. One day my son would be old enough to understand the whole story, without our editing of the negative aspects. He would wonder, "*Where was my school, my rabbi and my community while my sister was being excluded?*"

That realization would amount to a waste of hundreds of thousands of dollars dumped into a private Jewish education. If the school could not actually demonstrate Jewish values for my son, their Torah teachings were to no avail. If this were the example under which my children were learning, they could end up disillusioned by a community that fails to practice what it preaches. Ultimately, I feared, they could walk away from their faith due to the hypocrisy they saw practiced by its leaders.

It was time for us to move our children to another school, not out of intimidation, but to give them a proper example of Jewish values. I was saddened that with a school right in our neighborhood we would have to send our children to another community.

At that time we received a call from Rabbi Binny Kraus, principal of Salanter Akiba Riverdale Academy in Riverdale (SAR), just north of Manhattan. Rabbi Kraus told us that he had heard of our challenges.

"We have children with special needs at our school. We have never had a child with Down syndrome, but if you want to bring Caila to us when she is old enough for our kindergarten program, we will learn and we will do whatever it takes to make sure we are successful," he told us.

That day, we made the decision to transfer Meron and Temira to SAR. There, they would see Jewish values in action. We felt so welcomed.

I demanded our deposit back from the first school, which they issued right away after the rancorous few months. They were more than happy to banish the specter of the Samuels from their midst even at a loss of forty thousand dollars a year.

In the U.S. and many other countries, laws have been passed which make sure that children with disabilities can go to regular schools. The term is called "Least Restrictive Environment" – which means children with special needs should spend as much time as possible with their typically developing peers. The system itself promotes the inherent idea of inclusion. That law applies to public schools, but I knew of Jewish schools in Brooklyn, Riverdale, Long Island and several other American and Canadian cities that applied that law to themselves as well. Everywhere but Manhattan. Why? Could all these schools be wrong and our local school be right? I could hardly think so.

Coincidentally (or not), that year at the annual fundraising dinner, the school honored the parents of a student with special needs. When accepting their award, the parents commented that "other people" were criticizing the school for being closed to special needs. And yet there they were enjoying the full acceptance of the school who was educating *their* child with challenges. But I also wondered if it was an obsequious honor since the father was a successful hedge fund manager who made large donations to the school. In fact, I "wondered" this publicly on Caily's World, asking whether, if Gavin was a hedge fund manager, would Caila have been accepted? The mother of this other child commented on my post, arguing that it had nothing to do with money – her son was particularly "smart."

Wait. What? Did she just say that on my Caily's World? She explained that her son's syndrome was different than Caila's. But in doing so she was calling all people with Down syndrome *dumb*! This was not just outrageous to me as Caila's mom, but to every single person who read this. A war of words ensued between her and my supporters until she finally deleted her comment.

Meanwhile, we checked out the Chabad Early Learning Center, close to our 97th Street apartment for nursery school. I recall arriving for our interview so nervous that my lip was quivering. I had experienced enough rejection from the one school and several others around the city, and I could not stomach another one. I was just so weary and emotionally drained.

The nursery teacher and principal who met us were surprised – if our other children were already at the other school, why we were coming to Chabad?

"Because they don't want her!" I burst into tears.

Pearl, the principal, looked at me in shock. "Every Jewish child has the right to a Jewish education. Of course we will welcome Caila." Thankfully, Chabad received us with open arms. It was the opposite of our experience with the other school where the management did not believe that including a child with Down syndrome was in their best interests, and many of the parents sided with that viewpoint. At Chabad, from the top down, the school believed that Jewish children should get a Jewish education. This feeling extended to the parents as well. They set a welcoming tone.

It took us a while, but we've come to realize that perhaps the principal at the other school was correct when he said they didn't have the resources to include Caila: they lacked open hearts and open minds.

To this day, even though that battle is over, our rallying cry remains the same. Our mission is to see open schools and *shuls* in our community. We are all made in the image of God and we must all take responsibility to include our fellow Jew. Every Jewish child has the right to a Jewish education and inclusion at all levels of community.

This experience had exposed a high level of hypocrisy within New York's Jewish community and it permanently affected Gavin's connection with the city in general. He would walk past these same people – like "Mr. Half-a-Hamantashan" – in synagogue or on the street and be sick to his stomach. Were these our influencers and leaders? It was not just about inclusion, but we had also been personally *threatened*. Gavin questioned how we allowed people to hold regarded positions in the community while they blatantly disregarded Torah principles.

Though we were shaken, we did not lose our belief in the Torah. If anything, our commitment was strengthened. We sought out biblical principles of inclusion and God's example of full acceptance of His people.

But many of our relationships were strained or broken after that. It was a dark period and the beginning of the end of our time in New York.

Tales of a Modern Jewish Woman

Did you ever know that you're my hero?

During the dark days of our fight to get Caila into a Jewish day school, if I needed some encouragement, I would glance at an article I had framed in my office. In one of the sweetest honors ever bestowed upon me, a 13-year-old girl, one of our neighbors' children, wrote an essay calling me her hero.

Arianna Samet's essay won first place in an annual Jewish writing contest. Her piece was chosen from among three hundred others from all over the world. Ironically, at the time, she was a seventh grader at the school that would end up rejecting Caila.

The purpose of the essay was to feature someone (dead or alive, Jewish or not) who "exemplifies a core Jewish value that is meaningful to you." Arianna said I exemplified the value of hachnasat orchim, *hospitality, or welcoming guests into my home.*

We met Arianna's family when we first moved to New York — they were our neighbors across the hall from our first New York City apartment — and became immediate friends. They were impressed with all the entertaining we did and, eventually, we joined forces. We frequently hosted joint meals from across the hall: we set up the buffet at their apartment and the seating at ours. That way we could maximize the number of guests we could host on Shabbat.

All of this clearly had a huge impact on young Arianna. And to this day, her words boost my spirits when I am feeling down and motivate me to carry on. Here is the essay in full:

"*Jodi Samuels is my hero. Jodi is the mother of three young children and sets a great example for them all. She is a warm person, whose home is always open; even to strangers. This is someone, who was given a challenge in her life, but has chosen to embrace it rather than just deal with it. But, it doesn't stop there. She continues to spread awareness and has provided opportunities for those with similar circumstances at first throughout her community, but now, throughout the world.*

"*Jodi exemplifies* Hachnasat Orchim *by welcoming others into her home. She and her husband Gavin, moved to New York City in the year 2000. They both grew up in South Africa and came to New York after having spent a few years in Australia. They only knew a few people when they arrived and felt that there must be many other "internationals" in New York, who like them, were lonely in a new country and were looking for a sense of community.*

"*She co-founded JICNY (Jewish International Connection New York), to meet the needs of international Jews in New York City. Beginning with one Shabbat meal in her home, she and her husband Gavin have now hosted over ten-thousand guests from other countries for both Shabbat and holiday meals. The organization caters to Internationals in New York City hoping to give them a home away from home with opportunities such as Torah classes and classes on how to find your future spouse. Since its establishment, JICNY has led to countless relationships and at least sixty marriages! Jodi's door is truly open to all. If someone needs a place to stay, Jodi will make room for them whether for one night or for months at a time!*

"*Any Jew who has lived in New York City from another part of the world has been touched by Jodi and the JICNY. In fact, this past summer my mother and I were in a restaurant in Paris. The waiter asked where we were from and we were surprised to find out that he had lived in New York for a couple of year's right across the street from our apartment. We were not surprised however, to find out that he knew Jodi. When we asked him about her, his face lit up. He said that he had eaten in her home a few times and that he had attended a number of the JICNY programs. While he didn't think that Jodi would remember him, he would always remember her with appreciation for the community that she helped him to have while away from home.*

"A couple of years ago, Jodi gave birth to her third child. A beautiful little girl, Caily was born with Down syndrome. Many, if not most parents, would look at the birth of a special needs child as some sort of punishment. Not Jodi and her husband. Rather than saying, "Why me," they said, "Of course us!" Their feeling was that who else should God choose other than ones who open their home to all and strive to make a difference for all. From the moment that she heard the diagnosis, Jodi has been hard at work making sure to give her precious Caily every opportunity that her other children have. She has also worked tirelessly to make sure that all Jewish children with Down's have opportunities.

"Jodi is not only opening her home to people and working on JICNY, she is also spearheading an effort to make sure that all children with Down syndrome who are high functioning, have the ability to be mainstreamed at a Jewish Day School.

"Jodi was nominated as a National Jewish Community Hero and was a finalist. She sleeps only three hours each night; not because she is not tired but rather, because there is work to be done, work to change the lives of others, work to change the world for the better!

"Jodi takes the core Jewish values of Hachnasat Orchim *(having an open house to guests) and helping those in need to a new level. While she is only in her mid thirties, Jodi has done more good than hundreds could do in a lifetime. Jodi Samuels is amazing and she is my hero!"*

CHAPTER 12

Whoever destroys a soul of Israel, it is considered as if he destroyed an entire world. And whoever saves a life of Israel, it is considered as if he saved an entire world.

Babylonian Talmud, Sanhedrin 37a

After being ignored, rejected, discriminated against and threatened, imagine our shock when a school principal called us and invited us to a meeting regarding our daughter's potential enrollment at a school. What a breath of fresh air.

After all we had been through with that school, it was healing to our souls when we received that call from Rabbi Kraus, the principal at SAR, inviting us to sit with him and the associate principal and head of the school's early childhood department. They had heard about our woes getting Caila into a Jewish day school. And when we heard the magical words "we are willing to try to do what is necessary to make it work," we were moved to tears.

That magical word *try* is all we ever asked for. Every professional that has ever assessed Caila has told us that she is an excellent candidate for inclusion. No one could be sure that inclusion would be the right long-term solution for her, but we knew that we were obligated to at least try, and especially at the beginning. After everything we had been through in our fight to have Caila included in a Jewish day school, we felt that SAR, an institution with the same size class and resources as the previous school, reflected true Torah values. *This* was the school that we wanted educating all of our children.

Meron and Temira were thriving at SAR their first year, so we decided we would enroll Caila too after her year at Chabad was over. I realized that with Caila, the transition would be much more intense. In the four-year-old class, pre-literacy skills are taught, behavior requirements are stricter and children begin noticing differences between them. Inclusion was about to get more serious.

I am passionate about inclusion. But I am also terrified. I always knew that the younger years would be the easiest. Caila was a cute toddler, but cute can only get you so far in life. As children get older, the social challenges get more complicated, especially for a child with disabilities. During that first year at SAR, the other children's language and play skills leaped ahead. They quickly became aware of differences between them and Caila. What was more distressing, however, was that Caila too became self-aware. My mother's heart broke for my baby.

While self-awareness is an excellent developmental milestone to achieve and is important for successful inclusion, it is a double-edged sword. I'd been warned by pioneers in the world of integration of people with Down syndrome that first to eighth grade is the hardest time socially, as your child becomes aware of his or her challenges. If Temira was having complicated social situations at ten years old, imagine what Caila would face.

Yet we pursued inclusion because of the long-term benefits and the positive examples of those who have gone before us. A friend's daughter with Down syndrome, who was mainstreamed through high school, graduated, found a job and got married! Her mom has been my guide and mentor, and I held her story as my beacon of hope. Through her, we know that inclusion works; it *is* worth it. If we could navigate the early years, the social challenges would improve.

The challenges of mainstreaming Caila on an academic and social level were ours to face along with the school partnering with us. But I believed the challenges of inclusion must be dealt with on a moral level by the wider community. As someone who did not grow up observant, as I became religious I spent a great deal of time defining who I am and the world in which I want to live. The opposition we encountered in trying to mainstream Caila at a Jewish school caused me to question the religious world in which I found myself. This world was dominated by money, politics and power games. This did not jive with the Torah that so inspired me.

In such a hypocritical setting, many hang on to *chesed* (kindness) projects to condone their lack of moral clarity. While the concept of *chesed* is obviously biblical, the projects become a crutch for people to help them *look* more religious and to check a box for their conscience (or their schools). This is why I loathe these projects. Most yeshivas require their students to go out and help a "needy person" in society such as the elderly, the homeless, the hungry or children with special needs. In our case, two girls came to "play" with Caila once a week. They felt good, they completed their requirement and, *tick*! Mitzvah accomplished. Later in life, they will probably send a nice donation to a special-needs organization. *Tick* again! More *chesed*. But they may never learn to open their hearts, home and schools.

What we fail to teach our children and what the community fails to see is that we need inclusion and acceptance, not superficial *chesed*. I'm not looking for someone to come and sit with my child, call her cute and feel like they've done something good. No, I need people to come alongside us during the hard times as well. You don't just get to host my child for a meal or a night and check a box that you've done integration. True acceptance is completely integrating my child in all aspects of society.

Such as our schools and synagogues.

And this might mean making structural changes to an organization's building or learning new methods of pedagogy and classroom strategies. True inclusion means my child will have equal access to education, community, religious services and social opportunities. I realize that may not be easy, but it is *right*. Inclusion is our calling as a society.

The Judaic concept of *tikkun olam* (repairing the world) goes beyond feel-good projects. We are striving for lasting change, to make a difference that will resonate through eternity. This is much more than an hour of volunteering.

The expression *tikkun olam* is used in the Mishnah in the phrase "*mipnei tikkun ha'olam*" (for the sake of repairing the world). This practice is important to help avoid social chaos. The phrase itself is included in the *Aleinu*, the Jewish prayer that is recited three times daily. This prayer, said to have been written by Joshua, praises the Lord for allowing the Jewish people to serve Him, and expresses hope that the whole world one day will recognize God and abandon idolatry. The phrase *tikkun olam* is used in the longer expression "*letakken olam bemalchut Shaddai*" – to perfect the world under God's sovereignty.

I once read a book that examines how different cultural and societal perspectives influenced educational experiences. In Italy, an American observer watched as a teacher helped each child put on his or her jacket before they went outside to play. The American suggested that the children could learn the independent skill of putting on their own coats like they do in the United States. The Italian teacher smiled.

"If the children dressed themselves then I wouldn't get to do this to each one before they went outside," and she kissed each child on the cheek before sending them on their way.

At a school in China, the American observer saw how the children wore smocks that buttoned at the back, which seemed inconvenient, and again hindered the children's independence. Until the Chinese teacher noted that this way the students relied on the help of their peers to button their smocks. The observer also saw a group of children playing with one toy car and offered to send the school more toys from her class in United States. The Chinese teacher opened a closet to reveal a pile of toy cars. They didn't lack for resources, she explained, but by giving access to just one car at a time, the children learn to play collaboratively. It was a matter of perspective.

Educational environments can offer meaningful life lessons taught through simple yet purposeful constructs in the classroom. And these small variations change the world one student at a time by building character. Classroom teaching methods can be utilized to achieve desired outcomes such as building character in our kids. And inclusion should be part of this design. This is how we can achieve *tikkun olam*.

Even after Caila was accepted at SAR, Gavin and I continued to raise awareness on the importance of inclusion. We realized the story is broader than us and that first school that rejected Caila – it was about individual hearts and communities.

We encouraged Jewish institutions to live up to their Torah mandate of unqualified acceptance by making their facilities accessible. We empowered families to take a stand and not take no for an answer when trying to mainstream their children. And through Caily's World we sought to change the negative, knee-jerk reactions to people with Down syndrome, that they are scary, ugly, retarded. We have an opportunity to educate the world about the possibilities and, hopefully, create another world for Caila when she gets older.

This is the example of our forefathers: *ke'ish echad belev echad*, as one person with one heart. Based on this we are to view every Jew as equal and as an equal receiver in our holy inheritance. Being less abled does not make one less Jewish. No, disabilities are ancillary to one's personhood and Jewishness. As much as it pains me to admit, Caila will always need support, but that does not mean she cannot or should not be afforded the opportunity to play *her* role in our community.

At the end of Caila's first year at SAR, we celebrated success. Though welcoming, the staff had initially been apprehensive about accepting a child with Down syndrome and uncertain whether they could meet her needs. However, the experience surpassed their expectations – not only for Caila, but for the other children as well.

The motto of SAR's high school is, "It's not just what you learn, it's who you become." In Caila's case, she was becoming a confident and integrated young girl. The staff said *they* had become better teachers. Other parents were able to overcome their skeptical responses to children with special needs in the classroom and, in fact, appreciate the diversity. And a class of young children spent their formative years learning that not everyone is exactly the same as them, and that they can, and *should* make friends with everyone.

Ironically, during those days Caila's favorite words were "me too." Our daughter had always wanted to be a part of the action. Her wish of "me too" was a message to the wider community, a plea for unconditional inclusion.

Tales of a Modern Jewish Woman

Outreach gone wrong, right or left

As part of our Jewish outreach we always want to see people returning to their heritage. But sometimes it doesn't always go the way we imagined. We've seen people change their ways based on our example, but sometimes they've taken it from one end of the spectrum to the other. Here are two such stories.

Once a year we took a JICNY rafting tour to upstate New York. The bus company we hired employed drivers who were Hasidic. They were so devout in their uncompromising beliefs that they wouldn't even look at me – the tour leader – because I was a woman, even when I had to give them directions on where we were headed.

One year, we returned to the bus after the rafting outing and we could not find our driver. Eventually someone located him swimming in the river – fully clothed in his black and white attire.

The following year we happened to have the same driver. Again, after rafting we returned to our bus and, deja vu, we could not find him. We knew to look in the river first and, he was swimming there, but this time stripped down to his undershirt, with his black pants rolled up. And he was even speaking with some of the people from our group with the slightest bit of eye contact.

A year or so later, Gavin and I attended a wedding that had mixed dancing. One man in particular got everybody's attention. He was obviously secular in jeans and no kippah, grooving on the dance floor. But oddly, he was dancing like a practiced Hasid, which was so incongruous to how he was dressed.

I said to Gavin, "Look at that man, he's dancing like a Satmar."

Later this same man came up to us and said hello, like he knew us. I was very perplexed since I had obviously never met him before.

"Hey, I'm Yoelish," he told us.

With a typical Yiddish name and a strong Yiddish accent on his English, I was incredulous.

"You don't remember me? I was your bus driver for your organization's rafting trips!"

I nearly fainted. This was the man under that black hat and bushy beard who had driven our bus?

"After coming on your trips I decided I wanted to be more like your people," he said.

Well, I'm glad he wanted to be like us, but he certainly had gone a bit farther than any of us would have!

The other side of the coin was the love story of Avi and Daphna. A southern belle, Daphna had moved to New York and was strolling through the Upper West Side when a couple sitting at a bar got her attention, since the man was wearing a kippah. It happened to be Gavin and me.

"Do you have any idea what is going on in this part of town for Jewish singles?" Daphna asked us.

Little did she know who she had stumbled upon.

Daphna met Avi at one of JICNY's Torah classes, and these two secular Jews eventually got married and even became Orthodox. Successful outreach, right?

The story usually ends there. But some years later, a man with a black hat and a long bushy beard, obviously Ultra-Orthodox, greeted Gavin and I at an event. I drew a blank. I did not know this man.

"I'm Avi!" he insisted.

It took awhile, but when the realization set in I could not believe my eyes. Avi and Daphna had become Hasidic. We were thrilled for our reunion and sent photos to our mutual friends.

"Why is Avi wearing a Purim costume?" one of them responded. Nobody could believe their transformation.

We ran into Avi and Daphna again years later at the Milan airport as we were catching a connecting flight. Avi called over their five children, all traditionally dressed in the same frum outfits in which the Hasidim normally clothe their children. Meanwhile I was in jeans and Gavin in casual travel clothes. Avi introduced us to his wide-eyed children.

"Tate and Imma wouldn't be together if it were not for these people," Avi used the Yiddish word for father.

These children, who probably rarely encountered people outside the Hasidic community, were aghast that a woman with uncovered hair and wearing jeans could have had anything to do with matching their pious parents!

By the way, they now live in Israel.

Chapter 13

In the place where there is no man, strive to be a man.

Hillel, Ethics of the Fathers 2:6

I often look at Caila and thank her for making me who I am.

Before this crusade for inclusion in Jewish day schools I was not the candidate for leading a movement or becoming a public speaker. I was known from the earliest age as the shy one. I never raised my hand to answer a question in school and, rather than socialize, I would rush home and bury myself in a book or *Fortune* magazine while strategizing business plans, whether my next lemonade stand or tutoring service.

As a teen in South Africa leading youth groups for a Jewish heritage organization, I was considered a reliable leader who dotted all the I's and crossed all the T's. However, I doubt any tour participant would remember me – I was not the bubbly, fun tour guide.

When I started the Shabbat dinner outreaches in Australia and New York, I made the effort to invite people, hanging signs and spreading the word, but once people arrived at my home I retreated to the kitchen. I didn't mind the cooking or the work it took to put on the event, just as long as I wasn't the one greeting, hosting and leading the prayers. Gavin led the *lechayims*. The purpose of the event was important to me and I made sure it happened – just as long as I didn't have to be the public face of it all.

In any leadership role, I was less like the sun, bright and unavoidable, and more like the moon, which is less visible but quietly affects the tide. As a leader in business and in my organization – and even taking Jewish teens on tours when I was a young adult – I had tenacity. I was tireless, reliable and passionate. Those are essential qualities. But I came to realize that they alone could not propel me in the fight for inclusion and Caila's rights.

If you met me after Caila was born and heard about our public campaign for inclusion, you would presume that I was always an outgoing public figure who seamlessly moved in public settings with extreme confidence. If you've seen me leading massive events with hundreds of people, and even speaking on stage, you'd assume I'm thriving in that setting. Not even close. I was successful in business because I got to hide behind partners who fronted the company and did the necessary schmoozing. My business partner closed the contracts face to face with the clients while I happily hammered out the details back in the office.

It was the same with JICNY. My passion drove me to create the organization, but I did so with co-founders who would take the lead during public events. I preferred planning and running the events in the background.

It wasn't until Caila was born that I began my reluctant sidle toward center stage. I remember the exact moment when defensiveness as a mom trumped my shyness and the mama grizzly emerged. I was at a bar mitzvah with Caila, who was attached to me in the infant carrier, facing out, as was my habit. While there, I noticed a woman openly staring at us. It made me extremely uncomfortable, but even more so, defensive and angry. I couldn't believe someone had the gall to gawk at me and my princess. I stewed for a while until something snapped inside me and I did something I had never done in my life – I approached a total stranger ready for all-out confrontation. Advocacy on my daughter's behalf basically took control over my being.

As I stormed over to this woman, all timidity dissipated. But the woman caught me off guard.

"You're probably wondering why I'm staring at you," she greeted me with a smile. "I'm a member of the tribe as well."

Something you would quickly learn as a new parent to a child with Down syndrome is that, just like Jews identify Jews around the world, so do family members of people with Down syndrome. The Samuels were now members of two tribes.

After having a lovely conversation with this woman, whose daughter had Down syndrome, I reflected on the sudden surge of audacity that arose in me, enough to overcome the panic of confronting a total stranger. It was so rare for me to feel this way and yet the feeling rose up so powerfully and naturally.

I knew at that moment I could no longer remain silent, especially when it pertained to Caila. As the parent of a girl who may never have a voice in society, I realized I had to become that voice. It would mean advocating for Caila when no one else was standing up for her rights or battling injustice. This required me drawing from my inner strength in order to overcome a paralyzing fear that had long ruled my behavior.

"In the place where there is no man, strive to be a man." This passage in *Ethics of the Fathers* spoke to me, to be the man. Moses tried several times to pass off the crown of leadership to someone else. But God insisted he was the one for that task and required him to speak up for his people. He asked him to "be the man" for the children of Israel. I understood from this that I too needed to trust God to overcome my own fears in order to take a stand. It was the righteous thing to do.

Not one person who knew me from before Caila was born could've imagined me as the community activist that I've become today. We call it "Jodi BC" and "Jodi AC" –before Caila and after her.

"Jodi? Surely not our quiet, shy Jodi," a rebbetzin from my youth group in South Africa exclaimed when she saw me leading an event decades later.

Even my own parents were in shock when they saw me in action in New York City. They were dizzy from watching me running the show and welcoming guests from the stage at one of my JICNY events. This was totally out of character from the sheepish Jodi that grew up in their home.

Years later, after I made aliyah, my ulpan teacher brought an article to class that featured the seventy most influential female immigrants to Israel. And there I was, one of the profiles. I could just feel the skepticism oozing from the other students. *Her?? She makes a difference? She doesn't even answer questions in class!*

Ironically, I have always been an extrovert and I enjoy being around people. I am driven to accomplish my calling. It was just that in many circumstances I am too intimidated to open my mouth and engage around people I don't know.

Before the inclusion battle, I subconsciously began finding my voice and a reason to speak up in public. After Caila was born, I determined that I would speak at her *simchat bat*, the traditional Jewish celebration after a girl's birth – something I did not do at the birth celebrations of my other two children. Gavin was more or less the family spokesman and I was quite content with that. But with Caila's arrival I felt it was imperative that people hear my voice so they would be certain I was okay with Caila's diagnosis. As we decided from the beginning, Gavin and I would control the message about how people perceived our daughter. If I didn't open my mouth, I held no sway over it.

Caila began to draw a voice out of me I didn't know I had. I've always been confident in myself in private, but it was public life that stymied me. As I started to go public, to recruit supporters and to speak to the media, this new and different Jodi came out, spurred on by my inner mama grizzly. I had to "be the man."

What helped me overcome my own weaknesses was to look to Moses who, as the quintessential leader, led the children of Israel out of Egypt to the Promised Land. In addition to learning from his empathy and humility, I took comfort in the fact that he had a form of a disability – his speech impediment caused him to question his ability to fulfill God's calling in his life. As a person who still stresses out in a public setting, I could relate to this.

People rightfully would assume I must be outgoing if I'm running an event or speaking at one, but what they don't know is it still takes a little Dutch courage to calm my nerves before I go on stage. Once before an event where I was expected to teach, I had two separate friends inform me, "The vodka is ready for you under the counter." Those are people who know the real me. Yes, that wasn't water in the bottle!

In the years since Caila was born I've had to consciously take a stand even while petrified. I've accepted that tenaciousness and reliability are not enough to change the world.

Tales of a Modern Jewish Woman

Hacked!

For weeks leading up to our JICNY heritage trip to Poland in 2019, I was more anxious than I had ever been about a tour. I had committed to a twenty-person minimum. No problem, I assumed, since the previous year the trip sold out fast. However, for some reason, that year it was like pulling teeth to get people to sign up. And every unsold spot would cost $1,600 out of our own pockets. I frantically advertised the event on any channel I could and, somehow, we scraped to the end – the last person signed up at 11:05 on Monday night and the group flight leaving New York was at 4:00 on Tuesday afternoon.

My relief would be short-lived, however.

After a five-hour flight delay, I arrived in Poland to several missed calls that had come in while we were flying. As the gracious host, though, I wanted to first greet all of our attendees, some who flew in from South Africa and Israel. I would deal with the calls later. But they kept coming, and finally, about an hour away from the hotel, I got the head of Jroots, our tour operator, on the line. He was screaming at full volume.

"Do not let anyone off the bus until you release the payment! You haven't paid and we cannot cover your group's expenses!"

I blanched at his accusations. "What do you mean? Of course we paid!"

He did not let up. "I am so sick of your excuses! Every day it's a different story about the money. Now you are in Poland without paying, and your group is not getting off the bus! The hotel will not release the rooms."

Trembling, I quickly got off the call to find the email from his bookkeeper confirming payment. I also opened my bank account and took a screen shot of the payment to Jroots. We had paid! What was his problem? We had worked together for years and he knew I was reliable and always paid my bills.

Meanwhile the bus had stopped at Treblinka extermination camp, one of the most somber memorial sites in all of Poland where up to 900,000 Jews were murdered during the Holocaust. My phone rang again, but I refused to speak while walking through Treblinka. The tour operator texted me – he didn't care where I was, "Call now!"

"The reason we didn't get the payment was because that wasn't our bank account you sent it to – your money went to a different bank account and not to our organization," he explained.

I immediately called Gavin in New York and he ran to the bank to stop the payment. They told him he was the third person to walk in that day who had been the victim of cyber fraud – but it was too late. The money was gone.

In the post-mortem analysis, we found that my inbox had been hacked in the weeks leading up to the payment. The tech people found on the server an invoice that came in from Jroots at 8:09, was intercepted at 8:10 and replaced with a new email, containing an identical looking invoice with different bank account details, a few minutes later. The scam had started about two weeks prior when the hackers sent a fake email from Jroots saying they had changed their bank account. So we didn't question the new number when we received the counterfeit invoice.

An entire shadow conversation transpired between Jroots' real bookkeeper and fake me – while I was having a shadow conversation with a hacker who was pretending to be their bookkeeper! The hacker sent responses in my name with a litany of excuses of why I hadn't yet paid. Meanwhile, I received thank you notes and "payment confirmed" as if from the bookkeeper.

If only we would have spoken, we could have avoided this, but we only corresponded by email.

My people were getting back on the bus after an emotional day at this death camp. Wiping my tears and putting on my best face, I decided I was not going to let my worries affect their trip. We were approaching our hotel and I wasn't sure if we were getting off the bus. But I carried on as normal, every so often consulting my phone, trying to sort out this disaster. My head was spinning, my stomach churning.

Jroots was also scrambling and came up with a donor who agreed to front the money if we paid it off in monthly installments. I hastily agreed – there was no way I could let my tour participants suffer after paying their own way and already having made the journey to Poland.

For the next seven days, my stomach remained in knots as I wondered whether JICNY would survive this financial blow. How would we pay off the loan? JICNY raises about $80,000 a year so $34,000 was nearly 50 percent of our budget.

But the participants had no idea. The trip went off without a hitch and without indication of my distress. On the last day of the trip, I told my group what had been going on behind the scenes. They were astounded that I had buried my anxiety, continued to guide the tour, plus managed to connect with them personally. Somehow, I maintained my composure and remained effective and present despite the circumstances. My leadership had truly been put to the test. And we eventually paid off the loan, partly from JICNY donations and partly out of our personal funds.

CHAPTER 14

I wouldn't change you for the world, but I'd change the world for you.

Unknown

Three years later when we were considering making aliyah we visited a few kindergartens in Jerusalem, including Nitzanim, a bilingual Hebrew and English *gan*. We were looking for a school that would take Caila if we came to live in Israel. Gavin and I spoke to the teacher through a translator, and we steeled ourselves as we leveled the bomb: that our daughter has Down syndrome.

Dreaded silence followed the translation.

"Az mah? Ani lo mefachedet," the *ganenet* shrugged her shoulders, *So what? I'm not scared.* She wondered why this was even an issue.

Just like the one school rejected Caila sight unseen, this Israeli teacher was willing to accept Caila who at that point did not speak a word of Hebrew combined with all the challenges any child would face when moving countries. You can imagine our shock when this happened after all the trauma we'd been through in New York. It made us wonder if Israel was perhaps not more open minded toward including children with disabilities in regular education. We would eventually find that out firsthand.

As for us, though, from day one we've believed that inclusion is a right even if it is not the easiest thing to do. We believe in Caila's potential. The people who do not believe in her also fail to envision her continuing her studies post high school and getting married. We do, and Professor Feuerstein did.

I remember once at an evaluation of Caila's IEP (individualized education plan) in New York, the district administrator, who held a Ph.D. from Columbia University, was pleasantly surprised that Caila had a normal IQ. She was five at the time.

"But you know," she peered over her glasses, "all people with Down syndrome plateau by age six."

She proceeded to lecture us on how earlier IQ tests are based on concrete variables and that, later in life, when tests are more abstract, Caila would not score as high. When I started quoting research that suggested this was patently untrue, she simply replied that I should come to terms with "reality." She put "family counseling" on the list of suggested therapies, particularly for me, since clearly I was living in denial.

I still roll my eyes. This Ph.D. never met Reuven Feuerstein. And he knew firsthand the possibilities: His own grandson has Down syndrome, yet he finished high school and served in the Israel Defense Forces.

I wonder what kind of experts (if any) the school board consulted who had such strong opinions against admitting Caila to the day school in New York without even meeting or assessing her. It was discrimination based on a diagnosis, without even the most basic attempt to consider Caila as an individual.

In the *parashah* when the Jews were counted in a census, disabled Jews were neither excluded nor separated. Every human is created *betzelem Elokim* – in the image of God. This is the mantle of responsibility that we collectively committed to at Mount Sinai. Until we come to this understanding, we fail our community.

I also believe that inclusion is more than just accommodating people who are different. It means extending them *dignity* as well. Rights can be enforced. Dignity must come from the heart. That is a much harder battle to wage. Whether it is therapists, psychologists and doctors rendering verdicts on your child's future or the higher-ups at a school refusing them entry based on their diagnosis, we are constantly fighting a mindset that disdains people with Down syndrome.

Down syndrome is the most common genetic disorder at one in seven hundred births. It can also be diagnosed in the womb. In many countries, when the baby is diagnosed in the womb as having Down syndrome, the termination rate is 90 percent, including in the United States. A few countries – such as Iceland and Denmark – boast a near *zero percent* Down syndrome birth rate. In America, 90 percent of women who have pre-natal screening that identifies Down syndrome choose to abort, according to several data sources. Emotional phrases such as eugenics, reproductive rights and murder are bandied about.

Even with all the genetic testing, doctors still cannot identify all possible diagnoses before birth. So, it feels that Down syndrome – easily identifiable with increasingly sophisticated prenatal screening – is targeted from the outset.

My choice not to undergo amniocentesis was influenced by my religious beliefs and my conservative South African upbringing. I believe that every child has the right to life, happiness and love irrespective of any challenges.

But what has contributed to the rush to "eliminate" this syndrome? In studies, Dr. Brian Skotko, director of the Massachusetts General Hospital's Down Syndrome Program, found that 97 percent of people with Down syndrome said they like who they are, and 99 percent said they are happy with their lives. More than 96 percent of siblings said they feel affection toward their sibling with Down syndrome and 88 percent said they were better people for having a sibling with DS. When you are in the situation it is easier to see the positive side.

Not all the world sees it our way though.

After Caila was born we received what Gavin and I called "guilt offerings." People who had not given gifts after our other children were born bought expensive presents for Caila. And worse, *they left them with the doorman*! I saw this in one of two ways. One, they themselves didn't know how to speak to us about this. And two, it was their way of thanking God it didn't happen to them. These were nothing more than sympathy gifts which made the *givers* feel better. They avoided looking us in the eye. If they were really concerned with our feelings, they would have met us face to face. But people don't know how to cope with Down syndrome.

When people did come visit there was often the proverbial elephant in the room. I would always be the one to break the ice. For example, they'd make small talk like, "Are you nursing?" I'd reply, "Yes, they say nursing is *great* for babies with Down syndrome!"

Since Caila's birth, Gavin and I have been drawn into several conversations about genetic testing. As we became more outspoken and led community events about inclusion, we became the go-to couple to field calls from families that gave birth to a baby with Down syndrome and wonder if they should keep him or her. We've received many calls from women who received diagnostic confirmation that they are carrying a baby with Down syndrome and have to decide whether they will abort. A close friend of ours who struggled to get pregnant expressed to us her dilemma about whether she should do genetic testing when she finally got pregnant and whether she would keep the baby if it had Down syndrome.

Here is what we do not say: "*Caila is great! She is the light of our family and we could not imagine life without her so, absolutely go ahead and have the baby!*"

While I have my own beliefs that inform my personal opinion, my goal in these conversations is to help people make an informed choice and not just have a knee-jerk reaction either way. We live in a world of information overload, yet we remain uninformed. So, when we speak with people about raising a child with special needs, our goal is to provide more than just sound-bite answers. We give a broad view of the issues from possible medical problems, therapy sessions and time commitments plus the joys and accomplishments. I always then give the parents the blessing that they should get their own clarity to make a decision with which they are comfortable.

Now with the prevalence of social media, these debates always seem to be in the forefront. One such row was in 2014 when a woman posted on Twitter, "I honestly don't know what I would do if I were pregnant with a kid with Down Syndrome. Real ethical dilemma." She tagged famed scientist and atheist Richard Dawkins who responded rather crassly: "Abort it and try again. It would be immoral to bring it into the world if you have the choice."

When defending himself later he noted, "Apparently I'm a horrid monster for recommending WHAT ACTUALLY HAPPENS to the great majority of Down Syndrome fetuses. They are aborted."

Which is true.

Most babies born with Down syndrome are born to women who didn't do invasive prenatal testing for financial or religious reasons. I am happy to be part of the minority that did not do invasive testing or abort.

In Third World countries, many people with disabilities are hidden, subjected to terrible living conditions in institutions and, in some cases, are tethered to posts unable to move. While this is appalling, the Western version of hiding people with Down syndrome is through "sophisticated" means such as pregnancy termination and exclusion from the public arena. It's a hard comparison but, to me, the abuse of Caila's rights and of her dignity in our informed and resourceful community was just as shocking as what we see in some underdeveloped nations.

You would assume that in the wealthiest Jewish community in the world, we would be more advanced in our approach than, say, in some African nations where there isn't even a word for Down syndrome, such as in the Swahili language. It is unconscionable that in *sophisticated* Manhattan, our children have limited or restricted access to Jewish education, inclusion programs in synagogues and physical access to our institutions.

Until it affected us, I was unaware of the existing discrimination. But once we experienced this personally, Gavin and I committed to fight it. We crusaded for real change through a campaign of advocacy and awareness. This shouldn't be difficult considering there are laws and state-supported services for inclusion. What we encountered personally was part of a widespread problem in the Jewish community (and society as a whole) of segregation of people with disabilities.

But few people outside the child's circle of therapists and family members are concerned.

When I started my Jewish journey more than twenty years prior I was captivated by the dictate to be "a light unto the nations." After our personal battle I see that we cannot bring clarity to the world if we fail to be a light for our own people.

It is only when the world in general, and our Jewish community in particular, stops talking about "those children" and appreciates the intrinsic uniqueness of every person that we will emerge as a whole, good and inclusive society. We must take action to eliminate discrimination and demand change. It is biblical!

In the *parashah of Ki Tisa,* the children of Israel are required to take a census. God implements an interesting method. Rather than counting all men over twenty years old one by one, he tells them to donate one half a shekel, then they would just count the money. That way God shows how he considers everyone an equal: Not only is each person counted, but there is no discrimination based on the size of the donation. Each person is equally valued. And each person is *counted.*

Now I wait in hope for this thinking to conquer a wider majority of people. We should work together for the best of each other. Instead of assuming our children with disabilities will fail, we should set high benchmarks for success and then help them reach these goals. Let us together strive to help them reach for the stars.

Let us give them the dignity they deserve.

Tales of a Modern Jewish Woman

Life

When we were living in New Zealand, we became friendly with an Israeli couple who were based there for their work. On one Shabbat during dinner, the topic turned to abortion, and Gavin explained details of the procedure including some of the more gruesome components.

We lost touch with this couple after they took another posting overseas. Ten years after this conversation though, the woman became pregnant and the doctors suspected the baby had anencephaly, a serious congenital abnormality involving the absence of a major part of the brain and skull and not compatible with life. All of the doctors said the best thing to do would be to terminate the pregnancy. So did her parents who were both doctors. They flew back to Israel for further consultations and the consensus continued along the same lines – abortion was the best option, they were told.

But they remembered the discussion we had at our Shabbat table and Gavin's words about the procedure and they made a decision: Whatever God gives us He gives us for a reason. We will deal with whatever.

Even though in this situation, an abortion would probably even be permitted under Jewish law, and against everyone's wishes – even their own parents – they decided to have the baby. And after that stressful pregnancy, they gave birth to a perfectly healthy child!

Years later this couple found a way to contact us so they could tell us how Gavin's words resonated with them – and saved their baby's life.

CHAPTER 15

When we are no longer able to change a situation, we are challenged to change ourselves.

Viktor Frankl

Having a child with special needs invariably prompts people to say the most irritating things to you in an ironic attempt to bring comfort.

"God chooses special parents for special children."
"You must be so strong."
"She doesn't look like she has Down syndrome."
"Down's kids are always so happy!"
"God only gives you what you can cope with."
"Why didn't you find out before she was born so you could do something about it?"

Some statements are outright disgusting, but I do realize that most people are well meaning. I usually bite my tongue, but sometimes I respond (because I can't help it): "How do you feel that God apparently does not consider *you* strong – or special – because He did not give you a child with special needs?"

I once commented to someone that I could not understand why people abort babies with Down syndrome. The person, who totally missed the point, responded, "Well, at least Caila's high functioning."

After all the inappropriate comments we encountered after Caila's birth and the ongoing battles we had for Caila's acceptance in several different settings, we were a bit…frustrated to say the least. So much so that Gavin wanted to print a T-shirt that would make a statement: *"I have an extra copy of chromosome 21 as a reason for my cognitive challenges. What's your excuse?"*

We would all wear these shirts with pride as a family hopefully bringing truth and clarity to the world and a heavy dose of sarcasm for people that just don't get it.

I stumbled upon a quote that aptly sums up how I feel about us parents of children with disabilities: "You never know how strong you are until strong is your only option."

That's more like it. Many days we are tired, and we don't want to put in the extra hours and resources – but that is simply not an option. This doesn't make us particularly "strong" or "special," but it certainly does take more out of us on every level.

What people could say is, "Wow, this is going to be a tough journey." "Is this hard for you guys?" "It is probably going to take more work as a parent." And most importantly, *"Mazal tov!"* Only one couple said that to us at the hospital. A child is a blessing no matter what the diagnosis.

When you first give birth to a baby with special needs you are inevitably forwarded the famous essay by Emily Perl Kingsley, "Welcome to Holland."

Kingsley, who herself has a child with Down syndrome, wrote the piece in 1987. The premise is that you were planning a vacation to Italy, but the plane landed in Holland instead. The metaphor being that you give birth as expected only to find out the child comes with a surprising diagnosis. Not going to Italy, your dream vacation, is disappointing if not devastating. Holland isn't what you planned for, but you come to find it is beautiful in its own way.

Meanwhile, all your friends do end up going to Italy and they tell you how great it is. *"And the pain of that will never, ever, ever, ever go away…because the loss of that dream is a very, very significant loss,"* Kingsley writes. *"But…if you spend your life mourning the fact that you didn't get to Italy, you may never be free to enjoy the very special, the very lovely things…about Holland."*

Parents of children with special needs have a love-hate reaction to this poem. On one hand, when I first read it, I agreed with the overall analogy. A lot of it is true – Kingsley would know. On the other hand, Kingsley should have noted that going to Italy would have been like staying at five-star hotels. The trip to Holland is like a budget backpacking trek where you have to plan each step, lug your own bags, cook your own meals, take public transit and face traveling challenges every step of the way. Being a parent of a child with special needs is hard work. Holland may be a wonderful place to visit, but in this analogy, it is no vacation.

I would quickly learn that my work was never done. The productivity and efficiency that I was used to in business and home life was extremely challenged after Caila's birth. For example, doctor visits which were routine for my other children – the usual colds, flus and odd broken bone – were intricate and numerous for Caila. We were swept up by a myriad of appointments after her birth to check for all possible medical complications related to or caused by the extra chromosome – from eyesight and hearing to possible thyroid issues and leukemia of all things! Many of these checkups would morph into annual appointments to make sure she was still okay.

Then we set out to discover what our rights were and what therapies Caila was eligible for by law. Procuring all the therapies and interventions – and ultimately cramming those into our busy lives – was the next challenge. Speech, occupational, physical therapy sessions are just a sampling of the new additions that crept into our schedules.

Another difference I found between having "typical" children and one with an extra chromosome was school registration. When I wanted to register my other children in a school, I filled out an application, sent a check and – voila! – they were registered. You read in detail about our struggles in finding Caila a school. It involved many steps, a lot of advocacy and a lawyer. Our public war with the Jewish day school notwithstanding, many other schools also rejected us sight unseen, recoiling at the mention of a child with Down syndrome.

But after we finally got Caila into a school, our work had only just begun. I became the self-appointed CEO of Caila's intervention team juggling all the aspects of inclusion. I had to maintain daily contact with teachers and therapists, attend meetings almost weekly and battle bureaucracy on a regular basis.

Just as one battle ended another one began. After we were warmly accepted at SAR Academy, we had to fight the Department of Education to make sure it provided Caila's support services: physical, speech and occupational therapy at the school, an aide and a special education plan. We met with countless officials to lobby for services.

The conversation went something like this:

"We believe Caila is doing great in an inclusive environment and we would like to continue," we would begin.

"Great, then she doesn't need as many services," the education official would say.

Um, that's not what we meant! We then would have to explain that she is thriving in an inclusive environment precisely *because* of the support she gets. Hence, her services should not be cut. Inevitably, the city's response is, "Well if she needs so much support then she should be in a special education environment and not in an inclusion class."

This repeated itself every year – the ongoing argument of rights versus success.

As parents, our goal has always been to make sure Caila gets what she needs and deserves by law. Under the Individual with Disabilities Education Act, a child is entitled to a Free and Appropriate Education (FAPE). Many times, what the Education Department deems as "free and appropriate" is at odds with what the parents believe. I heard one scary example where an administrator determined "FAPE" for a wheelchair-bound child was at a school with no elevators!

We hired a lawyer to fight for Caila's rights, but sadly, many parents could not. I met a mom who emigrated from Mexico. She didn't have enough money, time or English to fight the system and, ultimately, it was her daughter who suffered in a less-than-optimal school environment.

Every year, we had to argue that we believed that the most suitable education for Caila was in a private Jewish day school where she would get religious instruction. As practicing Orthodox Jews, we contended that the most suitable environment for Caila was in a Jewish educational setting. It isn't "inclusion" if she cannot attend a birthday party on a Shabbat because of our religious obligations, or if she would miss learning about the Jewish holidays at school.

And this was just the educational aspect. We also invested in Caila with additional opportunities and activities from swimming lessons, gymnastics, a tutor and when she was older, a sleepover camp. Our weeks became packed with therapies and activities.

To be frank, it was all overwhelming – and still is. When Caila was born we briefly dwelled on, *"Why us?"* Then with a surge of hope and inspiration we said, *"Of course us!"* But as the years progressed, many days we plead, *"Oh my God, please help!"*

We were drowning. In wanting to give Caila the best, we stretched our resources to the maximum.

Though it is harder on the parents, we believe the concept of inclusion in school is a kind of therapy too. My husband, "Dr. Gavin" quickly grew weary of approaches and treatments that he said merely packaged "hope in a bottle" and presented it to desperate parents who were willing to pay any price to help their child. When we found that the Feuerstein Institute – which works extensively with children with Down syndrome and autism – had published more than two thousand peer-reviewed articles and numerous books, we latched on to them. The primary belief at Feuerstein is that a person can learn and change with the correct intervention. Its goals are inclusion in society, community and school. Like I said before, Feuerstein spoke our language.

The Feuerstein philosophy is about actively accepting the challenge, believing your child can grow and constantly setting higher goals. But this also requires a lot of extra investment. From the beginning Caila has had about twenty hours a week of various therapies and tutors *in addition* to her hours at school.

While I call myself the CEO of her team, Caila is the one with the schedule of a CEO.

I believe that I adjusted well to Caila's diagnosis because we only found out on her third day of life. By that point I had cuddled her and had gotten to know her for the baby she was and not through a label. The social worker assigned to Gavin and I shortly after Caila's birth insisted that our lack of sorrow was abnormal and there must be something wrong with us. I did confess to her as we prepared to take a trip to South Africa to bring Caila to meet her grandparents that I was petrified... about the crime there. She threw her hands up in disbelief: "The crime in a distant country nags at you more than your daughter's diagnosis?"

My first concerns were focused mainly on how Caila's diagnosis would impact our other children and our fast-paced lifestyle. As time moved on, I began to see the world differently. Caila had challenges, but she was an adorable and interactive baby and toddler. And life was still "normal." Caila became the light of our lives and that of our extended community. Rather than typifying the generic "retarded" person with a series of physical conditions that I read about in those books, she was just another one of my children.

I developed a new philosophy: Life does not have to be perfect to be wonderful. Another hurdle for me was the high stock society puts on physical and mental acuity. Our Facebook and Instagram accounts are lined with snapshots of perfect families, dazzling success stories and enviable travel adventures. Contrary to that, the books I read about Down syndrome listed all of the potential *problems*. I presumed my own social media accounts would forever remain bereft of happy tales.

All people with Down syndrome will have different symptoms manifest due to the extra chromosome, but much of the information given to parents at the outset can leave them with the impression that their child will have every symptom! And that life would not be worth living. This mindset is patently wrong.

Caila came with physical and cognitive challenges, but she arrived with an already developed empathetic soul, something that is under-appreciated in our world. When she was just two, she noticed another young girl her age at the playground who was not yet walking. It turns out that girl had cerebral palsy and was apprehensive to play with the other kids. Caila walked over to her, held her hand and – with a hug – coaxed her to join in with the other kids.

That is one of the reasons I am writing *this* book. Hopefully a new parent will read our story and begin their journey with hope rather than horror and despondency, which we managed to avoid.

In fact, Caila's gift to me is the different lens I now have to view the world. She became my own *tikkun,* my correction. Before I had

Caila, I lived a fast-paced, high-stress life. I didn't stop to take a look at who or what was around me. Caila taught me it is okay to take it slower, appreciate life, to love unconditionally.

Having Caila has also changed my perspective of what I actually consider a challenge. I realized that while chatting with my grandmother in South Africa. She asked me about Caila and I shared some cute stories, the usual grandparent fodder. She enjoyed it, yet at the end she commented that even though Caila is cute now, I will need to look after her for the rest of my life. "What can you do when God gives you challenges," she sighed.

Her voice had the resigned tone of: "*The poor Samuels, their lives are full of tragedy.*" My grandmother had two grandchildren and a great-granddaughter with disabilities. I understand her worldview is rather pessimistic, but I do not consider raising Caila a burden. Many people resign themselves to the fact that they have a child with disabilities. We decided to reframe our world with a proactive approach.

One inspiring and thought-provoking movie that I saw confirmed our approach and our instincts of inclusion and treating your child as "normal." *Yo, Tambien* (*Me, Too*), is about a young man with Down syndrome who graduated from university and landed a regular job. He fell in love with a coworker and the movie was about their relationship and its challenges.

The heart-wrenching theme, for me, however, was the question, "*What is normal?*" In the movie the son asks the mother "Why did you want me to be normal?" She tells him – in my words – "I had no choice but to allow you to reach your potential."

That is exactly how I feel about Caila. It is why we invest so much in her, at a cost to our own time, money and, sometimes, sanity.

But I still struggle with all these questions. We strive to help our children be "normal," but is this fair to the child? And what is normal anyway? Is it fair to put Caila through so many hours of therapy? Should I also be investing this much in my typical children?

It is an exhausting mental and emotional process to revisit these questions on a regular basis. Going to Holland has been much harder than going to Italy would have been. But since that's where we landed, we are committed to make the most of it.

Tales of a Modern Jewish Woman

Mommy and her wine

We got a call from Caila's psychologist, one of the therapists who had been treating her for years and knew our whole family well. She asked to meet with me, and I should bring Gavin too, she suggested.

When we arrived, we made small talk and then she asked very seriously, "Can you close the door please?"

Uh-oh. I was waiting to hear something I didn't want to about Caila.

"I feel we've known each other for so long so we can be honest. When Caila plays with dolls, her role play always revolves around wine. The dolls always say to each other, 'Mommy loves wine.'"

I must have been turning as red as the finest cabernet I've ever had.

"Jodi, I know you've had a hard time since you made aliyah. But I felt obligated to ask you, do you need intervention?"

Of course I didn't, but my daughter was basically telling the world I was a raging alcoholic! If only the psychologist knew what happened that very night when a new therapist came to our house. Caila answered the door, and as we've taught her, she welcomed the woman.

"Do you need some water or something to eat?"

"No, thank you. You're so sweet!"

"Well, maybe you'd like some vodka or whisky instead?"

The therapist almost fell to the floor.

I could not have been more proud of Caila, however. Not only was she articulate and polite, she clearly understood that alcohol was for adults. She proved that when she started planning her own bat mitzvah about four years in advance. When she called our relatives in South Africa she would tell them she was planning "adult games" for her party and the prize would be wine.

While some therapists have inferred that perhaps I have unresolved issues from having a child with special needs, I like to note that the "unresolved issues" come from challenges way harder than our daughter. They stem from the rejection, the lack of resources and the exhaustion that accompanies our battles to get Caila what is due her by law and figure out what is the right support for her.

Chapter 16

We achieve greatness by handing our values onto the next generation and empowering them to go and build the future.

Rabbi Lord Jonathan Sacks

As a South African, I was inspired by my fellow countryman Oscar Pistorius, the South African who rose to fame as an Olympic sprinter – but is a *double-leg* amputee. Unfortunately, the "blade runner" as he was known, is now more famous for being convicted in the homicide of his girlfriend in 2014. But before the very public trial and conviction, he was known for overcoming a major disability and setting an extraordinary example.

After competing in the Paralympics, Pistorius fought for and earned the opportunity to enter non-disabled international competitions. At the London 2012 Olympic Games he ran in the 400-meter sprint making him the first amputee to compete in a track and field event at the Olympic Games. He finished eighth and he made history.

Pistorius was born without fibulas in his legs and had both legs amputated before his first birthday. His mother, who was a strong figure in his life, never treated him differently than her other children. She would say to the boys, "Cole, go put on your shoes. Oscar, go put on your prosthetics."

When he was interviewed by the media, he described how his family treated him the same as his siblings, and he did not realize that he was different, just that he had different shoes.

So maybe it's a South African thing, but in our family, we have always made a point of treating Caila exactly the same as we did our other children. We asked the same of her schools. Focus on Caila's abilities rather than on her diagnosis. We truly believe that Caila will flourish in a setting where she feels just like everyone else.

Long before Caila was born, Gavin and I had agreed on our parenting style. When Meron was born, rather than adapt our life to the baby's "schedule," he came along with us on our schedule. We didn't skip a beat. We still went out every night and traveled overseas. Same after Temira was born. We never declined late Shabbat dinners just because our children had a certain bedtime. We took them to the same restaurants we enjoyed going to before they were born, rather than the "kid friendly" ones. While we are very strict and disciplined at home, my children grew up feeling they were "allowed" to do "adult" things. Temira, when she was seven, told me her friends snickered about Gavin and I being strict parents. She defended us, noting that she would get to go out later and travel the world – privileges that she didn't see any of her friends enjoying. This perspective certainly suited us!

We never negotiate over homework or housework, but the tasks they are required to do come with these "adult" privileges and eventually resulted in our kids developing deep interests in world events, social and political issues and very sophisticated food preferences as well. And because we never catered to the babies' schedules, our children grew up to be flexible and adaptable to many different situations. What in modern life works according to a schedule anyway? So why train children to live by a schedule when that is not going to be their reality when they are older?

We decided on this lifestyle well before we had children. We saw divergent parenting methods play out in our own home with some guests while we were living in Australia. Group A held to a strict schedule. The parents freaked out when they were five minutes off schedule, and so the kids learned to freak out as well every time things did not go perfectly. There was a lot of yelling. Group B was relaxed about schedules and the baby was flexible and went with the flow. If we decided we wanted to go out at night, the parents simply picked up the sleeping child and came along. We decided to adopt the "Group B" approach when our time came. And we succeeded with our first two children.

Then Caila was born and for a few moments we wondered whether having a child with special needs spelled the end of life as we knew it. We quickly decided, "No way." Initially we were overwhelmed with all of the doctor appointments and therapies. But once we sorted out Caila's busy days, we just rearranged ours a bit. We still went out at night, we still traveled. Of course, it helped that Caila would turn out to be high functioning and could easily cope even with overseas travel. Sometimes people don't even realize we have a child with special needs.

It was a learning curve, but we also maintained and adapted several key non-negotiables in our child-rearing approach when it came to Caila. We are not laxer with her just because she has Down syndrome. Our expectations for her are high. She has responsibilities just like her siblings, albeit modified to her abilities.

Experts warn that it is very easy to inadvertently spoil a child with special needs. You might assume that is out of pity, but it is more out of convenience. Often times, we would prefer to do things *for* Caila than wait for her to do it herself. But if we did that, she would never learn for herself. We want to help her gain independence. We treat her as we do our other children, we just need more patience. With Down syndrome, milestones take longer to achieve, but most of them do come along eventually.

We've learned to give Caila chores that she can accomplish on her own so she will feel successful and will continue to grow in her abilities and responsibilities. Then we raise the bar every so often to challenge her to get to the next level. The goal, exactly like for our other children, is to keep her challenged but not to the point of causing her stress.

It really helps that Gavin and I are on the same page when it comes to…well, everything regarding parenting. And thankfully, having a child with special needs did not shatter our unity. We still approach parenting, even of Caila, with exactly the same mindset.

Parenting today is just hard even without the element of extra needs. Gone are the days when parents drew on the wisdom of the generations before them. Instead of our own mothers and grandmothers being the sole source of wisdom, we are bombarded by information, much of it good, but most of it sound-bite material that may or may not be relevant to our lives. I drew much inspiration from my friend and mentor Slovie Jungreis-Wolff, author of *Raising a Child with Soul*. She teaches about parenting and family life through timeless Torah values, which haven't changed with the trends or wavered throughout the generations.

Today, very few role models exist for our children. Politicians, celebrities and sports stars are all too often caught in various public scandals. Even religious leaders are constantly in the news for moral failings. How can we bring up our children to be righteous, moral, giving and normal in our crazy world? I have come to one conclusion: We, as parents, must be the light and the example.

The Midrash speaks about Joseph, who in one of his most challenging moments, had an image of his father come to mind. That gave him strength to avoid temptation. Moms and dads should be the image that keeps our children on track in an increasingly depraved world.

But that being said, let's be real. Life never goes as expected and disappointment always lurks around the corner. And so, Gavin and I have developed a principle that we use to our advantage: slick marketing. We as parents control the message that we give the kids, so we make everything sound *amazing*! Even the direst situation can turn into a dream come true if you pump it up just right. For example, once when we were traveling we made a reservation for the last room available at a hotel. Two queen beds and five of us. Some quick reframing of the situation was needed. We asked our kids, who, as a treat wanted to sleep on the special bed on the floor. We hyped it up so much that by the time we arrived at the hotel they were arguing about who deserved the special bed!

Whenever the kids had a new babysitter we did not allow it to be the stressful situation that many of our friends had to deal with.

Rather, we told them that if they were really well behaved all day, they could have a new babysitter as a reward. If they were not well behaved, we would cancel the new babysitter and call someone they already knew. By the time she knocked on the door my kids went running over to hug her and couldn't wait for us to leave for the evening.

We also hyped up dentist visits of all things, harping on the shiny teeth and prizes they would acquire after. Instead of an unhappy, traumatic time, it became the envy of the siblings who did not have a dentist appointment that day. Our kids actually nagged us to go again.

Admittedly these shining examples ceased to work at some point, especially as they became teenagers. But we emphasized the positive – and true! – side of otherwise unpleasant situations, and I believe it engendered gratefulness and flexibility in our kids. They once headed to school straight from the airport after a seventeen-hour flight from South Africa. Everyone asked them if they were tired.

"In our house we do not get jet lag," Temira replied matter-of-factly, repeating a small piece of indoctrination we had told them since they were very young.

Another time, Gavin was putting Temira, five at the time, to bed, when she spontaneously said: "Abba, when I get married, I really want a baby with Down syndrome. They are so special."

If nothing else, we are definitely good at marketing.

And maybe we are doing something right. When he was only five, Meron decided to forgo birthday gifts and ask his friends for donations to the charity he had recently heard about. Another time for school he was asked to write about the highlight of his holiday break. Unbelievably, he chose to write about the night he volunteered to help Gavin and I run a JICNY Torah class. I was so elated to see that he enjoyed being a part of what was important to us – and that it was meaningful to him as well. Not many children would find "volunteering" exciting.

But we've also had our share of parenting fails.

As teenagers traveling in Milan, Meron and Temira were arguing so much and so loudly that a nearby homeless man asked me if I needed any help with my children!

Our situations are never perfect, but sometimes they are really funny.

Tales of a Modern Jewish Woman

Model parenting?

Sometimes parenting takes the proverbial village. The Samuels children grew up with people constantly milling in and out of the house.

Temira loves to retell how one summer when we opened our apartment to several different guests staying at the same time, she was staying there with a friend, plus another couple and a recent divorcée who needed a place to stay. None of these people knew each other.

Meanwhile, from abroad I arranged for a contractor to come and fix something in the house. When he showed up, everyone assumed he was just another guest! He was also rather confused when no one in a house full of people claimed ownership or could tell him what the problem was that he was there to fix.

Later a rabbi stopped by for a meeting with one of the guests. He too was puzzled as to who everyone was and why we, the owners — of all people — were not there.

But this is our version of normal at Camp Samuels.

I had always pat myself on the back for the wonderful lessons I assumed we were imparting to our children with this open-home hospitality, juggling being a working mom, scheduling date nights with my husband and modeling activism on Caila's behalf. So it came as a bit of a surprise when Temira knocked me off my high horse with her own perspective.

"Imma, why don't you just admit you're the worst role model for a mother? You're wild, impulsive, irresponsible and always out partying!"

Gulp! Not what I was expecting.

I hope when she is older she will see it my way. Here's to hoping... lechayim!

Chapter 17

**A friend loves at all times, and a
brother is born for a time of adversity.**

Proverbs 17:17

I have another philosophy that I applied to parenting which proved to be extremely prescient.

I bought the children an ice cream to bide the time while we waited at the airport. Mind you, one ice cream for the three of them. Temira got a spoon and promptly shoveled in way more than her fair share. When Meron challenged her on this, she looked at him very seriously and said, "Meron, you know life is not fair."

I suppressed a laugh. Temira was just repeating what I would tell my children all the time: *Life isn't fair*! The sooner our children learned this concept, the sooner they would be able to cope with life.

And when you have a sibling with a disability, life can seem *really* unfair frequently. The emotions and stresses for siblings of children with special needs are numerous and complicated. They will navigate these feelings and evolve with them their entire lives. Every stage of life will bring new challenges to the siblings just as much as to the child with the disability.

When the doctors informed us of Caila's diagnosis, one of my first worries was how this would impact Meron and Temira. Would they have to take care of her later in life? Would they be shunned from the community because they have a sister with special needs? Would this affect their marriage prospects?

I consulted a rabbi who is also a dear friend and expressed my concerns. He put my fears to rest.

"Jodi, one day I was at a wedding and I saw this young woman with her sister who had Down syndrome. I watched her and I thought, the level of empathy and love she showed to her sister is something she would show to her husband and own children one day because it is a part of who she is. I said to myself, 'This is the woman I want to marry.'"

Indeed, he did marry her. And his response gave me hope and a new perspective.

When the children were younger, Meron and Temira adored and doted on Caila, and, for the most part, their relationship was just that of typical siblings. Later, in their teenage years, they still loved and defended their sister fiercely, but the requirements, responsibilities and social pressures placed on them were not typical for children their age. As they surpassed us in our Hebrew abilities, Meron and Temira started helping Caila with her homework when we, the parents, could not.

Siblings of a child with special needs also tend to become independent rather fast. That's because so much of the parents' time goes to the child with special needs. Ohel Bais Ezra, an organization based in New York that provides support to people with special needs and their families, produced a film about siblings of these children. When interviewed for the film, Temira observed how much time parents spend with their child with special needs, a theme echoed by many of the siblings interviewed in the video. No doubt, Caila gets more of our time than her siblings.

We had to be extremely conscious to spend one-on-one time with our other children, even scheduling dates with them. Gavin and I both had our special times with them. I'd take Temira for a manicure or a movie and, separately, I'd get a burger with Meron. They need to feel that they get their share of quality time with us, not the dregs at the end of the day when we were drained from work and Caila's therapies.

The siblings, sometimes even subconsciously, are aware of their parents' already heavy load and don't want to add to it. They make their own way and figure things out for themselves. One expert called that "internalizing issues" and warned that these siblings are "at a greater risk than average of developing emotional issues, anxiety, and stress." Avidan Milevsky, Ph.D. and a professor of psychology in both America and Israel, also noted "the double-edged sword of responsibility." Siblings tend to become extremely, if not overly, responsible. They seem mature and well- adjusted on the outside, but this may lead to emotional distress. Kids are still kids, and though a sibling may frequently be called upon to act more mature than their age, it doesn't mean they are emotionally ready to.

When Caila was a few years old, I took her and Temira to the playground just a day after we returned from South Africa. Jet lag and a late night had turned Caila into a really grumpy toddler. Another child at the park asked why Caila was whining.

Just seven at the time, and assuming the child was asking about Caila's "special needs," Temira's answer was curt.

"She has Down syndrome, and if you have any other questions, ask my mother sitting over there."

Temira was experiencing that "double-edged sword of responsibility" – defending her sister while explaining her behavior. Not easy to ask of a seven-year- old.

Caila once had an accident while in the carpool mortifying her brother and sister. Another time, she hid at the school and no one could find her for several petrifying minutes. These stressful moments placed Meron and Temira in awkward situations with their peers, torn between embarrassment and loyalty to their sister.

After receiving a diagnosis of disabilities at birth, many parents grieve the child they will never have. Too young to understand perhaps at first, siblings may undergo different seasons of grief later in life. They grieve the typical sibling experience they will never have. From anger, jealousy, guilt, resentment and sometimes even embarrassment, they experience a wide range of emotions. Many of them go through soul-searching of, "Why her and not me?"

Parents must pay attention.

Many times, siblings try to hide or suppress their own feelings because they understand that their brother or sister with a disability has more urgent needs. Some may try to act perfect in order to compensate, while some may outright rebel.

On the positive side, these siblings will develop empathy, compassion, a strong sense of justice and responsibility. I believe that by focusing on building and balancing these positive traits, we can raise healthy siblings. I see this in Meron and Temira. We have always been open with them and have allowed them to process their feelings along the way.

We sought out expert advice from the outset to try to make this road smoother for all of us. We learned that siblings need to know that the child with special needs supports *them* as well, whether that means attending award ceremonies or sports games. In our case, we travel extensively as a family and during that time all the children are engaging in the same activities. We are touring sites as a family and enjoying new places in the world together. It is a wonderful bonding experience. We also have Shabbat, every week, where our daily activities cease temporarily, and we can connect on a family level.

Another aspect we learned to monitor is assigning responsibilities. Perhaps it's not "fair" if we ask Meron to do the most chores and Caila the least, but we try to assign tasks according to our children's abilities. On one hand, we do not want to overburden Temira, but we also cannot frustrate Caila with tasks that are beyond her. Meron and Temira understand that they are more capable in many things, but we don't want them to be resentful either. It is a tough balancing act.

We also heeded some good advice to keep our children in the know regarding Caila's challenges from the cognitive to anything medical. The experts say that keeping your children in the dark, usually in order to protect them from scary information, actually backfires. First, they feel excluded. Second, their imagination can conjure up something worse than what their sibling is actually suffering.

When occupational, speech and physical therapists began a steady stream through our doors on a regular basis, the kids wanted to know why. We explained that Caila wasn't as strong as a typical baby and she needed extra help. We just explained it on their level.

Then there is what I call my impatient parenting style, which for better or for worse, I apply to all of my children equally. *"Come on, just do it, just hurry up!"*

My children see how I treat Caila the same as them. We never made excuses for her and we have always held the same expectations. We expected her to behave properly out in public just as we did the other two.

As they've gotten older it's been interesting to see how my children react with a healthy attitude to others with Down syndrome. When they saw a boy with Down syndrome at a wedding they got excited and ran over to meet him.

Our transparency has paid off and our children openly and honestly process their feelings. They also help educate others. Once we were with some friends and the children stumbled upon a video clip that had gone viral of a Labrador playing with a toddler with Down syndrome. The children were all watching the clip when our friends' six-year-old asked, "What is Down syndrome?"

Before any of the stunned adults could respond, Temira – eight at the time – promptly and matter-of-factly answered.

"Oh, it's just like Caily – someone who learns a little slower and sometimes needs extra help and therapists to catch up and learn better."

Good answer, Temira!

While I would've loved to have added a few (million) points, Temira's real-life example of her sister did more to explain than I, or even Google, ever could have.

Tales of a Modern Jewish Woman

Caila's Biggest Cheerleaders

When Caila was born we were given advice: Don't label; act normal and be transparent with your other children. From the day Caila came home from the hospital, we spoke about Down syndrome in front of the kids and we haven't shied away from speaking of her ongoing challenges. We were told that the level at which a child asks questions shows the level of their understanding.

So we proceeded accordingly – and we were pleasantly surprised to see from very early on how our children's perceptiveness and empathy were honed by Caila's presence in our lives.

At Caila's simchat bat, *Meron went straight up to the learned rabbi to ask him a question.*

"Why does everyone say Caila is special?" he demanded to know, and without waiting for an answer he continued, "All children are supposed to be special, correct?"

As children usually do, he ran off without waiting for an answer, but it showed his already burgeoning understanding and sensitivity just a few weeks after Caila's birth. At school Meron befriended the outsiders and the kids who were bullied. I was always floored by his sensitive soul.

Years later, I watched a film with Temira featuring a high functioning man with Down syndrome who was once an actor. I had read a book about him around the time Caila was born and, based on his successes, I shared with Meron and Temira all the amazing possibilities for people who have Down syndrome. It was so encouraging. But by the end of the movie, however, we saw how he was living at age forty – and I was utterly deflated. The man lived in a semi-independent home situation and worked a lackluster job.

"Wow, is this it?" I thought. I had so much hope that with all we do to invest in Caila — extra therapies, inclusion, etc. — she would thrive. But after I saw this movie, I wondered, will she only end up at a tedious line job while living a life supervised by others?

"No, Imma! She's so much more high functioning!" Temira insisted. She listed examples of how Caila was different from this person at every step of the way.

I thank God for all of my children, and I am so happy that Temira and Meron are growing up to be Caila's biggest cheerleaders.

Chapter 18

I am for my beloved, and my beloved is for me.

Song of Songs 2:16

Gavin likes to say he picked up his wife off a street corner. Technically, he did. On that fateful day in Jerusalem near Zion Square as I chatted with a friend, Gavin approached us and asked for directions. Gavin met a confused and idealistic young lady who hadn't yet found herself, but somehow this young medical student had the patience to press through my standoffishness and eventually got me out on a first date.

I'm not sure if it can be classified as a "date" since I was engaged to someone else. Gavin, however, would not know about that "minor" detail for months to come.

It was interesting that I was so comfortable with Gavin from the start. Normally I was shy and never started – or even continued – a conversation with someone I didn't know. From the outset something about him calmed my nervousness and discomfort with a stranger. Maybe the breathtaking vista overlooking Jerusalem from the promenade, the *tayelet*, in south Jerusalem helped, but I poured out my heart to this fellow South African. I excitedly told Gavin about the Fachlers, the lovely couple with whom I had stayed in London who opened their home to any Jews who were in need of a place to stay or a warm Shabbat meal. I told him how I wanted to be like them. I also revealed my passion for travel and my quest to see as much as the world as my entry visas would allow.

Gavin and I were aligned in every way from the outset. He loved the idea of Jewish outreach and travel spoke to him as well. We were both Jews who had recently become *baalei teshuvah*, and our respective outlooks plus our common upbringing were already unifying factors.

Decades later, Gavin is my anchor and soulmate, and we are still on the same page about almost everything. But that didn't just happen. Marriage is hard work. And, poor Gavin, being married to me is extremely challenging. For all my leadership skills and my toughness, I am both a princess and a crybaby at the core.

People ask us how we knew we found the right person even though we were so young when we met. One cannot know every scenario in advance. For instance, Gavin and I never discussed how we would cope if God gave us a child with special needs. But we held similar life values which transcend the situations that arise and challenge us. That was enough for us to "know" our relationship could work.

And thank God. Because the truth is, siblings aren't the only ones affected by the presence of a child with special needs in a family. When a child is diagnosed with a disability, the assumption is that the marriage will become way more strained than the norm. All kinds of extra stressors accompany this diagnosis – and those can affect your relationship.

After having lived in several countries together, traveling extensively and parenting two children already, Gavin and I had already built a strong foundation during our years of marriage. Nevertheless, the moments that unfolded after we heard the news about Caila were the make-it or break-it moments for our marriage as much as anything else. When I shared my thoughts with Gavin that I felt God gave us this child, Gavin agreed without hesitation. It was this decision that defined how we would parent her and how we would handle the stress and demands associated with that diagnosis.

Gavin, the astute man that I married, quickly observed that in families of children with a disability, an exaggeration of the traditional male-female roles often emerges: the mother usually takes on the bulk of the additional responsibilities of the child with special needs often largely to the exclusion of the father's involvement. This kind of gender fragmentation can well lead to additional tension and, ultimately, resentment between the parents.

Since we have always had an egalitarian relationship, we strove to keep it that way after Caila was born. Gavin and I are both career-minded, and so we decided when we started our family to share the role of raising our children and continuing with our respective careers. When Caila came along, this presented a new level of logistical complexity, but Gavin made it a point to keep this balance. We attend the numerous assessment sessions together, we share the countless trips to various therapies, we take turns doing Caila's homework with her (when it is in English) and we take equal responsibility for the never-ending hours of helping her inch toward her milestones.

Rather than drive a wedge into our relationship, having a child with special needs has created even a stronger bond between us. It gives us a common purpose and a shared responsibility for our child. It has caused us to find new and creative ways to work together and support each other. Gavin often encourages fathers of these children to get involved as much as possible for the benefit of the whole family.

We are two people with completely different ways of coping with stressful situations, but we make this work by giving responsibility to whichever one of us can cope best with a given situation. My friend, Deborah Grayson Riegel, who is a business coach, gives great advice in her book *Oy Vey! Isn't a Strategy*. Marriage consists of strategies tempered with flexibility that help us weather the challenging times. When we "assign" tasks based on our strengths in our marriage, we succeed better as a couple.

We also employ three principles: giving, being flexible and encouraging our shared passions. Giving is always number one. Embedded in the Hebrew word for love (*ahavah*) is a clue to the essence of a successful relationship. *Ahavah* has the same root as the word for "to bring" (*lehavi*). Relationships only survive when both people are focused on giving: What can I *bring* to the table? Gavin sets the ultimate example: He wakes up every morning and asks himself how he can make his wife happy today. I really need to learn from him. The essence of a relationship is not how I can make myself happy, but how I can make the other person happy.

The next ingredient in any successful relationship is flexibility. Marriage is all about flexibility. In Jewish philosophy and Kabbalah we have the concept of contraction and expansion. Every force in the world requires equal and opposite expansion and contraction. A good marriage operates like that. People who do not have the ability to expand or contract (be flexible) will have trouble in a long-term relationship.

Having shared passions creates opportunities for us to connect and to experience the world together. Our shared passions – from Jewish outreach and traveling to listening to jazz music, drinking good wine, advocating and changing the special-needs world – create moments of connection. Many couples live parallel lives failing to connect over shared passions and points of connection.

What's important to Gavin should be important to me and vice versa. We so often look at issues through our own eyes without seeing our partner's perspective. If it's important to the other person then we should be able to shift our priorities. I have traveled the world for Gavin's career and he has supported my tireless passion for community work.

Being in a relationship often means having to leave your comfort zone. One of the hardest adjustments for me when we first got married was getting used to Gavin's need to be silent and unwind. He is a big thinker and not a big talker whereas I need to talk and emote through every issue. When Gavin returned from work I would launch into a detailed description of my day and he would just grunt every now and then. I had to learn to give him some space to think in silence and Gavin had to recognize that his wife needed meaningful conversation. We met in the middle.

These foundational principles of love, flexibility and shared passions better prepared us for having a child with special needs.

We also learned early on how to balance each other. For example, Gavin was not in favor of buying our Upper West Side apartment which we absolutely could not afford on our credit card, which I thought was a brilliant idea. I have a huge appetite for risk, but that inherent unpredictability turns Gavin's stomach. On the other hand, Gavin matter-of-factly recounts stories of dealing with emergency room patients in Soweto with axes stuck in their heads. I can't look at my children's paper cuts or scraped knees! I have such a queasy stomach.

Actually, speaking of my stomach. It's not just blood that makes me queasy – so do diapers and anything, well, gross. Despite having had three children of my own, I have somehow managed to not change a single diaper in my life. Gavin agreed to be the solo diaper-changer before we had children. That means of the roughly ten thousand diapers that have been changed for my children, *none* have been changed by me.

But Gavin traveled a lot, so I called friends and neighbors in emergencies. Believe it or not, I even had a friend take a taxi to come bail me out in the middle of the night once in New York.

Aside from that, Gavin spoiled me in many other ways. Every Friday since we started dating, he has given me flowers for Shabbat. He started this tradition when he was a financially struggling medical student and has continued to this day – even if he or I are overseas. He simply arranges for a delivery of flowers to wherever I am from wherever he is. Gavin also insists on taking out the garbage when he is home. He says princesses don't take out garbage. But it is not about buying flowers or taking out the garbage – it is about making someone feel special. Gavin makes me feel special. He has made himself my prince and hero. And I leave him notes thanking him for all these thoughtful gestures, even the small ones, so he knows that I still appreciate him and I do not take his actions for granted.

Temira, when she was nine, observed that so many single women who came to our house would pine over how much they want to get married.

"Then when you suggest someone, they say no," Temira said. "Why don't they just marry someone like Abba? Not good looking, not bad looking, but a good husband and a great father!"

We have also always been advocates of "we time." Gavin and I go out almost every night. We noticed that many of our friends stop going out once they have a baby, but we decided to push through the exhaustion of having a baby. It is important to switch from the titles of "mom" and "dad" to becoming Jodi and Gavin, because that is how we started out and fell in love. "We time" is essential oxygen for a constantly growing relationship.

The humdrum of carpools, diapers (if you do change them), school lunches and homework can wear on a relationship. It gets boring and evaporates the adventure and fun out of life, degenerating into a purely logistical relationship. That's why we intentionally infuse fun and adventure into our lives. From midnight concerts to climbing Masada to watch the sunrise, to camping and wine festivals, we seek out the fun in life. These shared experiences create memories and keep passion alive.

These are the ingredients of a good marriage.

Gavin often says being married to me is like being on a high-speed car chase which never ends…except for the occasional crashes! I am always planning (large) events, opening new businesses and inviting dozens of people to our home. Nevertheless, we are moving in the same direction, even if our speeds vary, and that is of utmost importance. When I say Gavin puts up with hosting an average of fifty guests per Shabbat and hosting two hundred events a year, I mean, yes he deals with the enormity of it, but he also shares the vision of these outreaches and he is happy to lead the prayers and *lechayims* every week at Shabbat dinner.

An Israeli woman who had attended several of my Shabbat dinners in New York observed that Gavin and I were a strong couple because we were moving in the same direction. When you are moving in the same direction all your energy is mutually invested. When couples have their own individual directions, they need to come up with extra energy to realign themselves with each other, which makes a marriage feel like more work.

Clearly this does not mean we never argue or have disagreements. Our underlying desires and visions usually line up, but our ideas of how to execute them are sometimes different.

Only one time in our marriage did the word divorce come up. We had been married nine months and were living in a remote town in

Australia. Gavin was working long hours as a junior doctor, while I was left on my own in a new country with no friends and no job. I was bored! Keeping me home doing nothing is generally not a good idea.

When Gavin returned from one of his shifts, I told him I wanted a divorce.

"Absolutely no way," Gavin said. "We will work on it."

But I persisted. We didn't yet have children, I was still young and, with no strings attached, I could easily start over again.

That's when Gavin lost his temper. I've only ever seen the cool-headed Gavin get angry three times in my life. I was so scared I did not bring up the "d" word again and, here we are decades later, very happily married.

Gavin could have entertained the discussion, but he did not give it a moment's thought. Our philosophy has always been to work things out. Failure or mediocrity will not be entertained when it comes to our relationship.

Slovie Jungreis-Wolff teaches to ask yourself when you have a conflict, "Is this worth my *shalom bayit,* peace in the home?" Most issues are trivial, and just not worth chipping at the foundation of a marriage. Being in a solid and happy relationship has given me the strength to excel personally and as a family. We work hard at it and our investment is constantly put to the test. With the extra challenges of raising a child with special needs, being on the same page and having a united front has helped us become a more solid couple and a stronger team. Our investment in each other has paid off.

Tales of a Modern Jewish Woman

Princess policies

My I-don't-change-diapers policy is shocking to many people. As you may imagine, however, I found myself in some harrowing moments where my lucky streak of finding ways to not change diapers almost came to a messy end. These are those stories.

Caila was a baby when she and I were meeting Gavin in Orlando where he was attending a conference. Caila had been having stomach issues all week but seemed to be improving…until we walked into the airport lounge and I noticed a brown splotch all the way up her back. Now I was in trouble. I was literally shaking as we entered the women's restroom.

In a complete panic I came to grips with not just my first possible diaper change but an explosion of diarrhea. Holding back dry retches I strategized how I would tackle this. First, I decided I would simply throw away the soiled clothes. As I was poised to toss the perfectly good (but dirty) clothes into the trash, a cleaning lady walked in and gasped. To this day I cannot believe what came over me, but in that moment, I started crying and told her I was watching the baby for a friend who was attending the conference at the hotel.

"I've never changed a diaper before and I don't know what I'm doing," I sobbed.

At least that part was true.

"Well I have nine grandchildren, and I'm an expert at these things," this sweet lady explained as she took Caila from me, bathed her in the sink and changed her. She washed the clothes as well and kept cooing to Caila as she worked, "Are you going to see your mama?"

Boy was I glad Caila could not yet talk!

Around the same time, I flew to Israel alone with Caila. I was adamant in my assumption that if a baby can sleep through the night in a diaper, she can make it through an eleven-hour flight without a diaper change. However, the lovely young mother across the aisle from me pointed out that Caila was wet through. We still had three hours left in the flight and then getting through the airport and to our destination. She had to be changed. I gulped.

But this lady across the aisle was already in the middle of her own baby's Israeli-style diaper change – which is to say she just did it on her seat since the bathroom line was too long. This saint told me to hand over Caila.

"Pass me your baby and I will change her while I have the stuff out," *she said.*

Saved again! Thank you, God!

Chapter 19

Love work, hate positions of power, and do not make yourself known to the government.

Shemayah, Ethics of the Fathers 1:10

You would expect at least a chapter like "The Seven Highly Effective Habits of a Successful Wife-Mom-Entrepreneur-Non-profit Manager." But you won't find that in this book.

I like to say, I may be the most incompetent competent person out there. I can start a company, but I can never find my keys. The world may see an organized and composed Jodi. Gavin and my kids know the absentminded Jodi.

Well, sometimes the world also sees that side of me, and it can be slightly mortifying. Once at a rather large JICNY dinner, I whispered to Gavin that I was concerned because the speaker had not shown up yet. He reassured me the man was sitting right next to me. I glanced over. That man was thinner and shorter than I remembered, but maybe I had a bad memory.

Nevertheless, I got up on stage and read his bio hailing the speaker for interviewing all the Israeli prime ministers since Golda Meir and for frequently being called upon as an Israel commentator for news shows. When I sat down our speaker got up and thanked me politely, but noted that I had exaggerated his bio a bit and that he had not interviewed all those prime ministers.

The event carried on and the speaker was great. It was only when I sent him a thank-you note later that week that my huge error became apparent. I got a reply to my email from Tom G. who said he had not spoken at any of my events. *Ever.* My mouth dropped to the floor as I realized: I had confused two people with similar jobs and the same *first* name. All along – up till and including the event itself – I thought I was hosting Tom *G.*! It turns out I was emailing and had introduced Tom *W.* using Tom G's bio!

At least the latter Tom was extremely humbled by my invitation and introduction.

Another time Gavin asked what we were doing the following night and I told him we had a JICNY event I was running. The next morning I asked him to pick up some ingredients on his way home from *shul.*

"For what?" he asked.

"For a cooking class that I am teaching tonight," I responded.

"What about the JICNY event you're supposed to be at?"

I gasped. I had been organizing, planning and taking registration for two events that I had scheduled *and needed to be at* occurring on the same night.

Another time, I accepted an invitation to a Shabbat lunch at a friend's house. A few days before that, I received a message from someone else asking me what time was the lunch I had planned at my own house on Saturday. Thankfully she asked – I had invited thirty-three people to my home for the same time I accepted an invitation from my friend at her place! The reminder saved the day.

These sorts of things happen to me quite frequently. My children, since they know me, even worry I will forget to pick them up. In fact, I have. One time we got home from Friday service and were just sitting down for *kiddush* when we heard shouting outside our apartment, "Jodi! Jodi!" We had left Caila at *shul* and some kind neighbors brought her to us. We had not even noticed – *yet* – that she wasn't with us.

On another occasion, Temira had been at a friend's house for the afternoon and, suddenly, it was after Shabbat sundown. We had completely forgotten she was not home…until her friend's father walked her to our apartment after sunset.

I also once hid our passports so well that we never found them. Gavin was unimpressed when I noted, on the positive side, if we couldn't find the passports, neither could any would-be thieves. While traveling once in Ethiopia, we turned the hotel room upside down to find my credit cards that I hid over Shabbat.

Yes, I run an international organization. Just don't ask me to change diapers or put fuel in the car. Actually, I can't iron either. Once, early in our marriage, I ironed Gavin's shirt for work. When he arrived one of the nurses took one look at him and suggested that he should ask his wife to iron his shirts. He explained that his wife *had, in fact,* ironed the shirts. I have not used an iron since.

I am chronically running late as well. I always try to squeeze in a few more emails or reply to a few more messages. When I leave the house, I'm running. Running to pick up the kids from school, running to the subway, running to events. Makeup is applied on the go. Once, while walking with Caila in Manhattan, we saw a group of actual runners. I like to prompt Caila's speech so I asked her if she knew why they were running. I was hoping to introduce some new vocabulary about exercise.

"They are running because they are late," she responded.

In addition to my keys, which are misplaced several times a day, I have also lost several phones. Once I left my phone in a rental car after I returned it. One of the clerks there dutifully took detailed messages from all my phone calls before I returned to retrieve it. Another time, the manager of a venue hall found a phone and decided to keep it charged until someone would call and she could locate the owner. Months later, in a crazy coincidence, a friend of mine meeting with the manager saw an incoming call from a mutual friend and recognized the unique case I had on the phone. I had long given up on the idea of finding this particular phone.

My ability to overcome my shortcomings is partly due to my own tenacity, but it is also miraculous. I developed my own methods that work for me. For one, I write down everything that needs to be done in my life from details of an event to buying toilet paper for the house. From this master list, every night I create a must-do list for the next day. I also have thousands of notes on my iPhone because, knowing me, if it isn't written down, it will not happen.

The second thing I do is compartmentalize. I know myself and if I had to think about all the tasks I have to do simultaneously, I would stress out. In New York, sometimes I have seven events in seven days. I will not even think about the Tuesday event until I'm done with Monday's. On Tuesday morning I will break out the list for that night's event and get to work. Pulling out the Tuesday list sooner would spell certain failure for me. While I know I can pull it off, it certainly makes my coworkers, volunteers and family anxious.

I also strive for efficiency, which generally means multi-tasking or finding the quickest way to get something done well. I wanted triplets so I could give birth to all the children I wanted in one pregnancy. When Gavin warned me of the risks, I decided twins was more reasonable.

While I had little control over conception, this obsession with efficiency is best displayed in my "Shabbat in an Hour" cooking class. This is not a made-for-TV gourmet show, but it is a lot like me: It seems haphazard, but it is 100 percent efficient – and you *will* have a four-course Shabbat meal in an hour. Because I frequently host large dinners, I honed the preparation to my lifestyle. For instance, I do not chop or fry a single vegetable. Every item in each dish is cooked together. And I improvise on the spot, working with meat that is not fully defrosted or switching vegetables because a certain one was not available.

Ultimately, I love coming up with a vision, thinking it through and then doing. When I have a vision, I break it down into tasks and I'm willing to do whatever it takes to see it through. I don't need the glamor, I just need the job to be done.

Through all this, I came to realize that success is not simply defined as having made it to the cover of *Fortune* magazine, of which I had long dreamed. I redefined success as successfully balancing family, work and community – and trying not to lose my phone, keys and marbles in the process. And remembering to pick up my children from school.

I found that being both a businesswoman and a mother worked synergistically. As an entrepreneur, I was constantly riding ups and downs. One day I thought I was going to be a millionaire and the next day I was frantically wondering how I was going to pay the bills. I rode similar waves with parenting. One moment my children were adorable and precocious. The next moment I was rushing them off to sleep just for a respite from their squabbling and whining. As an entrepreneur, I pulled many all-nighters and I walked around perpetually sleep deprived. As a mom of a newborn, same thing. In fact, I may have slept more with a newborn than with my start-ups! Temira slept six or seven hours a stretch from the start – that was the most sleep I had gotten per night that year.

Just like an MBA only went so far in equipping me to deal with the real life of entrepreneurship, the parenting books barely prepared me for being a mom. Entrepreneurs must constantly innovate in order to stay relevant and, parents too have to roll with changes and think on their feet. How do you entertain three children when unexpected rain spoils your plans to go to the zoo? How do you respond when your child throws a question at you like, "Why did God make so-and-so ugly" *in front of* so-and-so? And not even managing a Fortune 500 company requires the same innovation and creativity as managing a public temper tantrum.

Entrepreneurism teaches you to go with the flow. There are no hard and fast rules, but there is a lot of intuition and winging it. That goes for parenting too. When I started jdeal with my business partner, we met with an investor who guided us in creating our business plan. Then he took the plan and ripped it up.

"Now you can discard all the numbers because reality will not play out that way. What matters is your thinking and your assumptions that went into the planning."

It's sort of like planning for a typical baby then finding out she is born with Down syndrome. Or planning a family vacation, but your three-year-old wakes up with chicken pox. Both entrepreneurship and parenting cause you to rely on principles, quick thinking and flexibility to carry you through the unexpected crises that life throws your way. As long as your principles are consistent and strong, you can weather the unexpected.

Being an entrepreneur – and failing at it – also prepared me for being a mother. The years of business start-ups, failures and successes taught me that mistakes are okay. You just make adjustments and move forward. Entrepreneurship has taught me to believe in myself and to come to terms with "imperfect." Same with parenting – I know that I am still a good mom and that one small mistake doesn't define who I am.

I loved the challenge of building a business. It's like taking a blank canvas and creating a beautiful work of art. The same with each precious child born into the world – from these human canvasses we create the most beautiful treasures.

Though I was never the typical Jewish mom, I like to consider myself a "real" Jewish mom. I try to be a good role model of what is possible if you work hard and use Jewish values as a compass for navigating life. And I worry and nag like a good Jewish mom.

I feel equally passionate about my "spiritual" work with JICNY. Strengthening Jews in their identity and in their connection to spirituality was heavy on my heart since I was a young *baal teshuvah* in my twenties. And so, when we made our work "official" in New York through a registered non-profit organization, I added another aspect to my already busy life. At some point, a rabbi of mine once asked, "Jodi does the world need another businessperson or does it need someone who can contribute to the Jewish people?"

The obvious answer he was looking for was to make a contribution to the Jewish people. My parents, on the other hand, never understood why I devote so many volunteer hours to my nonprofit. My dad even suggested I give up "the Jewish stuff" and focus on making money. But no apologies – I wanted both.

Wearing all these hats, I developed a mantra to keep me on course: Live, Love, Learn, Laugh.

"Live" meant going out every night because I believed – and I still do – that life is too short not to. This is how I maintained such long and meaningful relationships. At Meron's bar mitzvah shortly after we moved to Israel, we had at least forty guests that we had known for more than twenty years. That includes people from several countries and those were pre-email days! We had somehow stayed in contact with dozens of people who were still close enough to be invited to a family milestone celebration years later.

"Love" meant setting aside the time with my family and friends and doing the things I love such as eating chocolate because I *love* it and traveling. Both Gavin and I traveled a lot for work so we spent lots of quality time together when we were home and on Shabbat.

"Learn" meant keeping my brain engaged and me aware. I refuse to go back to the narrow days when apartheid was the only reality I knew. Knowledge is what helped me get that out of my system. I read prolifically, visit museums and learn Torah. By gaining knowledge we gain wisdom.

"Laugh" meant finding the humor in every situation, even if it meant laughing at myself, which is never hard. Humor helps me cope with stress whether its related to business, Down syndrome and inclusion or my JICNY events.

Tales of a Modern Jewish Woman

Jodi's future books

The self-help books you won't see on the bookstore shelves:

1. "All dressed up and nowhere to go!"
That describes me in many situations. One of my less proud moments was when I took a friend to a Broadway show that she had really been looking forward to seeing.

I take my relationships seriously and this was an opportunity to deepen my friendship and really bless her with something she had wanted, especially for this special birthday of hers. I went online to purchase the tickets.

On the big day we met outside the theater. We were all dressed up and stood on the long line chatting excitedly about the show we were about to see. But when I showed the clerk at the box office my printout, he noticed a problem: I had printed the screen before *the actual purchase. I had not purchased the tickets at all! I felt horrible as my friend and I stood there, the very embodiment of all dressed up with nowhere to go.*

Today this is something I can laugh at, thank God, but I was mortified for a long time afterwards.

2. "Discerning which voice in your head to heed!"
How do I function with the voices chattering in my head all the time? Gavin calls it The Council of Monkeys. The monkeys are barking out commands all the time. Intrepid Monkey tells me to take the risk. Sister Mary Monkey makes me feel guilty. Princess Monkey tells me I

can have it all. Passion Monkey is out to change the world. My main challenge is figuring out which one is right and when!

3. "I can't live if living is without... my security blanket!"

And to really shatter any image of a put-together Jodi, I am loathe to admit that I still use a security blanket to deal with my anxiety. My parents tried to break me of the thumb-sucking habit when I was four years old. They had me also throw out my security blanket in a "ceremony" designed to symbolize how I had moved on and didn't need one. They believed they had succeeded. I let them think that — meanwhile I snuck it out of the garbage and asked the nanny to wash it. My blanket remained hidden under my mattress until the day I moved out, and it moved with me.

Luckily, Gavin thought it was the cutest thing ever that I kept a blanket since early childhood. He also thought — mistakenly — that it was a great idea to show it to my father, that first year of our marriage when my parents came to visit us in Australia. My father was in shock — I had gotten away with hiding it from them for years. He did not share in Gavin's assessment that it was "cute."

By the way, my dear blanket has traveled with me to dozens of countries and, though only a small fragment of it has survived from the original, I have a replacement blanket with me every single night.

Chapter 20

Lech lecha! Go out from your country, and from your family, and from your father's house, to the land that I will show you.

Genesis 12:1

Hamas was our aliyah *shaliach*.

No Jewish ambassador or organization was as effective as the Palestinian terrorist organization in convincing us to immigrate to Israel. During the summer of 2014, Hamas was pummeling southern Israel with rockets while Hezbollah – the Shiite terrorist group based in southern Lebanon – started up in the north. Suddenly Israel had two war fronts. The country called up the reserves and every civilian familiarized him or herself with the nearest shelter even as far away as Jerusalem, where we were. Sirens sounded hundreds of times a day and the entire nation was on alert. Even Jerusalem absorbed a few rockets, which was very unusual, it being so far from Gaza.

We happened to be in Israel over that summer and being in a country at war is a compelling experience. In Israel, it brought out the best in its citizens. Spontaneous collections were taken up for those under siege: food and toothpaste for soldiers at the border, diapers for babies whose parents couldn't leave the shelters, blankets, food and money. Those who were located in the center of the country were doing their part to help those who were worrying for their lives in the north and south. Summer camps in central cities took in children while homes for the elderly and disabled opened their doors to patients from embattled regions. Extra prayers were called for at the Western Wall and religious and secular Jews would stream there to petition God for safety and deliverance of the nation.

I remember attending one of those rallies. Thousands of people showed up, from Ultra-Orthodox to secular Jews. It was so moving. We were really one people. *Am Yisrael chai*!

The Samuels were swept up in this war-time atmosphere that summer. Far from the First World worries of the Upper West Side, we were suddenly thrust into this mode of social responsibility and national camaraderie. One thing you notice quickly about Israel is how everyone gets involved in…*everything*. From wishing you *bete'avon* as you are eating at an outdoor café to strangers scolding you when your child is not wearing a hat in 50 degree Fahrenheit weather, Israelis throw themselves fully into everyone else's existence. And even more so during a crisis. Most native Israelis served in the army so you could feel their knowledge and expertise surrounding you. Everyone was extremely vigilant. Almost everyone seemed to know a reasonable amount of self-defense and first aid. These are qualities you don't see among the general population in America and other Western nations in which we had lived.

I tried to picture New York under constant threats of incoming rockets. I imagined the city would be frozen. Yet in Israel that summer, hours after the first rockets fell, fans crowded the bars to watch the World Cup semifinals. In cities that were not under attack, life continued as normal for those six weeks despite thousands of rockets flying overhead just a two-hour bus ride either north or south. The only difference was the spontaneous prayer meetings and donation collections.

It was all so impressive. Nothing about life in Israel was shallow. It dripped with meaning and purpose. A nation of eight million became one community when under attack. No one was a stranger or an outsider. The people were all united by a tacit pursuit of survival.

I dare say that the war, Operation Protective Edge, actually had a huge – positive – influence on us as we were considering our next move in life.

Around this time we were looking – against my will – to move to the suburbs where we could buy a house with more bedrooms and a yard. But I couldn't contemplate the thought of suburbs. I didn't want to give up my city life for a car and a yard. It wasn't me. I had friends that moved to the suburbs – and we didn't see them for years! Once someone crossed that bridge or tunnel, it was like the Bermuda Triangle. They just disappeared, swallowed up by the boroughs and loathe to battle traffic into Manhattan. I was resisting the move and remained antagonistic during discussions of which suburb would suit us.

Suburbs or not, my son, the idealistic child who takes after his father, had been telling all of his friends that he was going to live in Israel someday. For him, it was a sealed deal. Either his family would move as they often spoke about, or he would do so on his own anyway when he turned eighteen – and join the IDF. Meron had been instilled with a passion for Israel and aliyah – because that's how we raised him. It was only a matter of time until he would call Israel home.

That's what Gavin and I had been saying for more than twenty years now. It was the infamous "two-year plan." We were going to save money and move to Israel. First from New Zealand, then Australia, then from New York. But two years stretched into four and then seven, then ten and here we were twenty-three years after we got married, well established in New York, considering a home in the suburbs and not even really thinking about Israel.

How could I think about Israel? We had a great community. I had an amazing organization, JICNY, which was strong and influential. I had started several companies and was thriving in business. And we had finally settled into a great Jewish day school that accepted all of our children, including Caila.

Not only that, but the services we were receiving for Caila from the City of New York were some of the best in the world. She had a full-time aide with a master's degree at school and every therapy you could ask for including three speech, two physical, two occupational and one play therapy every week. New York City gave her eight hours a week with a respite worker who would take her to after-school activities or additional therapies. She was assigned a tutor for another eight hours a week. All of this *plus* we would receive $1,200 a year to pay for extra activities such as ballet or swimming. And to top it all off, the social worker would do the paperwork for all of this, submitting grants on our behalf for reimbursements and applying for summer camp – *for free*.

Let's just say, I wasn't thinking about making aliyah. I wasn't moving a muscle to go anywhere.

But the idealism of our youth hadn't been stamped out of Gavin. And, he had grown weary of Manhattan. After the battle to get Caila into a private Jewish school in New York, Gavin was scarred. He didn't want to live in a city where Mr. Half-a-Hamantashan was leading prayer in his *shul*. Gavin likened New York life to the cycles of a washing machine: soak, spin, dry. People eventually got out of the cycle because it was soaking, spinning or wringing them dry. Every year our Shabbat table was comprised of new and different people. I didn't mind, but Gavin wanted deeper, long-term relationships.

In addition to that, Meron presented me with a little math equation.

"There's a 25 percent chance I'm staying in Manhattan, 25 percent chance I'm moving to Israel, 25 percent chance I'll relocate to the suburbs and 25 percent chance my mother comes up with another idea."

I explained to him the prospects of moving to Israel were more like zero percent because Caila has to finish school in New York. Twelve more years, I told him. Meron then did another math equation. "Imma, in twelve years' time I'll be married with children and living in Israel anyway."

I hadn't thought about that. He was getting the exact education we were paying for: passionate, religious Zionism that, for him, meant going straight from high school to the Israeli army. Now, I hadn't thought of it that way, but if I waited for Caila to finish school, my other kids would already be long gone, probably in Israel, and I'd be torn between two continents.

Admittedly, I too was a little bit swept up by Israel during the war. In fact, on our anniversary, as we strolled through the streets of the city in which we had met, I confessed to Gavin.

"I know you're never going to believe what I'm about to say, but maybe we should move here. Maybe we should live in a more meaningful society."

Ah, the romance of wartime.

It wasn't long before my words were put to the test. After our summer abroad in 2014, Gavin gave me an ultimatum: the suburbs *or Israel.*

With that positive vibe still lingering, Meron's assumption he was moving to Israel anyway and after placing a few other conditions on a potential move, I agreed to "give it a try" and move our entire lives. My main noncommittal caveat was that we would not sell our New York apartment just in case Israel "didn't work out." I also said we would give it a one-year trial. My other caveat was that we would move immediately so we could get the kids into schools on time.

All of these negotiations culminated in a sudden decision in New York on September nineteenth: We would make aliyah.

Now.

Then in typical Jodi fashion, the race was on. Instead of a six-month long process, we got our immigration paperwork done in four days. Just like I organize my events at the last minute, I similarly moved our entire family to another country in days. With little time for packing or goodbyes, and in order to get our children into schools before the fall holidays ended, we were on the plane to Israel on October sixth – two weeks from the day we decided to make aliyah. After twenty-three years of talking about it, it was finally happening.

All the pieces began falling into place around me. Caila was accepted at an Israeli kindergarten (sight unseen) and we found a furnished apartment to lease for six months. I felt it was a conspiracy between Gavin and God to convince me this was the right thing to do.

I had come to the reluctant conclusion that, before we moved to the suburbs, maybe we should try Israel for a year. How bad could it be? At least the children would learn Hebrew very well.

I further reasoned that now was a good time since Caila was still young and at six years old one's brain is still primed to learn another language with relative ease. It would be easier for her to transition while still in kindergarten than in first grade. Even though this was, in my mind, a trial, we officially made aliyah and became residents so that Caila could receive services in Israel.

My life motto is *Lech lecha*. Go. Or, *just do it*. And that we did, with no wavering. When I decide to do something, it's all or nothing.

We left the Manhattan apartment as it was, frozen in time. Because, remember, we were coming back in a year after this little aliyah experiment. I didn't even clear my desk. The same papers scattered on the desk, the chair still askew, as if we had fled. We arrived with just our suitcases and moved into an apartment off of Emek Refaim Street located in the German Colony of Jerusalem, a very Anglo neighborhood.

Despite having long been Zionists who believe in the State of Israel and the responsibility of Jews worldwide to live there, it was the war that made us realize how important Israel was to us personally. That is what pushed us over the ideological edge to finally move. And for a few moments I found it thrilling. It felt right.

The year we left New York, more than 10,000 people from forty-two countries attended our two-hundred plus JICNY events. Our children attended the same, beloved Jewish day school that opened their arms to Caila. We had great friendships and were connected to a strong community. I had established empires of business and advocacy in the city. I could confidently say I had "made it there" in New York.

I loved the city. I loved what we built there. As we boarded the plane to Israel in that flurry of activity, I suddenly remembered the moment after we first moved to New York when I broke down because I didn't even know my zip code. I was about to go through that same process and learning curve. I was again leaving behind my comfort zone and everything I had built with little foresight and zero idea what awaited me.

All the excitement of moving was tempered with the reality that I was trying not to think about: I was going from everything to nothing. All based on idealism.

Tales of a Modern Jewish Woman

When in Rome...or Israel

Government offices in Israel can be frustrating, exasperating and down-right painful. As new immigrants, we were shuffled into these offices pushing paperwork for all sorts of things.

Years prior to making aliyah we had a little taste of Ministry of Interior bureaucracy when Gavin tried repeatedly to get certain paperwork in order to register as a doctor in Israel. I like to say that your first three trips to the Ministry of Interior are pilot trips where the person behind the glass tells you which documents you were supposed to bring but did not because no one told you they were required. The fourth time, maybe, is a charm. If you're lucky.

We were only in Israel for two weeks and so it was stressful to keep coming back and waiting for their vaunted seal of approval. On our third trip, after we failed again to get what we needed, we left in abject despair. And I broke down sobbing on the street in front of the Ministry of Interior.

A man walking by stopped in front of me and Gavin.

"Hey! I was at your Shabbat table years ago in Australia," he said, then, noticed I had been crying.

"What's wrong?"

Yuval, an Israeli, had found us when we were living in Tasmania, where the Jewish population was nearly nonexistent. He was traveling with a friend and had consulted a Jewish student travel guide which listed us as contacts.

Now, here in his hometown, he wanted to help us.

"Don't you worry. Tomorrow, we will go together and get this done," he assured us.

The next day we headed to the Ministry of Interior armed with Yuval, our Israeli friend. He got to work screaming and yelling right away. We were shocked to see our mild-mannered friend raising his voice like that. There was a lot of frantic back and forth, all at high pitches, until suddenly that same clerk from the day before slapped a stamp on our papers and we walked out victorious.

Moral of the story: You either need to be Israeli or you just need an Israeli to accomplish anything in Israel.

CHAPTER 21

By wisdom a house is built, and by understanding it is established.

Proverbs 24:3

It didn't take long for me to decide. I hated living in Israel.

As a Jewish community leader, I'm supposed to be positive and sing the praises of making aliyah. But I have to be honest, those first few months (which stretched into years) were the most challenging of my life.

In New York, I was connected, influential and could advocate and navigate any situation. My biggest challenge in Israel was that, without the language and the ability to express myself and understand others, my Type-A(AA) personality was stressed out. I could not independently communicate in Hebrew. I always brought a Hebrew speaker with me to official meetings especially where it concerned Caila's education. I couldn't read messages from the Ministry of Interior or the children's schools, ask shopkeepers for help or read my own mail. I needed someone else to fill out our forms and other paperwork, of which there was much.

Then there were the people. Rude, pushy and operating on raw frazzled emotions, Israelis are perpetually stressed, live in cramped apartments and drive like lunatics. Lines are nonexistent at bus stops and supermarkets where I quickly learned to guard my spot as others crowded around me. Zero personal space was allotted.

Living in Israel as opposed to just *visiting* were polar opposite experiences. Suddenly I was thrust into the culture headfirst and I felt like I was drowning. I learned that in order to be heard, one must yell and pound tables. However, my cultural upbringing stressed courtesy and decorum. I was appalled and couldn't raise my voice just to get what was mine by law. Several times in the Ministry of Interior, rude clerks told us we were missing paperwork and just shoved our files back toward us without even a glance. Apparently, that was an invitation to argue with them and figure out what we really did need, but it took a while to figure out how things work.

I was not cut out for this. In case I had thought Manhattan was a tough place, New York had nothing on Jerusalem.

We encountered so many cultural idiosyncrasies that, to me, were unforgivable. People chat incessantly through shows and movies. They arrive late to everything (although this was actually a good thing for me since I am chronically late). Loud and heated exchanges were the norm yet somehow ended with a wave and *shalom*. Just because someone was shouting at you didn't mean they were actually angry with you. To get anything you wanted – from a spot in line to the right school for your child – you had to be aggressive and pushy.

This irreparable chasm was on display at Meron's bar mitzvah in Israel. My nephew visiting from South Africa excitedly told me that Temira had taught him "so much" about living in Israel. I was intrigued by what she could have taught him just after a few months living in Israel, so I asked him to explain.

"Like how to get food!" he responded enthusiastically.

"How do you *get food*?" I asked quizzically.

"Like this!" He proceeded to raise his elbows at a sharp ninety-degree angle and headed for the buffet line where he forced his way past everyone else up to the table.

As I was processing this Israeli buffet table etiquette (or lack thereof), the caterer approached me with her concern.

"Do you know why these people are standing over there and not eating?" she asked.

I looked over. All of our South African family members who flew in for the event were politely standing in a line *that wasn't moving*.

Meanwhile the Israelis present at the event were already going back for their seconds and thirds – heading straight up to the food tables completely oblivious to the existence of a "line," as my nephew had learned.

These were the sort of things that made me laugh and cry simultaneously.

Another disturbing fact is that Israel is shockingly expensive. Salaries here are generally lower than in the United States, yet the cost of living is much higher. Even compared to New York City, which isn't cheap by any stretch, our grocery bills and basic items were astronomically higher.

The high cost of living was somewhat offset by the reprieve from the expense of Jewish day school tuition and with our U.S. salaries, we were suddenly considered "rich" by others. Enough to be sought after for donations and hosting parlor parties anyway. In New York we were not even counted in the parlor-party circuit.

The contrast became apparent in another way. For the most part, Israeli school fashion is more granola than in Manhattan. One of my children came home from school crying one day after learning they were considered the "rich kids" because of how they dressed. Meron, Temira and Caila were certainly not wearing designer clothes, which is the mark of "rich kids" in America, they were simply well groomed.

Another massive adjustment for me was the lack of delivery service in Israel. New York had me spoiled – I ordered everything we needed from groceries to party supplies for our dinners. Amazon, Google Express and Instacart all delivered to the front door of our apartment. Even my dry cleaning was picked up and delivered to the doorman in our building. Suddenly I was on my own in a foreign country where – trust me – you can never tick off your entire shopping list in one store. The schlepping, whether in searing temperatures in the summer and blustery rain in the winter, was dispiriting after years of shopping from the comfort of my keyboard.

Idealistically, scripturally even, I believe that Jews must build the State of Israel. I am ideologically and biblically in favor of aliyah. And, in my defense, it's not like I was twiddling my thumbs in New York either. I was contributing to the community and to the Jewish diaspora which cannot survive without idealistic people living in their midst. I had a good life there.

Not only that, but I couldn't find myself in Israel. My work began to fizzle out. And though I created events – all well attended and successful – I felt less impactful in Israel than in New York.

By nature, I have a resilient and buoyant personality. But Jerusalem was killing my spirit.

I was lost. I felt purposeless. I didn't see a role for myself. My mission is connecting unaffiliated Jews, but in the Jewish state, everyone is already connected to the geographic core of Judaism itself.

After one year, I announced our intention to move back to New York. Actually, it was only *my* intention by this point. We did Israel, I exclaimed, and the experiment was over. Now we can go back. I even paid the six-thousand-dollar nonrefundable deposit for the children to be enrolled at SAR the following year!

This was by far our worst year of marriage. The angst that I experienced in Israel compared to the sheer joy it gave Gavin placed a tremendous strain on our relationship. And we were too busy sorting out the practical things like Caila's therapies and school schedules to even deal with it. Plus, Gavin traveled for work and so he was out of Israel frequently, enough that he didn't have time to let the grating details bother him.

Gavin insisted one year was not enough to know if this was the right move. We would have to stay a second year to really test the waters.

"If we go back now and live in the suburbs, you're going to wake up one day and wonder if life would have been better in Israel," he warned. I had to hand him that, going back just for the suburbs would also be a challenge for me. I decided to give it another year.

After all, everyone else in the family had drunk the Israel Kool Aid. Meron only took a few days to acclimate to Israel. Then he never looked back. The language came to him fast and he found himself here at the age of twelve, making friends and joining youth groups, all with ease. Temira took a bit longer, a few months, and then she settled in nicely. She was ten at the time.

Caila, who is really the true hero of our aliyah saga, also adjusted amazingly relative to her specific challenges. She became bilingual and managed in a regular kindergarten, with twenty-six typical Israeli children. It wasn't seamless for her and she did have trouble making friends, but she was fully included in a foreign country and she made the transition look simple compared to me.

Idealism smooths over a lot of things, like a good wine. Gavin, for instance, would see a secular female soldier in her skintight army uniform reading the traditional Book of Lamentations on Tisha B'Av and feel inspired by the Jewish essence of the country. He would marvel at the security guard at the mall practicing the Torah portion for the upcoming Shabbat. These things make him swoon with wonder at the Jewish state and the Promised Land. I needed the *good wine* just to cope!

Gavin's grandfather moved to South Africa from Lithuania before World War II. All ten of his siblings stayed in Lithuania and ended up being killed in the Holocaust. Imagine how this man would feel now that his grandson was living in Israel and his great-grandchildren would be serving in the first sovereign Jewish army in two thousand years. It is profound from a generational standpoint.

I do admit, part of me is idealistic. I am enthralled that Israel is really the "Start-up Nation." I love hearing Hebrew on the streets, a testament to the revived and thriving language. The ingathering of the exiles to a land that we had lost then regained, is a miracle. I fully believe our DNA echoes in this land. But I prefer to *visit* the miracle rather than live in it.

On the day of our two-year aliyah anniversary the children made a cake and woke us up singing. I played along which made them happy.

"Imma, I was worried that you would not want to celebrate," Meron said. "You always remind us how hard it is here and how you wish you could go back to New York!"

Clearly, I didn't keep my feelings to myself. My struggles were not in vain either – all of my challenges inspired my dear friend Nechama to start her own organization. The Jerusalem Olim Center was born partly in response to years of me crying on Nechama's shoulder as I struggled to figure things out in Israel. She learned from me how the challenges facing immigrants can be eased, if not averted.

My response to feeling anchor-less was to do what I do best: build friendships, circles of influence and community initiatives. In fact, I jumped in just days after arriving. I knew that the South African Chief Rabbi's visionary program, the Shabbat Project, a global Jewish unity project involving more than thirty countries, was coming up. So I deigned to find out what was happening in Jerusalem – the epi-center of the Jewish world– for this event. Nothing, as it turned out.

I was aghast. I quickly forgot that I didn't know the language, that the *chagim* had just finished and my three children had started new schools in a new country. I sent an email to two dozen people that I knew in Jerusalem who were connected. I hoped to get a group together to create some sort of programming in Jerusalem for this event. I kept hitting the send-and-receive button awaiting their excited responses, but none came. I realized if it was going to happen, it would be up to me. As I like to say, *"Just do it."*

Two people stepped up to help me and, with loads of stress, a massive learning curve in Israeli event organizing and linguistic challenges, we organized a challah bake, a Shabbat dinner for young professionals and *havdalah* under the stars in the Old City. We had three hundred women show up to bake challah at the trendy First Train Station to kick off the events. Not bad for having just arrived in the country.

It took guts for me to "be the man," to "just do it" in the face of these new obstacles. But I put a stake in the ground, set a date and went into action. My comfort zone had always been planning events, especially if the event is getting Jews involved and connected with their faith. Despite living with nine toes still in New York, I slowly started doing this in Israel – planning events for *olim*, for young professionals, for lone soldiers. It helped me feel like I had more of a purpose. Keeping busy was very important for me. Eventually I established JIC Jerusalem and I also became involved with an organization that sets up tourists with Israeli families for them to experience authentic Shabbat dinners. It was exciting to host so many different people from around the world.

These were the kinds of things that made life in Israel palatable for me. This and the fact that I traveled to New York several times a year to run JICNY events. Otherwise I would've been downright miserable. Shortly after we moved, I was back in New York and I spent Shabbat with some friends. One of the guests remarked that the previous Shabbat they discussed families from New York who made the "big move" to Israel. She told everyone that the Samuels were an example of a family that made a seamless transition and were happy. It couldn't have been further from my reality. My positive Facebook posts of our adventures and my successful events were deceiving. The move was extremely difficult for me and I was far from settled.

I had a running checklist of life in Israel versus New York, hoping to one day tip the scales in Israel's favor. Israel got checks in the "like" column for:

1. *Nearly every restaurant in the entire country is kosher*
2. *Great beaches and spectacular weather*
3. *No soccer-mom schlepping*
4. *Shabbat and holidays that feel like actual Shabbat and holidays because the whole country is observing*
5. *Celebrating one-day holidays instead the two days required in the Diaspora*

Everything else – from the government bureaucracy, the school system, the lack of lines and the rude and pushy behavior I encountered daily – got a "dislike." But by Israeli standards we were living well, so who was I to complain?

I pretended everything was fine and coped those first two years. It was a learning curve – visiting Israel and living there were totally different experiences. *Living* here was much less spiritual, less fascinating. Actually, having to deal with the country's realities and challenges as a citizen was just plain hard.

In the Diaspora, especially in established and strong Jewish communities like in New York, many people are "armchair Zionists." They support Israel and believe that Jews should immigrate there and populate the Jewish state, but they want to hear *you* have done well in Israel, that you are thriving – mostly so they don't have to do it themselves. I struggled with how to respond to their questions about life in Israel.

Those first two years in Israel were the most difficult years of my life. What compounded the challenge was that everyone else in my family was happy. It was lonely and isolating. It also didn't help that Israelis were incredulous as to why we would make aliyah. How does one give up the American Dream and a Manhattan lifestyle to immigrate to Israel? I still don't know how to answer that. Behind the social media posts detailing our adventures was a person struggling with aliyah, with idealism and finding herself.

Tales of a Modern Jewish Woman

Crossing borders

I love how my life flows seamlessly among all types of people. I appreciate the diversity that they bring into my life.

This was on display during one of my milestone birthday parties. I had seventy guests, all close friends, ranging from "black hat" religious Jews, non-Jews, same-sex couples, people with special needs and other people of different religions and cultures. I effortlessly floated across the crowds, because all of these people were truly friends of mine and I related to each one in an individual way. I noticed that many of the guests, however, had trouble being in the same room as some of the others who were not like them.

My Shabbat table is equally diverse no matter where I am. In Israel, I hosted one Shabbat in Tel Aviv at my friend's apartment. She is extremely left-wing politically, yet our friendship transcends politics. Other people cannot imagine that the two of us can get along since we have such divergent views. Our guests included a good friend who is an Orthodox rabbi, skimpily dressed women, secular work colleagues and everything in between.

We once hosted a Christian Israeli who enjoyed hours of lechayims *at our table one Saturday afternoon before racing off – seriously inebriated – to a game in his Palestinian basketball league.*

In New York, I hosted a Shabbat dinner for the Council of Young Jewish Presidents and we had representatives from right-wing AIPAC and left-wing JStreet in the same room, at the same table even!

When we visited Israel during the summers before we made aliyah I sent my Modern Orthodox children to the YMCA bilingual Hebrew-Arabic camp with Jewish, Christian and Muslim counselors. In Israel we have friends who live in the "settlements," in religious neighborhoods of Jerusalem and the most secular areas of Tel Aviv. I have taken walking tours of Hasidic communities, tours that support appropriating Arab land to Israel and tours that explain why that same land belongs to the Palestinians.

My life got even more diverse thanks to Caila and the special bond that is shared by parents of children with Down syndrome. This was evident in a home group meeting with fellow moms of children with Down syndrome. Here I was in Jerusalem, the only Modern Orthodox woman with a secular Jew, a Haredi woman, a Muslim and a Christian. We came from neighborhoods across Jerusalem to meet and discuss our mutual challenges and struggles of which there were many. It took us becoming parents to children with special needs to cause our paths to cross — and to break down the walls that might have otherwise existed between us.

Chapter 22

We are as great as the challenges we have the courage to undertake.

Rabbi Lord Jonathan Sacks

We were meeting with the eleventh grammar school we visited for Caila, this time a Modern Orthodox school in the Old City. Disappointment welled up in my stomach as it was becoming clear, for several reasons, that this school – like the ten before it – was not going to be able to take Caila. As the reasons continued to mount, I began sobbing hysterically right there in the principal's office. I was inconsolable.

Caila had spent her first year in Israel at a bilingual Hebrew-English kindergarten we had found in the Rehavia neighborhood of Jerusalem. Remember the Israeli teacher I mentioned in a previous chapter? She was unfazed that Caila had Down syndrome. Thanks to her, Caila had an excellent first year, but little did we know that teacher's attitude was the exception not the rule. We had been in the country just three months when we already faced the looming fact that registration for first grade opens and closes – *in January*! No sooner was Caila settled in her kindergarten class than it was time for us to find her an elementary school. We scrambled to meet with the principals and staff of every Modern Orthodox school in the city in a short period of time.

I was beginning to have flashbacks. The trauma of our New York saga was still fresh – and it was going to continue in Israel. The opposition and rejection we experienced to get Caila into a mainstream Jewish school in New York came rushing back to my mind quite vividly. The pain, the isolation, the mother's heart that ached for her child to be accepted and included. Now walking back from this last school under the hot Middle Eastern sun, I couldn't believe that I had uprooted my life in New York only to relive this same nightmare in Israel.

"We have no room."
"The classrooms are already at the maximum number of students."
"We don't have the resources."
"We have no experience with those *children."*
Etc., etc.

Who knew there were so many ways to say "no." If we thought we had it bad trying to find a Jewish day school in New York, Israel proved to be just as difficult, if not more so. Here we were, in the Jewish state, where *all* the public schools are technically "Jewish day schools," so we seemed to have a broader scope of choices here. Yet the rejections were pouring in and we were running out of options.

When we were in New York, I had been enthralled with the idea of inclusion in Israel and how wondrously legal it was to have the choice to send your child to any public school. In my blogs and articles, I upheld Israel as an example of an inclusive and tolerant society that supported differences and disabilities. It was only when I got to Israel that I realized the law, good as it may be, has many holes, is woefully underfunded and makes inclusion in education a near impossible feat.

Gavin and I called school after school. Many of them outright refused to even meet with us. Most of the ones who did gave us a cold if not rude reception. One school *had* to meet with us because Temira was enrolled there and in Israel, schools are legally obligated to accept siblings. But before the meeting started, one of the staff – a woman who attended JIC events when she lived in New York – pulled us aside before we entered the office. "I feel it's my duty to warn you, they don't want her here." The icy response of the principal made that obvious although his words were couched.

"This is not a good school for her," he said.

Silly me, I thought it was the *parents* who get to decide what is a good option for their child.

"Look at other schools," he suggested. We had, we told him, and I brought up the law about schools accepting siblings. His face registered shock. Clearly, he thought the law applied only to "real" or "regular" siblings, not siblings with special needs.

In any case, it was the school in the Jewish Quarter that I had my eye on. I believed it was the perfect choice for Caila as we had friends who sent their children there and the school was experienced with inclusion. The staff listened to us, and even agreed with us, however, they were already maxed out on aides per classroom and by law could not include another child that would come with a shadow.

That's when I broke down. I was a wreck and I couldn't handle another no. By that point, I had pulled out every contact and networking connection I had made in my life. It's amazing that despite being new *olim*, we turned out to be quite connected. I placed calls to the mayor's office, the education ministry and Knesset. But the rules were set in stone more ancient than the city of Jerusalem itself. There was no budging. The classes were physically small, they were already maxed out with students and no law or connection in all of Israel was going to part this Red Sea for us. I felt so defeated in our quest for inclusion.

All of this was happening in our first few months in Israel with zero Hebrew and even less knowledge of the law and our rights regarding inclusion. On top of that we had to find new therapists for Caila outside of school. This was also time consuming and expensive. In addition, we were still sorting out our immigration papers and discovering those rights and requirements all while settling our family of five in a foreign country. To say this first year was extremely stressful would be an understatement. I was perpetually on the verge of a breakdown and I began feeding my emotions with tons of Israeli junk food while I sobbed hysterically and/or cursed the country several times a day.

Caila was finally accepted at a mixed secular-religious school. Designed to include secular and religious families, the school also successfully included children with special needs, which was a plus. It was not our first choice, however, because none of the children from our religious community attended. Caila was the only religious student in her class and the only girl with special needs in the entire school. Just a few weeks after Caila began first grade, it became clear that the balance sat heavily on the secular side of the population. This became more apparent at the parents' meeting which revolved around whether birthday cakes for in-school parties should be kosher. Though that is what the school demanded in order to ensure that everyone was comfortable, one mother argued furiously for her right to bring any cake she wanted. This made us uneasy and was an early warning sign that perhaps this wasn't as tolerant a place as we had hoped. After a few other questionable incidents, we started looking for a new school. Again.

Ultimately, Caila transferred to the Modern Orthodox school for which she was zoned. When Israeli schools say they "don't have the resources" to educate your child with special needs, it is true. The same *dearth* of resources plagues every school – even the one that does finally accept your child. In our case, the school welcomed Caila and staff members tried their best. But this school, just like every other, was underfunded and the staff not trained in integrating children such as Caila.

I came to understand the schools' resistance to including a child with special needs. What teacher who already has thirty or more students would want to accept one with more challenges? Without a budget coming from the Ministry of Education, no school is more equipped than the next. In New York, I could have chosen to educate Caila on Mars and the lucrative basket of services would have followed her there. Here in Israel, the funding doesn't back up the law. As angry as I was, I couldn't be upset with the Israelis schools. This wasn't discrimination against Caila. The Israeli schools' decisions to reject her were based on their already meager budgets and overworked, underpaid staff.

This was another area where the idealism of aliyah began to quickly dissipate for me. I mentioned before how in New York, Caila received an aide, called a paraprofessional, for fifteen hours a week, and a special education itinerant teacher with a master's degree who was the case manager and teaching specialist twenty hours a week, coordinating all the other therapists. Integration and continuity ran through all of Caila's learning and everyone was up to speed on her progress, her strengths and the areas in which she needed more work. In addition to that, the class size usually topped out at about twenty students.

Suddenly, sitting in her rowdy Israeli classroom of nearly thirty students, Caila had none of this. She was allocated a shadow for twenty-five hours a week and we were told she couldn't be in school without one (which we later learned was untrue). The only therapies she was eligible for, once a week, were speech and occupational, however, the Ministry of Education didn't even have therapists to send to the school. And a good, but harried case manager came to school for about *one hour a month* to observe Caila, train the staff and create an individualized learning plan. She did this for every single child with Down syndrome throughout all of Jerusalem and she clearly did not have the same amount of time as the New York case manager who devoted twenty hours a week to Caila alone.

This might shed some light on my underlying angst at living in Israel – we walked away from these unparalleled services and rights in inclusion and stepped into a vacuum.

Knowing what is possible, based on my experience in New York, I set out to replicate that for Caila as best as I could in Israel. Not every person who makes aliyah gets to start off with a network like I already had. I realize what a blessing that was. All those years serving the Jewish community, plus my propensity for networking, gave me a fortuitous edge in my battles here. I was on top of all of Caila's needs. If I found out she was not receiving a therapy to which she was entitled, I went to the offices of the people in charge. Phone calls don't work in Israel. Screaming and shouting at the office, and sometimes breaking down in tears do. In New York, that was the school's job to advocate; here it fell to us. It was a big learning curve for me and was against my nature to behave like this, but the mama grizzly reared her head again.

I also relied heavily on advice from parents who have done inclusion in Israel, from the most veteran whose children had graduated to the ones like me, with young children just starting off. Those parents were a huge help and I started to understand the situation better.

Another crucial element to hammering out our action plan for inclusion was finding our "guardian angel." Tehila, an Israeli with a special education background and training at the Feuerstein Institute, came alongside us to help us navigate, translate and understand all our rights.

I still came up short…many, many times. For example, we never received more than twenty hours for a shadow for Caila. Twenty hours barely covers five full school days, Sunday through Thursday, but in Israel the children also go to school for half a day on Friday. I also couldn't even get a meeting with the principal of the new school when Caila started there. That was until a simple social media post went viral around Israel. It started the day before when Caila's shadow let me know her hours wouldn't cover Friday, so Caila would not be able to attend school. What did I know at the time except to say, okay? Instead, Gavin and I took Caila to the botanical gardens that day and I posted a photo of her on social media with a simple hashtag: #inclusioninIsrael.

Then I shut my phone for Shabbat not knowing what a stir I had made in cyberspace. Somehow, this post went viral reaching government agencies and advocacy groups that fight for inclusion in Israel – this despite the post being in English. I was unaware of the comments people were writing decrying a school that would ban the child with special needs of a new immigrant family from school.

Sure enough, first thing Sunday morning, the school secretary sent a message: CALL ME. We finally got our meeting with the principal, yet it was under rancorous circumstances.

"How dare you go straight to the Ministry of Education with your complaint and not come to us first!" She was livid. "How could you report us?"

Only we had not. My post apparently prompted the education department to send an inspector to the school. This incident was one of the few times Facebook did the screaming and shouting for me, while I enjoyed my Shabbat.

I always focused on what Caila was missing in Israeli versus New York schools, but Gavin had a different take. If there's anything Israeli schools teach the millions of students in its system, it is independence and true grit. The academic level and support for special needs might have been subpar compared to the school we were at in New York, but all of our children were certainly leaning other life lessons. Ironically, before we moved to Israel, I always used this motto for my children: "You get what you get and you don't get upset." Now it was plaguing me and I wanted to cry! Never did that ring more true than it did now in the Israeli school system.

"See how hard it is for her without the support? She is much more stressed." I would whine to Gavin.

He would counter. "Look at Meron and Temira. They are thriving! And they are better children for living in Israel."

Gavin also noted how Caila was thriving. With all of Caila's services in New York, she constantly had professionals hovering over her. She was handed from one therapist to another. Even her shadow, when it was suggested everyone ignore Caila's violent outbursts in an effort to get them to stop, worried she could be sued for taking her eyes off of Caila for one split second! Perhaps Caila was "over supported" in New York and didn't have a chance to learn key skills such as independence and self-reliance. Helicopter parenting – and schooling – even for a child with special needs, can have an adverse effect.

In Israel, Caila found herself operating without a shadow much of the time. She went from an environment where it was forbidden for staff to turn their backs on her to essentially being responsible for herself. Gavin argued that because of that, Caila was learning resilience by default.

Gavin and I did agree, a good compromise would be somewhere between the plethora of services given by New York private schools and the lack thereof in Israel. We call this fictional system London which sits geographically between our two worlds. And in the meantime, we just coped with what we were given.

Along the way we found several organizations that promote and advocate for integration. What Israel lacks in services from the government it makes up for through *tikkun olam* and the 45,000 not-for-profit organizations that meet a variety of needs in society. We depended on Bizchut, Feuerstein, Chabad's Friendship Circle, Shutaf and Beyahad, all whom helped us in some way or another to reach our goals of including Caila in public schools.

I went from being "merely" an advocate and concerned parent to now filling the role of the master's-degree educated case manager who coordinated a team of professionals responsible for the care of my daughter. I could start up and manage a company, but I had zero experience in writing curricula and coming up with behavioral strategies. I had to find, recruit and make sure Caila's therapists – both in and out of school – were on the same page. This gave new meaning to the concept of being a CEO.

And all of this in a foreign language.

In order to match what Caila was getting – for free – in New York's education system, we spend thousands of extra dollars a month to get tutors and therapies to get her the support she needs to be in a typical school environment. In addition, I was suddenly the one doing the schlepping. In New York, all therapies were given at the school and Caila didn't return on the bus until almost 5:00. In Israel, we bring Caila to school and pick her up when it ends at *2:30*! Then the afternoon crush of therapies and after-school activities begins. Again, all on us, with zero government support for the financial burden, transportation costs and no respite workers.

Instead of solving these issues, education officials push parents of children with special needs who are included in regular schools to transfer them to special education schools. There, all of our services, including therapies, transportation and after-school programs, would be provided. But we had always been staunch advocates of inclusion and we decided to plow ahead with the hard work of making it as successful as we could.

Chapter 23

How good and pleasant it is when people live together in unity!

Psalms 133:1

Maybe if I had known a few dozen (or million) things before I moved to Israel, the transition would have been easier. After three years in Israel, I was still in shock with just about everything, but what especially bothered me was the rampant inefficiency of the so-called Start-Up Nation.

A few years ago, I went on a trip to Ethiopia. As I was waiting on an interminable line just to activate my phone, I was able to appreciate Israel's efficiency compared to Africa. But since I had emigrated to Israel from Manhattan, I was far removed from my African roots.

When we made aliyah some people said it would take a year to settle in. Some said three, others seven and one person even ventured twenty. Three years into the journey I realized I still had a long way to go. And so as part of my own *chesed* project I compiled a list for anyone interested in packing up their lives in the West and moving to the Holy Land – the things you really should know before relocating to Israel. These are not going to make the glossy Zionist brochures. And I wish I knew a few of them before I got here!

1. "No" does not really mean no. No is actually a starting point for negotiation. Whenever I handed in one of the million forms

during the aliyah process, I was invariably told "no" straightaway. I naively thought that was the end of that particular request, but I learned it was actually the beginning of a protracted discussion that would ultimately result in "yes." Native-born Israelis know this, hence do not fear the word no. True Israeli chutzpah is "the absence of the fear at hearing 'no' for an answer."

2. Rules seem to exist merely as suggestions. The only real rule is: When in Israel be Israeli. "No camping on the beach"? Pitch your tent with hundreds of others who are blatantly disregarding the sign. "No fires"? Does not apply if you are in the mood to have a charcoal barbecue. "No parking on red and white?" Prohibited, until everyone else is doing it, then feel free to join them.

3. Everyone in Israel knows more than you…about everything. And everyone is perfectly comfortable dispensing unsolicited advice from neighbors and close friends to taxi drivers, shopkeepers, the beggars of the Old City of Jerusalem and perfect strangers walking by as you sit at an outdoor cafe.

4. Screaming is a volume, not a disposition. Yelling at someone does not necessarily mean you hate them and are about to kill them. In fact, after many an argument at the checkout counter or a traffic collision, everyone goes on their way with a wave and "*Shalom, achi.*" Bye, bro.

5. Lines are nonexistent.

6. Helicopter parenting is scorned. From young ages, children walk to school by themselves, ten-year-olds come home well past midnight after youth group activities and teens take the bus alone.

7. Despite #6, sending your kids out in 55 degrees Fahrenheit without gloves, scarf, a hat and a down anorak is considered a form of child abuse. Though they have no idea what cold actually is, Israelis dress their children like Inuits as soon as the temperatures are less than blazing hot.

8. Germophobia was nonexistent in this country before the outbreak of the COVID-19 pandemic. A soldier sitting next to me on a bus asked for a sip from my water bottle! Teachers are too harried to enforce hand washing. At events, salads and food platters are placed on tables with no serving spoons, so double dipping is a given. At playgrounds, parents allow strangers to hold their newborns – so opposite of America where infants are shielded from everything. Israelis think of themselves sort of like one massive (and somewhat dysfunctional) family.

9. Nut allergies are (almost) nonexistent. Coming from America's fervent nut-free policy, it is shocking to see children – babies even – eating peanut butter and Nutella, as if they were staples. Meals at events always feature salads with cashews or sunflower seeds and pistachio ice cream for dessert.

10. RSVPing is nonexistent. While planning a bar and bat mitzvah in my first few months in Israel, I endured some massive panic attacks when only 5 percent of the invite list – all expats – bothered to respond. Meanwhile almost all the Israelis showed up anyway on the day of the event.

11. Start times are elusive to nonexistent. Only sabras – those born in Israel – instinctively know the true start time of concerts and shows. We've been on time to many shows…which have started ninety minutes later than advertised. Somehow all the Israelis, however, showed up late and didn't miss a thing. Next time, somehow, everyone got the memo that this show is starting on time and were there for the start (except for us who didn't want to waste ninety minutes waiting again!)

12. Blinkers are optional, and lanes are interchangeable without warning.

13. The one rule taken with utmost seriousness is the pedestrian traffic light. Suddenly an entire population of ADHD Israelis become patient and wait for the green light to cross the road.

14. Miracles occur daily. From the Iron Dome missile defense system blocking rockets fired from enemy territory to nine-year-old children surviving unsupervised bonfires on Lag B'Omer (the Jewish holiday marking the counting of the omer observed by lighting bonfires around Israel) and the six-year-old leading his younger siblings across a busy intersection, we have constant proof that there is a God and He is protecting Israel. In fact, a T-shirt slogan said it all: "In Israel we don't believe in miracles, we rely on them every day."

15. Native English speakers are strictly banned from translating menus and street signs from Hebrew to English. There are ubiquitous – and sometimes hilarious – spelling and grammar mistakes all around the country, and *not one* of the million Anglos in Israel are consulted to help translate.

16. Driving directions are the same to get to anywhere: "*Yashar, yashar.*" Just go straight. "*Kol hazman,*" the whole time. Whether they don't know or they are averse to details, Israelis just direct people who ask for directions to go straight.

17. Age in Israel is irrelevant. Both toddlers and the elderly can be sitting at a bar or dancing at a concert until two in the morning.

18. Prepare for the country to shut down in inclement weather. Unbelievably, Israelis head out to bars and cafes after a missile attack, but school is canceled over the mere *threat* of snow.

19. After living in Israel, the rest of the world seems affordable. Israelis are prolific travelers and now I understand why. The same two-dollar beer overseas costs you eight dollars in Israel.

20. Just when you are down on Israel, the advertisement on a passing bus wishes you *Chag Same'ach* or blesses the soldiers or encourages charity.

21. Your children will grow up with a sense of purpose and idealism. They will feel part of something bigger than themselves and develop more empathy and awareness that their peers overseas who are worried about fashion, parties or which brand of beer to drink.

22. Israel is probably the only place you will find an off-duty soldier walking on the beach in a bikini…with her M-16 slung over her shoulder.

23. "God grant me coffee to deal with the things I can and wine for the things that I cannot," will become your mantra.

24. Google Translate is a must. Without it my children would have missed many birthday parties (announced on WhatsApp with one day's notice) or parent-teacher conferences.

25. Never trust Google Translate. A verbatim translation from my son's Bnei Akiva group informed me: "Young lovers, funny, huge and very dear to us! Today will be an action teaspoon at 6–7:30, we will be in a synagogue." Not to mention, my name Jodi is always translated "Goody."

26. Six months after making aliyah, you are expected to be a veteran. That's mainly because another wave of new immigrants has arrived by that point and you are old news. At six months, Israelis no longer applaud you for moving to Israel. Not being able to speak Hebrew buys you scorn, not sympathy.

27. Your life becomes a string of memorials countered by celebrations. Israelis are obsessed with memorials and mourning, while they are equally obsessed with partying. From Pesach seders to Purim *megilot*, remembering is etched into the Jewish consciousness. Yom HaZikaron (Memorial Day), one of the saddest days, is immediately followed by the rowdiest day of the year, Yom HaAtzmaut (Independence Day). The juxtaposition of mourning and celebration are embedded in daily life.

28. After living in lawsuit-conscious America, Israel feels a bit… lax. When tens of thousands of Israelis cram together to pray at the Kotel for the priestly blessing and, with everyone pushing and shoving, it becomes obvious that only the Holy One above can protect us from ourselves.

29. The postal system in the Start-Up Nation is stuck in the dark ages. It once took nine weeks for a check mailed *within the city* to arrive. An invitation mailed from the United States in October arrived only in April. The only exception to this rule is the army call up letter, which is issued when a child turns sixteen and a half. Without fail those arrive exactly on that day.

30. It rains mud. After the first rainfall everything is dirtier than after the summer drought.

31. Security is tight everywhere in Israel…until it isn't. At schools for example, security guards work until three o'clock in the afternoon. After that, the school is unlocked and open all night long and anyone can walk in.

32. *Savlanut*, patience, is the famous last words of Israelis. When you want something from someone you are supposed to have *savlanut*. "*Le'at le'at*," slowly slowly, they tell you. But if the same person wants something from you, they expect it yesterday. And drivers honk before the light has even turned green.

33. Nothing in Israel happens until "after the *chagim*" (holidays). Renovations, paperwork processing, work projects, even learning at school are all paralyzed until after the major holiday period. School starts on the first of September, but students don't start learning until the day after Simchat Torah. A few months later, there's Hanukkah, then Purim, followed by Pesach, Independence Day and then Shavuot. Plan large projects accordingly because "after the *chagim*" occurs several times a year!

34. Requesting ice at an Israeli restaurant can result in near shock for the waiter or waitress. And you only receive about three cubes at a time.

35. Israel is disparagingly called an "apartheid state," yet go to the mall or a supermarket and you will see Jewish and Arab shoppers walking around in perfect harmony. Same with hospitals where the Arab and Jewish medical staff and patients seamlessly interact.

36. Israelis have no qualms about staring. They size you up as you enter the bus or while you are eating at a restaurant. If you walk into a meeting or a class you feel all eyes on you as you make your way to a seat. Of course, if you are Israeli you stare back so it is not uncomfortable. But it makes me squirm with self-consciousness and I get defensive especially if the staring is directed at Caila.

37. Personal space is not a thing in Israel.

38. Play dates are scheduled mere minutes beforehand, which was weird and refreshing after coming from New York where they had to be scheduled two weeks or more in advance.

To add to my list here are a few "Only in Israel" encounters:

1. Gavin was in a minor traffic accident with a man riding a scooter. A few days after the accident Gavin got a phone call: "Hey, it's Moshe, from the accident. Can you give me a ride to the police station so I can file a report on the accident?" Gavin gave him a ride, and then they went out for coffee together.

2. I took the kids on a bus from Jerusalem to Tel Aviv during rush hour and we could not get four seats together. No one would even move to let me be with young Caila! However, the passengers seated next to the children helped them with their seatbelts and, when Caila complained that she was cold, the young man next to me asked all the

passengers for a sweater. Soon enough a sweater was passed forward and Caila was comfortable.

3. Though we were all squashed like sardines on a bus, I watched with utmost fascination as a person who entered the bus from the back door passed up a two-hundred-shekel bill through dozens of hands to the driver and his change made it back in its entirety. I've seen this happen many times and with all sorts of change. Never would this occur in New York.

4. We took a taxi back home after a hike when the kids started squabbling over sips from my nearly depleted water bottle. The taxi driver heard the commotion and insisted that I take his water bottle for them. "*Geveret*, Ma'am, I insist that your children drink! Your children are in *my* taxi and they are *my* responsibility!"

5. Another taxi story. We returned to Israel after an overseas trip, but our luggage didn't arrive and the keys to get into the apartment were inside one of the suitcases! In the taxi on our way home, I started crying. The taxi driver, who had been listening to our conversation, interjected. "*Geveret*, please don't cry. You and your family can sleep at my house and your children can wear my kids' pajamas. Don't be upset." Can you imagine *that* happening in New York?

6. I went to enroll Temira in a horseback riding camp. When I asked for the forms I assumed would be involved, the clerk told me he just needed my phone number. "If she has medical issues, I assume you would want to tell me. If someone else is picking her up, you will tell me. It's my job to make sure there are horses and fun," he told me.

7. Despite an announcement of a suspicious package and a mandatory evacuation of the Jerusalem bus terminal, no one moved. *Not one person was willing to lose his or her place in line even at the risk of losing their life*. It literally took a team of dozens of law enforcement officers to get people to move to the lower level. Contrast this to South Africa where I recall being at a shopping center when a bomb

threat came in. Mass panic and a rapid evacuation ensued. We took our fire drills, bomb drills and civil defense preparation drills seriously. But then again, we didn't have to guard our place in line as vociferously!

Israel is a crazy, chaotic country, full of chutzpah, but equally full of meaning and grit.

I tried so hard to adapt to it all. I hoped that before long I would adjust to this new lifestyle and everything would be okay. I had transitioned before to other countries and cultures. I had rebuilt my life. I had figured it out and found success. It would be no different in Israel, I assumed. But you know what happens when you assume.

Israel is not like any other country on the planet.

Chapter 24

That person is like a tree planted by streams of water, which yields its fruit in season.

Psalms 1:3

Not only was inclusion in Israel way more challenging (as was everything I was starting to realize), but as Caila got older and proved to be unusually high functioning for a child with Down syndrome, the complexities of raising her multiplied exponentially.

She had become aware that she was different, and she even knew that what she had was called Down syndrome. Sometimes she owned her differences. For instance, when we asked if she knew what it means to have the syndrome, she jumped right to it.

"It means I'm special," she beamed.

At other times, being different seemed to perplex her or even hurt, such as finding it difficult to keep up with the fast-paced banter of the group of girls in her class or when months passed without a single invitation for a playdate.

Each year it was getting harder to be Caila.

I'm not sure how much we as parents contribute to that. I'm definitely guilty of being the typical Jewish mom who sets the bar high for my children and then pushes them to achieve. Caila was no exception. We set high expectations for her and scheduled her life accordingly. Eventually Caila's schedule rivaled that of Israel's prime minister. As we settled into Israeli life, Caila was getting therapies in both Hebrew and English and was being run from school to activities six days a week.

We also began encountering various behavioral problems at school as Caila got older. As her feelings and awareness matured, it became increasingly harder for her to control her impulses. Her communication skills were adequate, but sometimes she could not express herself quickly enough. Once at school, some of the kids told her she was ugly, so she hit them. Caila was sent home for this.

While we don't condone violence, I was hoping the staff could understand that without the tools to communicate fully and express her feelings, Caila was just overwhelmed and responded in the quickest way she could. Another time at the beginning of the school year she got punished for not returning to class after the bell rang. There was a commotion at the school as the staff searched for her. After she got home she explained to me what happened.

"Imma, all the kids ran away and I didn't know where to go," she cried. "I was just lost."

My heart just broke for her.

She was fully aware she was "different" among her classmates and was starting to feel socially rejected. This led her to act out – and many times she was accused of bad behavior. She was misconstrued as being "mean" when many times she was merely seeking attention and lacked the skills to adequately express herself.

It is hard to understand Caila's perspective sometimes, but I wish people would stop and wait for her to explain. Many of the times Caila got into trouble she was simply overwhelmed with the challenges she encountered, and she responded out of stress.

We thought putting Caila with other children who have special needs at her youth group would give her a break from keeping up with typically developing children all day at school. But Caila protested.

"Imma, I want to go with the real people," she said.

"Who are the *real people*?" I asked her.

"Like, *not* Leah," Caila named a friend's daughter (not her real name), a much younger girl with Down syndrome. Caila had already delineated the world and she was going to try hard to land on the "right" side of the chromosomal spectrum. She wanted to be "real," a euphemism really for just being "typical."

Whether she was getting this message from school, society or even us, Caila knew that she was the exception and she seemed to make it her life quest to be "normal." I often wonder, with all our pushing for inclusion and setting high goals, had we created unhealthy expectations of her? This is a guilt I deal with on a regular basis.

But on the other hand, she is more advanced than her peers in a special education school too. After she finished third grade, Caila told us that the following school year she wanted to stay in the classroom for all lessons rather than be pulled out for one-on-one work for certain subjects. Caila even suggested that she study extra over the summer so that she could be with her classmates more often. She realized that getting pulled out for tutoring made her different. And she did not want to be different.

What I find most difficult in raising Caila is watching how she fluctuates with her high abilities and functioning and her sometimes incongruous behavior. For example, she is at grade level in math, she speaks two languages fluently (something that her parents without disabilities have not mastered) and shows an amazing ability to understand her environment and the people around her. You can ask her what is 20 times 30 and she'll answer 600 immediately. A minute later ask her for 2 plus 2 and she'll respond 3! I don't understand why.

She can be on top of her game one hour and melt down the next. She will keep up with her class in math then go and play with toddler toys at a friend's house.

While I frequently stress out that I am putting too many expectations on her, she also consistently proves our instincts correct about her potential. In third grade when Caila was struggling to keep up with her class in math, even her personal tutor said that maybe she had peaked and that we should set modified expectations. I stood my ground, however, and demanded that we continue to push her to class level. I'm so glad I did – by fourth grade Caila had a breakthrough and she was yet again on par with her class.

I love proving the naysayers wrong. And I love seeing my daughter succeed. She is also elated when she does and beams in her success, and it gives us all the motivation to keep pushing ahead.

On an emotional level she also continues to shock us. When she was four, a friend of ours took her to a Shabbat lunch. She must have heard us discussing whether to take her bag with a change of clothes in case she had an accident. But ultimately, they didn't take the backpack. My friend told me later that when they sat down for Shabbat lunch, Caila gasped.

"Uh oh! I just had an accident!" After my friend looked over in shock, Caila started laughing. "Just kidding!"

This sly sense of humor at such a young age showed us that she had advanced emotional development. Understanding and making jokes shows a high level of mental acuity.

She also began to show a strong desire to be married someday from a young age. I couldn't believe my ears when on one blazing hot day she asked me, "Imma, you know what I am dying for?" I was expecting her to say she wanted a cold drink or ice cream. Instead, she said. "I am dying for my husband to kiss me on the lips!" After nearly choking, I asked her to explain why she wants that so badly.

"I just want a husband who will love and cuddle me and look after me."

Her nuanced answer showed that she is fully aware of her own needs and desires. She looks adults in the eyes and has sophisticated conversations. She shows incredible empathy and high emotional intelligence. She compliments people and flashes them her winning smile.

And yet, she can have an accident because she freaked out at seeing a bumblebee.

It is also hard to discipline her, but not because we feel bad for her that she has Down syndrome. For instance, once Gavin was scolding her for something and she got really sullen. After he was done, she asked him, "Abba, are you unhappy? Do you need a hug?"

How are we supposed to be serious about discipline when we are on the floor laughing?

Many times, when Gavin and I squabble, Caila will interject and try to put the matter to rest.

"Guys, stop!" she once commanded. Then she addressed me, "Imma, he is your husband and right now he's tired and grouchy. And despite that, you love him anyway. So, behave yourself!"

With Caila around we never know what we are going to get. Though she might be struggling to keep up with her peers academically, many times she acts like the adult in the room.

She also unconsciously evokes a gut-wrenching groan of helplessness with her own observations from time to time. One random morning, she just piped up with this zinger: "Imma, I really don't want to be special needs anymore. I just want to be a regular kid."

What am I supposed to say to a child who thinks like this? Even with all the investment we pour into her, we realize that her independence will be limited. Clearly, she sees what is meant to be in the "normal" world and is frustrated by her inability to achieve that. Caila's days at school are essentially spent standing on tiptoe, arms outstretched trying to climb up to everyone else's level socially and academically. She lives between two worlds: She doesn't fit 100 percent into her inclusion environment, but neither does she fit into a special education setting. These are some of the complexities of raising a high-functioning child with special needs.

We knew that starting from first grade, one of the more challenging aspects of inclusion would be the social component. As children get older, they socialize more by talking and less by playing. This is difficult for children like Caila who process at a slower pace. As these issues began to emerge with Caila, I realized that the battleground of inclusion had changed for us. We had fought to get the broad spectrum of services that were due Caila by law, then to include her in various schools. As she matured, we found ourselves waging a much harder and less tangible battle – social inclusion.

One Purim, Caila delivered *mishloach manot* to her school friends at their homes. Then she waited at our apartment for her friends to bring her a gift for the holiday. But only one girl came. Caila was crushed.

On Lag B'Omer, when every teenager in Israel is busy building a bonfire – hence no babysitters can be found in the whole country – we declined an invitation to an adults-only barbecue. When the hosts found out we had no one to watch Caila, they made an exception so we could bring her. Gavin asked Caila on the way if she knew why she was the only kid invited. He was trying to make her feel good and was going to say that it was her exemplary behavior that got her an invite. But Caila already knew the real reason.

"I know," she said matter-of-factly. "Because I have special needs."

Then there was the Yom Kippur I'll never forget. I spent the day in a continual flow of tears, and not because I was struggling with fasting or that I had some revelation of deep repentance and atonement wash over me. No, it was because of what I saw from the synagogue window as I tried to focus on the prayers. I sat in line with the window so I could keep an eye on Caila while she played outside, but every time I glanced out the window, I saw her sitting alone while all the children were playing. And she looked so sad. It is hard for her to manage the dynamics of a big group in an unstructured environment. Our telltale sign when Caila is anxious or stressed is that she picks at the skin on her lips. And on Yom Kippur, her lips were bleeding. By the time services were over I was a wreck. As soon as I saw Gavin, I just burst into uncontrollable sobs in front of everyone. Watching Caila struggle so much for the social inclusion that she craves was just too much for me.

I understand it is difficult for girls her age to accommodate Caila. They too are trying to fit in and manage the complicated group dynamics. When one particularly sensitive mom noticed the disparity, she asked one girl at a time to pair with Caila one-on-one – and it worked so well. Caila was beaming and she felt included. It was the best part of the day.

These are some of the perplexities that we deal with as we raise Caila. Gavin and I were given Caila for a reason, but we are no better than any other parent who has a child with special needs. We are all scraping for reserves of our energy and will to try to rise to our challenges. I constantly need to pray for wisdom to know how to help Caila and to find the delicate balance between challenging her to progress, but not stressing her out at the same time. Some days are a little harder than others.

I am so thankful that we have a strong connection to God. From those early days, which were so stressful setting up doctor visits and therapies, coming to terms with our new reality and dealing with people's stupid comments, to our present challenges with a preteen, it has always been our trust in God that kept us going. After Caila's birth, I often wondered if I would ever truly feel happy and light-hearted about life again. The moment crept up on me about four months later when I realized that I *was* enjoying life and was totally in love with my little princess. I was confident that I would still lead a happy – yet challenged – life. There would be difficult moments along the way, but I knew we would ultimately be okay. This has all proven true.

Actually, we have been better than "okay." Parenting a child with special needs teaches you patience, humility, determination, resilience and acceptance. It's a constant rollercoaster of emotions you didn't know you were capable of, ranging from a fierce love for your precious child to frustration at developmental delays, medical complications, failures in the education system and social settings. You experience greater pain with the hurts and challenges, but a far greater joy than you thought possible at the routine milestones, because they were so hard fought.

I remind myself that our *Imma'ot* (biblical mothers) endured trials and tribulations from barrenness to marriage issues to challenges raising their own children. If life was meant to be simple these matriarchs would have been drinking mojitos on a Sinai beach. The Torah never promised that God would grant us a life of perfection or free of challenges. In fact, most biblical heroes of the faith became such precisely because they faced and overcame obstacles that were in their paths.

Inclusion will get harder as time goes on and we are constantly being reminded of this daunting fact not only by educators, therapists and doctors, but also by social realities. But we believe we must press on as long as Caila keeps achieving. We have seen Caila's capabilities and her character change people's knee-jerk reactions to Down syndrome. She challenges their perceptions of people with special needs.

Raising Caila has been a lesson for me every day in what is possible to achieve, for all of us.

Raising Caila has also been an exercise in raising my consciousness, my compassion, my appreciation for life and, sometimes, my blood pressure as well. But I constantly remind myself what I learned in the early days: Life does not have to be perfect in order to be wonderful.

Tales of a Modern Jewish Woman

Becoming Israeli

You know your children have acclimated to Israel when...

We were flying back to Israel after a ten-day jaunt to Greece, waiting to board our plane, when suddenly it became obvious that yes, we were returning to Israel – everyone had taken up my "favorite" Israeli pastime of pushing and shoving.

I warned Caila to be careful to not get pushed, but she shrugged her head.

"Don't worry about me Imma, I push back harder," she said.

Yes, Caila had officially become more Israeli than me.

Another funny Caila story. I left Meron to babysit Caila while I attended a class. Meron decided it would be okay to leave Caila, who was eleven, for a little while alone while he went for a jog. He gave her my phone number and left.

Caila immediately called me to see if it worked. I answered and reassured her she was going to be fine, but that maybe she should call her grandparents first if she had any questions since I was in a class.

"Okay, I will," she said.

Then, she thought of another question.

"Oh wait, Imma. One more thing – are you in Israel or in New York?"

Even my baby girl knew it was impossible to keep up with my schedule. I really could have been anywhere.

Caila wasn't the only one far outpacing me in acclimatizing. Gavin was doing pretty well himself. When he first started working for an Israeli company, he raised an idea during a conference call – and one of his colleagues wasted no time in expressing his contempt at the notion.

"What are you, meshugah?*" the man demanded to know if Gavin was crazy. Though shocking to a Westerner, it is normal for Israelis to express their strong and plentiful opinions even in business meetings.*

Gavin took the lesson to heart. A few years later, when I was in Australia visiting family and he was in Israel, he arranged for flowers to be delivered to me before Shabbat. They arrived nearly wilted and with the price tag attached.

When Gavin heard about this, he went into full Israeli mode and called the company, threatening the apologetic woman that if I didn't receive a bouquet worth of a night at the Oscars or a full refund within the hour he would go on social media and destroy the company. The woman – who hastily agreed to both a refund and a replacement bouquet – actually started crying! That's when Gavin realized, he wasn't dealing with an Israeli company and he could have toned down the aggression to a level more appropriate for the customer-centric Australian culture.

I, however, am a wimp. After my first personal encounter with Israeli chutzpah, I broke down and cried. The man I was working with at the venue for one of my events started screaming at me, in the usual Israeli custom of having a disagreement. He was mortified at my tears – because he was expecting me to scream back! That's what you do in Israel.

A year later, the same scenario occurred with the same man. This time I was ready and I screamed back.

Then, after I got home, I cried.

Chapter 25

He gives power to the weak and strength to the powerless.

Isaiah 40:29

My wake-up call came when nine-year-old Meron made an observation as we were traveling through France as a family.

"I have a secret," he whispered conspiratorially. "Imma's having another baby!"

Gulp.

From out of the mouths of babes.

I was not even close to being pregnant and it was three years after Caila's birth. Meron's innocent observation became the knell for me to look in the mirror and face facts: I had gained so much weight that I could have passed for being pregnant again. It was ironic because with my Type-A personality I was in control of so many other areas of my life. Businesswoman. Entrepreneur. Special needs advocate. Founder of a not-for-profit. Super mom. I left no stone unturned. While I knew I was overweight and had continued to gain weight for years, I was less obsessed with that aspect of my life as with other areas. My clothes had gotten smaller, but I didn't have time to really process that new and nagging reality. I would simply throw on a jacket or compensate somehow. Denial prevented me from making changes.

Those few words from Meron became my clarion call. If my own child thought this, what were others thinking? Up until that point I had not been concerned by what others thought about my weight. For all of my insecurities, being overweight was never an issue for me. I wasn't inhibited by my looks. My staggering frame did not compound my panic in front of an audience or negatively impact my self-image.

But facts are facts and when I finally faced them head on in the mirror, I knew I had to lose weight. I had to strive to be healthier and make better choices. I had to find a solution to become a healthier mom and community leader.

That began what would become a six-year "diet" or attempt at it anyway. Every Monday morning for the next six years I started a new diet. I woke up with determination after a weekend of Shabbat meals and decided that *now* I would be hardcore. The resolve usually lasted until about nine o'clock in the morning when the first hunger pangs set in. I would break down and eat something, maybe "healthy," at that point, but usually by midday I was back to my old habits until the following Monday rolled around and my diet began anew. It took years for me to get my act together and actually succeed in losing weight. In fact, it wasn't until after living in Israel for three years (and gained an additional twenty-five pounds) that I found some mental real estate to seriously focus on dieting and getting my weight under control.

The problem was I really had no plan when I started out. With the start of every diet each week, my resolve melted away like butter on hot toast with the onset of hunger. Not having a plan meant I turned to anything that would satisfy me. I also did a lot of "stress eating" in those days. I worked late and slept little, so I reached for the closest food, whether a bag of potato chips or, many times, chocolate. Chocolate was going to be part of my life no matter what. But it didn't help that while starving myself on a "diet" that I reached for chocolate more often and at bad times. And I was addicted to junk food because it was easy and tasted appropriately great.

I had a busy life, I couldn't be bothered to prepare healthy foods and I was also feeding my emotions. Whether dealing with the challenges presented by special needs, Caila's rejection by Jewish schools, launching a new company or managing the debts of my organization, I fed my stress and anxiety with sugar and junk food to ease my turbulent feelings.

216

When I mentioned to people that I wanted to take charge of my weight, everyone around me suggested I start exercising. The only problem was, I'd been exercising religiously since the year 2000. I have made it a point to spend a minimum of four hours a week exercising, whether running or walking, weightlifting or using a treadmill. I treated exercise with the same natural obsessiveness with which I approach everything. The moment I settled on this requirement of four hours a week in 2000, I only missed three weeks – and those were the three times I had a C-section. I took a week off for each birth. Then I returned to my four weekly hours albeit with a slightly modified schedule so as not to rip any sutures! When I broke my leg, I still managed to meet my four-hour-a-week quota by focusing on upper-body routines like lifting weights from a bench. Even when traveling, to this day, I exercise in the hotel room or take long walks.

I even applied a unique and pedantic system of calculating my exercise hours. For instance, walking is lower impact than running. I would have to walk one and a half hours in order for it to count as an hour of working out.

My biggest problem was that the muscles that worked hardest in any given week were my stomach and mouth muscles, endlessly engaged in food consumption. And after a workout, I always rewarded myself with way more calories than I burned. Clearly, my consistent exercise routine was not helping lose the pounds. It was all about my eating.

It became particularly apparent one Tisha B'Av. I woke up with a migraine and the shakes for a coffee. I prepared food for my kids throughout the day and had to stop myself from picking at the food as I made it. It became evident how I chronically picked during food prep. Another time when I took the kids for ice cream, I didn't order my own, fully knowing I would be eating half of theirs. My daughter commented, when I was picking off her plate, "Imma, you should sit and eat a meal, not stand and eat." Only then did I realize I was not eating, just gleaning from the leftovers. These random incidents made me realize how atrocious my eating habits were, and so was the message I was sending my kids.

I continued to gain weight after we moved to Israel, perhaps even at an accelerated pace. I had reasoned that if I was going to live in Jerusalem against my will, I would reward myself with enjoying the food. I was finally living in a place where nearly all food outlets were kosher. Delectable items such as *burekas* or *rugelach* were readily available every couple of storefronts. And since I was frequently traversing the neighborhood on foot I could buy a croissant or cheese pastry while passing by and finish it before I reached my destination. I had to eat anyway, so I may as well enjoy the good stuff. This tasty food became a way to gloss over my unhappiness.

Eating became my comfort to an even greater extent in Israel – and it was starting to show. I had a major shock that rattled me from my junk food coma. Facebook started tagging me as someone else – a family member who is a few decades older and who is overweight. Facial recognition doesn't lie and it was telling me that I too was obese. At first, I thought Facebook was just being glitchy, but then I looked in the mirror. I was no longer who I thought I was. I had been married almost twenty-five years and put on fifty-five pounds. Even Facebook no longer recognized me.

It was time to get serious.

I knew from experience though that I needed a system, and one that would suit my lifestyle. I had to be completely honest with myself: I could not adopt a program that involved meal prep and shopping for nutritious ingredients that needed to be cooked. I hate cooking and I loathe shopping. If this was going to work, I needed a regimen that avoided putting the onus on me to provide the healthy food for myself.

I sought out people I knew who had succeeded in losing weight until I found friends who used a method that would suit my lifestyle. One friend in particular who lost a significant amount of weight in a short period of time used a program that was based on protein bars and shakes. The ingredients kept him satisfied and prevented him from reaching for the foods that would derail his diet. This sounded like the very method I needed. All I had to do was order the products (that was the only food prep involved) and just stuff these bars in my purse, my pockets, my car and anywhere else I thought I'd be when I needed a quick bite. Now this was a plan I could stick with.

I threw myself into this as I do with anything, obsessively. I ordered the low-calorie, on-the-go (and kosher) protein bars and shakes which were excellent options for me.

Then I adapted the products and the method to my lifestyle. I have a very active social life – something I won't compromise on. Basically, I was vigilant during the day, eating my bars and shakes and controlling my calories. Then I splurged in the evenings when out with friends.

The goal was to consume the bars or shakes every three hours, even if I wasn't hungry, to maintain an even metabolic rate. I would always have a protein bar on me because I didn't want to depend on my own lack of discipline to make good food choices. I also had the company's high-protein pretzels on hand for late-night snacking since I slept so little and often worked through the night.

I remember after I started, when the first Monday morning rolled around – and for the first time in six years, I succeeded in keeping to my diet. I was elated. Finally, I had found my solution.

I stuck with this plan and, slowly but consistently, the results came in. Over seventeen months I lost forty-six pounds. I never actually read the book *The Secrets of Skinny Chicks*, but I could sum it up in one sentence: Skinny chicks eat less and exercise more. During my journey to drop the pounds, I thought of this book a lot. Because suddenly I was eating less and losing weight! It was very simple science.

This "simple science" also helped me while traveling. Weight issues aside, traveling as a kosher family has always been a challenge. With few kosher restaurants outside of cities with large Jewish populations, we rely on eating canned tuna and crackers that we schlep in our suitcases. As a result of this we are perpetually unsatisfied and frequently turn to junk food to satisfy our hunger. With my protein bars and shakes, I was able to avoid so many unnecessary calories and actually be more satisfied than I ever had been.

Some people challenged me that these bars were not nutritious compared to raw fruits and vegetables. But I look at it this way: They were way healthier than all the chocolate, Danishes, croissants, potato chips and fried food that I had been eating. Protein bars were, for me, a nutritional upgrade.

It was a long road. I realized this after those arduous first few weeks when I dropped twenty-two pounds – and *not a single person* even noticed I had lost weight! That showed me just how far out of control I had gotten. Thankfully I was doing this for myself, so the only approval I needed was my own. But still, it was amazing to me that after all those months of discipline, it was *that* unnoticeable.

All those years while I was packing on the pounds – and as part of my denial – I kept my clothes no matter how tight they became. As I lost weight, it was exciting to progressively fit back into my "skinny" – but now outdated – clothes again. With each milestone of dropping a size, I happily donated my larger clothes. It was like making a vow that I'd never need them again because I refused to gain that weight back. For me, the symbolism was important.

With all that I had accomplished in life, this was one of the battles I wasn't sure I could win. To finally tick this box of achievement, was a great feeling. It also caused me to appreciate a few things about living in Israel. I was never able to find the time or energy to accomplish this in New York. But in Jerusalem I was able to scrounge together some energy reserves to succeed despite all the challenges I encountered here.

Somehow, living in this hard place had drawn out of me an inner fortitude that even I didn't know I had.

Tales of a Modern Jewish Woman

Worlds collide

I looked at fifty-four apartments in Jerusalem before I found a place that met all of my requirements. I was adamant it should be wheelchair accessible, have an open plan with a large enough space to host fifty people and be located in a neighborhood close to the center of Jerusalem where I could reach my regular spots by foot. I did not want a coveted garden apartment because of security issues and my lingering trauma from burglaries in South Africa. Naturally, there wasn't much available that met all of my demands. Hence we traipsed from apartment to apartment.

In other countries, homes are staged so they look desirable to prospective buyers. In Israel, you need an active imagination. You walk into real life – toys, laundry, food on the stove and sometimes a person passed out on the sofa. Eventually, Gavin and I walked into an apartment that I fell in love with at once.

The woman selling the place gasped when she saw us.

"You look so familiar," she said wondering how she knew us, until the penny dropped. Suddenly, she went bright red and her eyes got really wide. "Oh my God."

From Israel, she was visiting New York before she got married and someone told her she needed to go to the Samuels for a Shabbat dinner while she was there. She was secular at the time.

"You got me so drunk with all those lechayims *I ended up throwing up on your bathroom floor! I crashed on your sofa."*

"Seriously? That's how I met the Samuels too!" The real estate agent chimed in.

Both the seller and the real estate agent had passed out on the couch in our New York apartment at different time. That was a not uncommon occurrence at our dinners. Now both of these women were religious.

Well, it was well worth all those Shabbat dinner preparations and clean-ups afterwards because, despite receiving higher offers on the apartment, the seller told her husband they must sell it to us. She knew we would use their home for good – she had experienced it personally.

And we surely do. Our Shabbats continue in Israel with all of the lechayims *and hospitality for which we are known.*

CHAPTER 26

We live in a wonderful world that is full of beauty, charm and adventure. There is no end to the adventures we can have, if only we seek them with our eyes open.

Quote on my hotel room door in Greece

I was showing a friend of mine photos of our family trip to Germany and proudly noted the picture of my children standing outside the Wannsee villa where the Nazis made the Final Solution official.

Located just outside Berlin, this infamous mansion was host to the Wannsee Conference in 1942. There the "Final Solution" – the plan to systematically annihilate all of Europe's Jews – was given the approval to continue massacres of Jews that had already taken place across Germany and other parts of Europe. For my children to be standing there was a special moment for all of us, as the great-grandchildren of the only survivor on Gavin's side. We all stood there as survivors.

My children were twelve, ten and six at the time. On this particularly emotional journey, we visited concentration camps, Nazi headquarters and old communist sites as well. My friend smiled politely, then I finally asked what she was really thinking.

"Shouldn't you take your kids to the zoo instead?"

The thought had not crossed my mind. We never considered shielding our children from truths and horrors such as these. On the contrary, I believe that with opportunity comes responsibility. If my children have the chance to travel the world, they have a responsibility to learn about it – to learn from the good, but also from the mistakes of history. We have no qualms about bringing our children to Holocaust museums, concentration camps, war memorials and the throne of Satan. The imagery, smells and somberness resident in these sites is more impactful than reading about then. They've learned about genocides carried out against Cambodians and Armenians, the ramifications of communism in Cuba, violence caused by the drug trade in Colombia and, of course, the Final Solution, this is the sort of knowledge my children walk away with after a family trip abroad.

We've never fit into a box culturally or religiously, and our type of traveling is no exception. I don't have many friends who would stay at a Catholic pension just to save some money. And our kids have developed a passion for intrepid travel too. They would rather experience life in an off-the-beaten-track village than go to the zoo anyway.

Gavin and I were always obsessive travelers. It was one of those passions we shared and developed together. We love to absorb other cultures, learn the history and religions of each land and understand the world a little better. We did not compromise on this when we had children. We sought instead to find a way to bring them with us. From infancy to teenage years we carried on as we'd been going. Whether schlepping through India with a toddler or rowing a canoe on the Amazon with a baby in tow just to get to our hut, we refused to modify our destinations.

From when I was a young girl, I dreamed of traveling the world. Later, when I lived in Israel for my gap year, I was able to travel to nearby countries in Europe and the former Soviet Union. Then after Gavin and I were married, we lived in Australia and New Zealand, which afforded us proximity to Asian countries. When we moved to the United States we explored many of the fifty states. After moving to Israel, I found one of the advantages was being at the crossroads of three continents. Being so close to Europe, Asia and Africa made it easier to travel and for me to "escape."

I had a secret goal of seeing forty countries before I had children. But unbeknownst to Gavin and I, our entire community was conspiring for us to have children. We were honored at every *brit* we attended to be the *kvaters*, the people who bring in the baby. As a *baal teshuvah*, someone newly returned to Judaism, I had no idea this was a *segulah* – an action that brings spiritual positivity. Gavin and I were always touched that so many people regarded us as such good friends, meanwhile they were doing it in the hope that we would start having babies of our own. They had no idea I was purposely holding off so I could hit up forty countries before giving birth.

By the way, I did visit forty countries beforehand, as I'm writing this book, I have been to eighty-seven countries, with no plans to slow down.

Our traveling is anything but glamorous, however. Our three months of travel one year cost the same as one family's weeklong stay at a five-star resort. Our extremely low budget means spending a lot of time on long layovers at airports and driving on back roads to reach our destination. We stay at pensions, hostels, convents and sometimes even in huts or tents. This is especially challenging at times because quite often, Gavin is not able to travel with us because of work commitments or can only join us for a few days of a trip.

Gavin and I came up with a philosophy on our traveling: The Cherry Pie Dilemma. Imagine your mom bakes you a delicious cherry pie, but she forgot to remove the pits. Would you still eat a slice, or would you forgo it? And would you choose a big slice, which would mean more pie – but also more pits? This is the perfect analogy for our family's travels. We choose to eat a huge slice and deal with the pits. It is worth it for the delicious bites and flavor in between.

Understandably, not everyone wants the pits. One friend told me our trips sounded more like her worst nightmares.

Sometimes our travel really is the pits. The photos I sent to our family and the Facebook posts of one particular trip were truly deceiving. While everyone saw the highlights, what they didn't see were the mosquitos that feasted on us and the hours of uncomfortable travel, which included a boat ride to our nauseating budget accommodations. When we arrived at our *rancherio*, a small shack, we found the bathroom full of garbage and poop floating in the toilet!

In Thailand, I was a victim in an elaborate jewelry scam. When we reported this to the police, we discovered the hard way that they were involved! I left the country as quickly as possible, fearing for my life. Another time, at an Incan ruin in Peru, we were held up at gun point and mugged. In Budapest, Gavin was marched around at knife point late at night forced to withdraw cash from several ATM machines for his captors.

We've lost or have been robbed of small items like sunglasses to big-ticket items such as laptops and, once, my American green card. That occurred in Costa Rica even after we were required to sign a paper that we were made aware of a certain scam aimed at tourists. Street savvy that we were (not), we didn't even get far from the airport when our rental car got a flat tire and some locals were conveniently nearby to help us. When we arrived in the next town I realized they had swiped my green card – the only document I could use to get back into the United States. Between the Easter holiday and bureaucracy, I had no way to prove I could legally return to America. Gavin had to leave me there and fly back to New York to mail proof of my status to the United States embassy.

In the Balkans, I got an infection in my nail bed. We found a rural medical clinic that looked like a communist relic. The "healthcare professional" cut, squeezed and dressed my finger with no gloves and no local anesthetic in less than five minutes. She called Caila a *Mongol* – the outdated term for Down syndrome – and then gave her a half-eaten roll of candy. It was a little rough, but again, what a life lesson.

We have also been victims of anti-Semitism. A group of us at a pension in Greece were kicked out just five minutes before Shabbat began after one of our friends mentioned we were from Israel. The man suddenly snapped.

"We don't want Jews here!" He demanded we leave. When we refused, he brought his extended family – brothers, uncles, etc., all burly Greek men – to forcibly remove us from the place. We found ourselves stranded in the streets of this far-flung mountain town on Sabbath eve. Our leader had to explain to other hotel clerks the cultural and religious reasons why ten of us as, Orthodox Jews, couldn't carry our suitcases, didn't use money and were just kicked out of another accommodation simply based on our race and religion. One finally bought our story and we had a place to stay.

My most petrifying experience occurred as Gavin, a friend and I were driving through the Jordanian desert on our way back to Israel. I had a nagging feeling that the driver was going the wrong direction. Suddenly two jeeps came out of nowhere and blocked our car. Armed men jumped out and demanded money. I thought for sure this was the end. Our driver was in on this and left us stranded in the desert. We waited hours until another car passed. For an exorbitant fee and a lot of hope that this driver wasn't involved in the previous scam, we got a ride to a border crossing.

The story got worse, however, after the Israeli soldiers freaked out upon seeing Jews at a border crossing meant for Arabs. They separated us for intensive questioning and didn't care that we had just been held up and robbed in the desert. After we were finally released, we discovered the only transportation out of there were Arab buses that required men and women to travel separately. I refused to split up with Gavin after all that happened, so we decided to walk to a distant bus stop the Israeli soldiers told us about. As we walked toward it, suddenly the watchtower guards sounded a harrowing alarm. Walking there was forbidden because of *land mines*!

That was it for me. I crumpled in a heap on the ground. As if by providence, just then a phone company worker was driving by. He asked what happened and offered to take us where we needed to go.

Thankfully, most of our less-than-glamorous experiences can be chalked up to inconveniences rather than dangers. In Vanuatu, a Pacific island, we drove the car into a sand bank off a deserted road and Gavin had to comb the area to find villagers to rescue us. Once we spent sixteen hours stuck on the side of road in Ecuador. In India we slept in beach bungalows, which sounds enchanting until you face the reality that there are neither air conditioners nor running water, but, hey, we were on the beach and it was super cheap! I have slept in hammocks, in cars, on a beach, in a park, with bed bugs in Ireland and in a roach-infested train station. We have stayed at many "hotels" with no showers, electricity or even proper toilet bowls. I've had to pee in the sea on several occasions.

Most establishments we stay at have no elevators, so Gavin schleps a lot of bags. Despite being an adventurous traveler, I have not figured out how to scale back my bags. Princess that I am, I always bring my own pillow and a bedsheet.

We also save money by taking buses or trains. In Turkey, we waited for over three hours at the bus station for our *third* twelve-hour overnight bus in seven days – *with* kids! When we finally arrived at our destination, sweaty, exhausted and irritable after an overnight train or bus ride, we hit the road straightaway, touring as though we had a restful night. Amazingly, the children go with the flow. Adaptability and flexibility are two important life skills that have to be experienced in order to learn.

Traveling is an opportunity to broaden your perspective. That happened to me in a small village in Colombia where I used Google Translate and lots of hand gestures to ask the hotel proprietor for an extra towel to use as a bathmat. He looked at me like I was crazy, but he finally brought me a towel. The next day I saw his wife and young children hand washing and wringing out each towel. My request was clearly extravagant in his world.

I always tell my kids, just one twist of fate and we could have been living in the streets rather than jet setting around the world. With privilege come a responsibility to be a better citizen. Traveling gives us a different perspective, empathy for people in different situations and an appreciation of our own blessings.

Despite all of the dangerous and inconvenient scenarios we have faced, I have no regrets. When I mention to friends or family that I am going to places like Myanmar or Ethiopia I get reactions ranging from, "Isn't it dangerous?" and "Why would you go to a rundown place?" to "Are you crazy traveling alone?" which I sometimes do when Gavin is on a business trip.

But if I stayed only at resorts, in world capitals and big cities I would never have witnessed a wedding in an Indian village, a funeral procession in rural Indonesia or the induction of an African chief. These are the experiences that infuse our trips with a flavor we could never find on a tour or at a resort. I love making unplanned stops and discovering a quaint village where locals are drawing water from a well or filling up bottles with homemade wine. I love walking around neighborhoods and shopping at the markets. City parks and public transport allows you to mingle with the locals and get to know the people.

Checking out Jewish communities around the world and learning their fascinating history is also high on our list. Thanks to Chabad we have experienced Shabbat, Sukkot and Pesach in cities from Shanghai to Nova Scotia and Bangkok to Rishikesh, India.

I asked the kids if they would prefer sleep-away camps instead of our family trips. After all we don't stay at luxurious hotels, we change accommodations almost every day and we do a lot of schlepping on unpleasant forms of transportation. Nevertheless, they unanimously agreed they prefer the Cherry Pie type of travel we do. The more they travel, the more they love it. All three of them reached thirty countries before their bar or bat mitzvahs.

That makes me happy because, by far, my favorite thing about traveling has been the conversations it sparked with our children. Religion, poverty, geopolitics and economics are not your usual child-friendly topics. My kids gain vast knowledge on these trips. They are keen to observe how different cultures react to people with disabilities. It's become personal for all of us and my older children are sensitive to how people in different countries treat their sister.

For Caila, the constant input expands her mind in ways that school lessons and therapies cannot. She is a visual learner and so the images she encounters on our trips make a huge impact. However, we do keep up with her homework even while traveling. She's done many a math equation on trains across a foreign country and during layovers between flights.

We passed on the travel bug and we definitely created little maniacs out of our children. When he was ten, I saw Meron perusing the globe and then writing down how many oceans and seas he had swam in. Now he plans many of our itineraries for us.

"Mom, in Baku we can stay further away from town for $15 less a night, or right in town and save on cabs," he will inform me after mapping out our next trip and comparing hotel prices versus cab fares.

No matter how much we study or read, experience is a more valuable education. When we were leaving Ethiopia, fourteen-year-old

Temira said the best part of the trip was our visit to The Red Terror Martyrs' Memorial Museum in Addis Ababa. The solemn museum displays graphic photos and torture instruments involved in the killing of more than half a million Ethiopian dissidents, intellectuals and pro-democracy activists during the brutal reign of the Derg Regime. Our guide, himself jailed and tortured for eight years, displayed intense, raw emotion as he took us through the building. We would have never have even heard of these atrocities had we not visited this place. Now the memories will remain vivid, the lessons etched onto our souls.

But leave it to our feisty and witty middle child to bring it all back down to earth as well. One Shabbat, in Croatia, we left our cheap pension for a walk along the gorgeous shore. We took in the ocean view and the beachfront resorts when, quite decisively and with zero hesitation, Temira threw all our compelling life lessons out the window.

"When I am older, I want to be rich and stay here instead," she said.

Both with travel and with kids, you win some and you lose some!

Tales of a Modern Jewish Woman

Down and out in Africa

The children and I went to Ethiopia when they were fifteen, thirteen and nine years old. Gavin had a business trip and was unable to come with us. We flew into Addis Ababa, but wanted to also visit Gondar, the northern city once home to centuries-old Ethiopian Jewry, known as Beta Israel.

From this already far-flung city, we went on a rough off-roading drive three hours deeper into the country to a hiking trail that wrapped around breathtaking cliffs overlooking the land. Absent from the hike were any warning signs or guardrails and, at any moment, we could have just slipped off the side. My stomach churns to this day when I see the photo of Caila standing precariously near the edge, posing for the camera.

Along the way I started feeling extremely weak. I looked at my children who were powering through the hike, even nine-year-old Caila. If anyone should peter out first, it should be her, I thought. But she was going strong – and I was feeling really ill. How was I going to finish this hike?

We sat to eat lunch on the rim and I peered into the ravine. "Wow, I may fall headfirst into Africa," I mused. As I backed away from the edge, the world started spinning. I quickly warned Meron, "I think I'm gonna die. Call the guide"…something you probably should never say to your children. And then I passed out.

After I came to, I started throwing up and felt generally terrible. The guides got me into a car and rushed me back to the town. Thankfully, within twenty-four hours I was feeling better. When I spoke to Gavin *later that night, he thought it most likely was some kind of local virus to which we had not previously been exposed. Luckily, it lasted only a day.*

The next day we agreed to teach English for our tour guide who had a class of university students eager to improve their spoken English. Even Caila took a few students and led them in conversations, an amazing travel activity for our family.

Afterwards we were crossing the busy street where cars were coming from every direction when Temira said she was feeling sick. "Oh no, this is not happening again," I thought. A few seconds later, Temira fainted in the middle of the chaotic street and the guide frantically helped us get her to the side.

Now that I was feeling better, I was able to think more rationally: How are we going to get Temira help? Will insurance pay for a helicopter if we need to get her to a hospital? But thankfully, Temira came to and almost immediately she and Meron started arguing, which assured me she was going to be fine.

However, this brought up an important discussion for our family: In case of an emergency overseas, who should we call? We set up a family protocol: First, contact Abba, since he is also a doctor. Then, call the closest Chabad House because Chabad will stop at nothing to save a Jew. And then call an embassy, but which one? Since we hold three passports – Israeli, American and Australian – we faced a geopolitical quandary of which embassy to contact in an emergency.

All of these far-out incidents and discussions are just a normal part of Samuels family travel.

Chapter 27

If you change the way you look at things, the things you look at change.

Quote in an Indian train station

Traveling while maintaining Orthodox Jewish customs is another side of the story and makes our journeys a lot more challenging. And sometimes hilarious. Never was it better on display than while on a cruise with my parents, a rare vacation together. Gavin, the kids and I reserved ahead for kosher meals for our family during our time on board. What you get are wrapped trays of pre-made food, similar to the kosher meals on an airplane. Meanwhile everyone else on board indulges in the sumptuous, freshly made gourmet meals.

On the Friday evening, we had our kosher wine and matzah that we brought on board with us so we could do the Shabbat blessings. We all stood for *hamotzi* and my father put a napkin on his head in place of a *kippah* – us with our foil trays next to my parents with their lobsters.

It was all so hilarious to see as well as bizarre – a family of Jews at the same table, some with lobster and some with wrapped, prepackaged kosher food, all partaking in the same blessing at our different levels of religious observance.

Yes, traveling with the Samuels can certainly be interesting. A friend of ours once declined to join us for a camping trip.

"No thanks. Our people camped in a desert for forty years," he said. "Now we stay at the Hilton."

We don't always sleep in a tent, but we do always, somehow, keep kosher and maintain our Jewish identity on all of our trips – thereby killing off any notion of glamor during our travels. You could say that our travel obsession often challenges our Jewishness, or even emphasizes it.

Maintaining our beliefs, customs and traditions is often put to the test while traveling. It is not easy to be Jewish in most countries, and not because of anti-Semitism. It is difficult to find a kosher restaurant outside of cities with large Jewish populations. They are pretty much nonexistent in the Far East and rural European villages. Whenever we travel, we pack suitcases full of kosher products to sustain us during our journey. Imagine living on canned tuna, peanut butter and crackers for two weeks.

We lug with us ready-made packs of kosher Indian and Thai food which we can warm on the radiator (if there is one in our room) and instant couscous. On one trip the flight was delayed because our seven suitcases, which were loaded with food and wine, were too heavy for the commuter jet. The customs officer nearly choked when we declared twelve bottles of wine (the limit was four), meat and dairy products. After an inspection and explaining to the officer this was all for religious purposes, we were admitted into Canada with all of our food – and wine – thank God.

The same menu every day for weeks gets old fast though and, invariably, we resort to junk food and dream about the first real meal we will eat when we get home. Being self-proclaimed foodies, it is hard to miss out on all the local cuisines. Hence, we spend every second Pesach in South Africa and we are indulged with great kosher food thanks to family and friends. The next Pesach we will travel, and our meals will be more like an episode of *Survivor*!

The drudgery of the food issue got to me on one backpacking trip when I was single. I was looking forward to meeting my father at the end of that trip where he was treating me to a stay at a fancy old Colonial-style hotel in Zimbabwe. He was bringing me a bag of kosher food I had packed in South Africa and I couldn't wait to dive in. Unfortunately, my father forgot the bag at home! I was so hungry and protein-deprived by this point, I bought a pot across the street, brought it to the fancy hotel dining room and asked them to make me hard-boiled eggs. Minutes later, a white-gloved waiter arrived with a silver-domed dish. He opened it with a flourish to reveal one lonely hard-boiled egg. All that fanfare for one egg! I had been dreaming of the whole dozen. The fasting would clearly continue a bit longer.

We also keep Shabbat wherever we are. Usually this is not too difficult. One Friday in New York, however, we got stuck in unexpectedly glacial traffic on our way to the Hamptons. We had left the city at one o'clock and it was winter, so the odds should have been in our favor. Nevertheless, we encountered a massive snowstorm and several accidents on the highway while the sun was setting very quickly. At the very last minute before Shabbat started, we had our friends drop us off on the side of the highway and continue on in the car with Meron, who was a baby at the time. Gavin and I walked *nine miles* to our friend's house. I was still in my work clothes – including high heels. It was so dark we couldn't even see ditches on the side of the road and it was below freezing. At one point, it was so dark that we tripped over a dead, frozen deer! We obviously lived to tell the story, but this particular Shabbat was a serious challenge to keep.

If we are traveling overseas during a holiday, we base our destination on accessibility to seder meals for Passover, a sukkah for Sukkot, Torah learning for Shavuot and general parties for Hanukkah. This usually means we are orbiting near the local Chabad house. We have been to sixty-four Chabad houses at the time of this writing around the world. We spent one Pesach with Chabad in Pushkar, a pilgrimage town in India for Hindus and Sikhs. Eggs, meat and alcohol are banned in the city due to religious restrictions. That made observing Passover an even greater challenge.

In general, I have learned that one can make do when forced to be creative. I've made coffee cakes and omelets on a sandwich machine. I even prepared matzah ball soup in a pot without a lid – in total violation of my mother's orders to leave a lid on for twenty minutes straight.

At a national park in the United States during Sukkot, we opened our pop-up sukkah so we could have a meal inside. Only problem – it was forbidden to pitch tents. During lunch, a park ranger drove up and we thought we were in trouble.

"Shalom," he started out. "Ah, you think I don't know what this is? I went to Jewish day school."

He wished us *chag same'ach* and allowed us to keep our "tent."

In a game reserve in South Africa, we did not encounter the same "no tent" rule, but the monkeys used our sukkah as a playground.

We have enjoyed Chabad hospitality in many small towns, and I can tell you it is a small Jewish world. At a Hungarian Chabad house, where nothing in the place has changed since the 1930s, the rabbi had a South African accent and it turns out we were in the same class in high school. That was before we were both religious.

I am always blown away by the personal sacrifice that Chabad families make to live in the middle of nowhere with no Jewish education for their kids and the challenges of getting kosher food. I laughed at the contrast when I saw a rabbi at a Tel Aviv Chabad house wearing roller skates and a top hat, dancing around in the boiling sun just so he could encourage some Israelis to put on *tefillin*.

Traveling kosher is a beautiful reminder of who we are. We are Orthodox Jews no matter how far we travel. Our principles travel with us, they define us, wherever we may be. It is an important lesson for our children. We could be any of the millions of tourists, but when our stomach calls for a meal, we know we are Orthodox Jews.

That said, we do not always advertise the fact that we are Jewish. We play that one by ear since being a Jew and being Israeli can spell danger in certain parts of the world. Gavin and Meron wear baseball caps instead of *kippot* in some places. But except for that one incident in Greece where we were kicked out of a hotel for being Jewish, we've received some of the warmest welcomes in some of the most surprising places. In India, on the affectionately named "humus trail" for the myriad of Israeli travelers who traverse it, the signs are in Hebrew and every restaurant promises genuine Israeli food. The shop keepers even play "spot the Jew" and they once engaged me in Hebrew that was way more proficient than my *kita alef* beginner's Hebrew.

In Turkey, we also hid our Jewish identity, but our disguise was quickly stymied when on Shabbat we needed help to get into the room as the door required an electronic key. Gavin fumbled for words to explain our dilemma to the concierge, however the man quickly grasped the situation.

"Oh! Are you guys Jewish?" He figured it out on his own. He was more than happy to help and we learned that even in a small town in Turkey, people know of Orthodox customs.

We were also astounded by how the merchants in Casablanca knew we were Jewish. We would stop to admire a work of art or some souvenir and the store owner would say, "*Shalom aleichem!*" And as we walked down the street, a boy got our attention.

"Synagogue," he pointed to a nearby building. I have no idea how they pegged us for Jews.

Then in Jordan we heard soldiers at each checkpoint refer to us as *yehud*, Jew in Arabic. Again, we were at the time simply South Africans traveling in a car, with no identifying Jewish or Israeli clothing or ID. How did they even know?

In Cyprus one weekend with three girlfriends from Israel, we asked for our fish cooked in an oven, triple wrapped in foil. We didn't mention it was for kosher purposes, but we were trying to make sure it was done according to our specifications. The chef cocked his head at our requests. "Where are you from?" We all answered separately: United States, Canada and South Africa.

"Hmm, that's funny. Usually only Israelis ask for their fish like that," the chef said. We all laughed.

By keeping our customs while we travel, we have reinforced our Judaic values in our own lives. Also inspiring has been experiencing how Jewish families in remote parts of the world live and practice their faith. In the outback and in far-flung villages, we are amazed to see how our peers – who do not have access to Jewish life in the same way we do – are so committed to their faith.

It is also a reminder to us as parents to be a good example for our children who are constantly watching us and learning from our actions. This is frequently tested during travel. Gavin and I have had to put on brave faces many times, whether upon entering a filthy hostel room, encountering delays at airport or train stations or dealing with a nasty taxi driver who is trying to rip us off. Our reactions will determine how our children respond as well.

We definitely use our traveling as good family time and we have many teachable moments. We see the beauty in the world and we see a lot of crazy situations. The result is that many times our children are more adaptable than we are. And they'll probably be better Jews for that matter!

Tales of a Modern Jewish Woman

Our first – and last – day trip to Mea Shearim

We traveled regularly to Israel before we moved here. One Shabbat we thought it would be nice to take a stroll through Mea Shearim, home to a dense population of Haredi Jews in one of Jerusalem's oldest Jewish neighborhoods. The streets are barricaded on Shabbat and Jewish holidays barring any vehicular traffic.

On the main road, Strauss Street, we happened upon hundreds of Hasidic Jews dancing in the square and we thought, how nice, they must be celebrating a special occasion. We tried to ask a few people what was going on, but no one would speak with us. We were dressed modestly for Shabbat and were clearly Jewish, but it was also obvious, we weren't one of them.

Undeterred, we continued our stroll down a windy and narrow road – Gavin pushing Caila, who was one, in a stroller and my sister-in-law and I holding Temira's hands. My brother-in-law and Meron were slightly ahead of us.

When we turned a corner, we thought we had entered a war zone. Garbage was strewn everywhere and the road was in shambles. At that moment I recalled hearing that the city's sanitation workers had recently refused to go into the neighborhood because they were being attacked. Perhaps this wasn't such a good idea, I thought.

As if on cue, some young children menacingly approached Gavin and threatened us to get off the street. As tension rose, we noticed a mob behind us – hundreds of people were following us.

Then suddenly a man ran toward us and started screaming, "Pritzus! Pritzus!"

I knew enough Yiddish to realize these men were more or less calling me, my sister-in-law and my five-year-old daughter prostitutes, or, literally, "loose women"!

The mob chimed in: "Pritzus!"

This was going bad fast.

Some older men sensed the imminent danger. Since we were clearly just tourists and had children with us, they discreetly tried to create a gap between us and the mob while Gavin told us all to maintain a walking pace – running would only cause the mob to attack. Nevertheless, the rioters were throwing garbage and bottles at us while keeping up their cries of "prostitutes!"

It may have taken about four tense minutes for us to get to the bottom of the road, but it felt like four years. One of the older men told us where to go and we exited in the direction of Damascus gate, into an Arab neighborhood. Never had we felt so safe. Gavin wanted to plead to them, "Cousins, save us! Our brothers are trying to kill us!"

For years, Temira was so scarred that every time she saw someone wearing a shtreimel, *the fur hat worn by some Hasidic sects, she went pale. We have never been back to Mea Shearim and I am absolutely terrified of that neighborhood until today.*

Chapter 28

**Keep this Book of the Law always on
your lips; meditate on it day and night,
so that you may be careful to
do everything written in it.**

Joshua 1:8

I was sitting at Aroma cafe across from the building that a group of us were eyeing for a potential new synagogue when a friend, who was heavily involved in another Jerusalem synagogue passed by. He had heard through the grapevine that a group of us had plans to establish a new *shul* and he popped in to share his opinion about that.

"Jerusalem doesn't need another synagogue," he scoffed. "How long do you think you'll be 'in business'? You must realize it's going to fail."

Even after I explained my reasoning, he was antagonistic. But as I have previously mentioned, telling me "no" is a bad idea. This man's dour prognostication of failure set the wheels – already in motion – into overdrive. I recounted this conversation to my three partners in this endeavor – all women, all of us expats – and we decided to move up our timetable. Instead of giving ourselves a reasonable amount of time to establish a new community synagogue, we decided to push this through before the High Holy Days, which were just two short weeks away.

The thing is, while I love proving the naysayers wrong – like when it came to JICNY and mainstreaming Caila among other things – I had a lot of doubt that this would work. Practically speaking, who were *we* to start a synagogue? We were all relatively new to the country and we didn't know how things worked here. We also happened to be women – not the typical founders of a synagogue. And, I for one, spoke very little Hebrew. Nevertheless, this is something we all desperately needed and wanted. The synagogue we were planning would fill what was a dire need in our lives in Jerusalem – community.

One of the things that surprised me when we moved to Israel was the lack of community we encountered. Now that might sound strange to a *sabra*. Native Israelis are extremely family oriented, and, on any given Shabbat or holiday, dining room tables are warm and crowded. Israelis also have strong bonds that are built in the army and last a lifetime. But if you've moved to Israel and you lack that same familial network, you can start to feel lonely and disconnected when Shabbat rolls around.

I was expecting it would take a few weeks until we felt settled and part of a community. After we made aliyah we had a lot on our plates with work, school, inclusion and just getting our bearings. What I didn't expect was that after two entire years we still would not have many new friends with whom to enjoy Shabbat. We did have friends we already knew before arriving here, but not many new bonds had been established. How ironic that the same people who hosted foreigners every Shabbat in New York and even founded an organization dedicated to that specific purpose, were now the ones sitting on the outside. In New York, I was known as the "dinner queen" and could have written the Who's Who of Shabbat dinners. I know New York has the reputation of being cold and unfriendly, but I found Jerusalem to be an even tougher place to connect. Here I was invisible. For us Samuels, driven by the notion that no Jew should be alone for Shabbat or a holiday, we were surprised that an efficient network to connect Jews within the Jewish state did not exist.

We were disappointed that after *shul* on Shabbat, congregants rushed home. No one stayed after to chat or hang out. Everyone just muttered, "*Shabbat shalom,*" and ran out the doors after the service. Being shy and not having a grasp of Hebrew, I certainly didn't try to approach anyone either. Most likely they were going back home to an extended family or network of friends. We were still trying to build ours.

Israel is really one big village, however, newcomers have to earn their way in. And it can take a long time. Sabras have grown up together, served in the IDF together, their children go to the same school. They have so many levels on which to meet and stay in contact, and of course live near their families. New people like us have a much harder time, in a transient city such as Jerusalem, making connections.

Admittedly, I was blindsided by this. Moving to Israel, I knew that language and inclusion would be obstacles to overcome and I was prepared for those. But I certainly didn't expect that I would not have a community. How could it have been easier to create camaraderie in outback Australia than in the Jewish state?

Israelis are largely oblivious to the plight of new immigrants and outsiders. When my friend recruited some young Israeli men to help us haul equipment to our venue in Tel Aviv, they were incredulous that we were planning to host new immigrants and lone soldiers for a Rosh Hashanah dinner. My friend explained that these people had nowhere to go for the holiday. The young men did not understand that not everyone gets invited to someone's house for holidays and Shabbat.

The government of Israel pushes aliyah and Israelis cheer on the efforts. Everyone collectively says, "Yeah, come build the country with us! We love *olim*." The government provides tax breaks, Hebrew classes and housing stipends for immigrants, so there is a good amount of logistical support. But emotional support is another subject. No one seems to consider what these new immigrants will do on their first few lonely Shabbat weekends after they arrive. I went through this myself – from New Zealand to New York – and yet in every place but Israel, our family successfully established ourselves in a community in a short time.

For me, the most obvious solution to finding community would be to find a compatible synagogue. But that was the main problem.

First of all, Israeli synagogues begin and end earlier than those in the Diaspora. We would find ourselves done by ten o'clock on a Saturday morning and twiddling our thumbs for the rest of the day. Also, there were no activities for the children at *shuls*. And last, there was the language barrier. We were new and, with little Hebrew, we could not understand the rabbi's sermon.

Those first two years, we wandered from *shul* to *shul* trying to find one that suited us as a family. And after two years we were still homeless. During this time I did meet some other new *olim* who had this same frustration. We spoke of these challenges at length and actually, inadvertently, became our own community of disconnected people.

Four of us got together and pinpointed exactly what we were missing and what we could do to fulfill that need. Hands down, what we missed most was a sense of community exemplified by the hot *kiddush* common in Diaspora communities, consisting of a communal meal, singing and schmoozing after the Saturday service. This was probably the reason we weren't making any new friends either. We also sorely desired to have a program for our kids which ran simultaneously to the service.

The service, we also agreed, should begin at nine o'clock rather, which was later than many Israelis synagogues. And lastly, we preferred to have a rabbi who could deliver his message in English so that the Anglos – of which we expected to appeal – could understand.

The more we spoke of this, the more we thought we had to try. Informal surveys of our mutual connections revealed that other residents expressed the same desires. But until we opened our doors, we could not be sure how many people would actually come.

I was spurred on by that man's comment after he spat out his incredulity that "Jerusalem doesn't need another synagogue." We decided to move up the opening of our dream-*shul* to take place before the holidays.

Of course, rushing this through meant sacrificing on marketing efforts. With less time to recruit potential attendees, we lowered the chances of a successful launch. But I'm a risk taker and I actually enjoy the challenge of a gamble such as this. And risk prevailed here.

In record time, we rented a place (that building I had been gazing at across from Aroma cafe which I had previously used for JIC events), we borrowed a Torah scroll and, with the blessing of a nearby rabbi, we created a satellite branch of his synagogue. It was September 2016 when we opened the doors of Shir Hadash on Emek.

That first week, we expected seventy adults plus children, which would be a good turnout for a first service with minimal time to advertise. What we did get was *two hundred adults plus children*! Then we had to decide quickly, with Rosh Hashanah only ten days later, whether to do High Holy Day services. If so, we would have to find a *chazzan* and sell seats. Again, we went with risk: We decided to do it and, within only three days of promoting, we sold all the seats!

This established us: Shir Hadash (New Song) on Emek was here to stay.

Clearly, we had tapped into an unspoken need. Shir Hadash on Emek, named after the street it is on – Emek Refaim – attracted a wide swath of Anglos and other immigrants. Located in the German Colony, we also attracted a number of Israelis who had lived abroad and missed that sense of community overseas that wasn't as prevalent in Israeli synagogues.

People wanted fellowship and to hear messages in a language they could understand comfortably. By starting later in the morning, we enabled people to arrive in a relaxed manner and then feel free to stay afterwards. Most people would linger for a good hour over hot cholent, kugel and *lechayims*.

Many of our congregants didn't realize what was missing in their new lives in Israel until they came to Shir Hadash on Emek. Four years later, the community is still growing strong and that proves it was sorely needed.

As for me, within a few weeks, I had widened my circle of like-minded people. I made new friends. And as a family, we had a synagogue we looked forward to attending together.

I am the same person I always have been – creating, building, identifying market needs, finding solutions and making connections. When I see something that isn't working ideally, at least in my opinion, I think of how I would do things if I had it my way.

Strategizing how to build something bigger or better is what I like to do for business, my family and my social life. It was the same with this synagogue, and I was honored to join with like-minded women in establishing Shir Hadash on Emek. What started as a quest to fill a personal need for each of us became a wider mission to meet a massive gap in a small community in Jerusalem.

In the start-up phase of the synagogue, I contributed my marketing and recruiting skills, but after our *shul* got up and running, I took more of a back seat and just happily attended. To this day, I love what we created.

I don't take my involvement for granted. I was sixteen when I started adopting an Orthodox lifestyle, and, with my limited knowledge, I was overwhelmed by the religious world. However, I am so grateful for those families who reached out, invited me for a Shabbat meal and even simplified the discussion on the *parashah* so I could be included. Those small acts during the beginning steps of my journey made me receptive to learning more.

My journey to return to my heritage was intentional. I made a choice to embrace Judaism's value system and worldview. Sometimes though I had to learn the hard way. I'll never forget one of my first Shabbat meals with another family. Everyone went to do the ritual hand washing and then sat in silence as they waited for the head of the table to say *hamotzi*, the blessing over the challah. I had yet to learn the custom of not speaking between hand washing and eating the bread, and I found the silence quite sudden and awkward. To break the ice, I innocently blurted out, "Isn't silence golden?" Cringe!

The self-awareness that I experienced during that time – of being the only person who was totally clueless – has enabled me to make our home a comfortable place for many other "rookies." Our Shabbat table ranges from highly Torah educated scholars to the completely secular who cannot string together two words of the Bible, and even non-Jews. I've poured years of my life into community outreach, trying to connect Jews to Judaism and to other Jews and trying to staunch the tide of assimilation and intermarriage in the Jewish community.

What Gavin and I lack in Jewish education we have made up for in relationships and community outreach. We have a lifetime of tales from our Shabbat table. I have been privileged to have a hand in helping many of our guests discover their paths to faith as well. Most of the stories I told in this book began at our Shabbat table. Many of the people who sat at our table are now rabbis and rebbetzins and a few are living in Israel today. For some of them, their first Shabbat or holiday meal was at our table.

It is a privilege to see our children carrying the flame of Judaism *and* the knowledge. Unlike their parents, they are getting a solid Jewish education. I watched one Shabbat evening as my son, now a young man, and my daughter who attends a feminist Orthodox girls' school and has the same rigorous religious curriculum as her brother, did what I could not do myself: comfortably converse about the Torah portion and keep up with the advanced discussion. In just one generation we had closed the gap. Now our children are living an expressive Jewish life based on Torah values linking them to dozens of generations before them.

It reminds me God's command to our people: "Be careful to follow all the commands of the Lord your God, that you may possess this good land and pass it on *as an inheritance to your descendants* forever" (I Chronicles 28:8).

We have passed on our inheritance to our children. We've given them the Shabbat table, a Jewish upbringing and education and, now, a synagogue that would parse the lessons of our religion and provide like-minded community. Of all possible accomplishments in my life, of this I am most pleased.

Tales of a Modern Jewish Woman

The cast of characters

When you have an open home and an open table, you can't always control who comes through your doors. The cast of characters that we have shared meals with could comprise a book on its own. Some are hilarious, but we have our share of funny, appalling and tragic tales of people we hosted at one time or another.

*A Holocaust survivor once asked Gavin and me to take in her daughter, a recovering drug addict. When we came back from synagogue one Friday night this young woman was dancing around our apartment, blasting music. I'm pretty sure she was not high, but being unaffiliated, she was blissfully unaware that playing Def Leppard at top volume was not exactly conducive to a relaxed Shabbat atmosphere. And because she was Jewish, we could not ask her to turn off the music. So we had kid-*dush *and dinner with her heavy metal mix in the background.*

But we have also had guests who went on to make the worst kind of headlines becoming white-collar criminals and, tragically, even murderers.

On a positive note, many of our deepest lifelong friendships began at our Shabbat table, stretching back to our days in outback New Zealand all the way to New York. We can be very proud of the 126 married couples as of this writing whose relationships began at one of our JIC events, the first of which were a Belgian and a Hungarian Jew who met in New York. This dear couple and their children now live in Israel and they are regulars with us many Shabbats a year. Stories like this make the risks of hosting the masses entirely worth it!

CHAPTER 29

Certainly, then, a person should repent today, for perhaps tomorrow he will die–so that all his days he is repenting.

Babylonian Talmud, Shabbat 153a

Somehow, as I was still struggling to settle into Israeli life and find myself in this new place, this happened: I was deemed among the seventy most influential women of Israel. This blurb about me – among sixty-nine other amazing women in the country – was published in the *Times of Israel* in honor of Israel's 70th birthday:

"Originally from New York City, Jodi has over 20 years of management and start-up experience working in not-for-profit and for-profit businesses including finance, fashion and beauty sectors. Jodi successfully started two non-profit Jewish organizations including the Jewish International Connection NY (JICNY) in 2001 that currently boasts 10,000 members from 40 countries and runs sold-out events in the New York, Jerusalem and Tel Aviv. Jodi recently sold her online marketing business jmediaconnections where she had successfully built jdeal NY, Buy Israel Week, jgives and jblasts. In addition to being a community activist, Jodi has a passion for moving the needle on inclusion in the special needs world. Jodi has devoted hundreds of hours in making sure her daughter Caila is fully included in Israeli society and receives the support necessary to be included

in a regular school. To this end, she developed and maintain a Facebook advocacy page called Caily's World, and she writes a popular blog on Metroimma. Jodi is a mother of three great kids and she and her husband Gavin live in Jerusalem. The Samuels are world renowned for graciously hosting hundreds of people every month for Shabbat meals and events in their home."

Clearly the author of this blurb didn't know I was experiencing some serious adjustment disorder in Israel.

Yes, I dove into hosting and Jewish hospitality from nearly the moment we arrived. Just like in Australia, just like in New York, also in Israel, I saw a need to provide Shabbat and holiday tables for those who had no friends and family. It was actually a way for me to cope as well. It was a difficult adjustment but at least if I were keeping busy, I couldn't always dwell on the negative.

Ironically, people told me that if I left New York, I was in danger of shuttering JICNY. How would I maintain – from across the ocean – the two-hundred plus events that my organization sponsored annually with only one paid employee who works twenty hours a week? While everyone was still questioning JICNY's long-term survival, we opened an Israel branch of the organization, JIC, while the American one continued to thrive. In Jerusalem, we now host more than a hundred events a year including Jerusalem Day festivities, Shabbat projects, weekly Torah classes and dating workshops. We host regular dinners in Tel Aviv as well. On one particular Rosh Hashanah in Tel Aviv, we had a wonderful weekend of meals with dozens of people. One of the guests asked if I, as the coordinator, knew all the people at the table. He was astounded when I said I only knew one person. This prompted the usual question: "So why do you do this?"

Sometimes, in the midst of shopping, schlepping, cooking and stressing about the last-minute sign-ups, I will look at Gavin, my partner in crime, and ask the same question. But the answer is rhetorical: Hospitality and Jewish outreach are my life's passion. Only the location changes.

Separate from JIC, our family also became involved with Shabbat of a Lifetime, an organization that matches non-Jewish tourists with Israeli families for a traditional Shabbat dinner. This expanded the variety of guests we've hosted at our home including evangelical Christians from America and businessmen and women from China. The guests are moved to see our children discuss the Torah portion and participate in the prayers. It is a real-life example of how our connection with thousands of years of a rich and beautiful heritage enable Israel and the Jewish people to survive, even thrive.

Hospitality is a central Torah principle. In our first seventeen years of marriage, we had guests in our home every single night except for a few months after we moved to New Zealand. This is how we earned the name "Camp Samuels" in New York.

It is such a significant mitzvah to welcome strangers, as Abraham did, hence we don't vet all our guests beforehand. Many times we are meeting people for the first time over *kiddush* in our home. In New York, and then again in Jerusalem, we had our share of criminals, gang leaders and some who were just, well, *crazy*. One lovely Jerusalem day a woman, who was invited by someone who met her at *shul*, announced during our Shabbat lunch that she is a lesbian.

"I don't like what hangs between a man's legs," she loudly proclaimed while everyone else choked on their food. Later she threw one of her shoes over the balcony and then proceeded to cry and petition the guests for *tzedakah* to buy new shoes! We came to find out that this poor woman had a tough life and had turned to drugs, which seemed to have left their mark.

One time we had forgotten to turn off our refrigerator light so one of our guests trawled the streets for a "Shabbat goy." He found a couple from India who were touring Israel and asked for their help with the light. Then we insisted they stay for dinner – along with the forty students from a Birthright trip that were arriving. This had to be the cultural highlight of their trip. We had a great time together.

After we settled into our Jerusalem home, we opened our extra rooms to people who needed a place to stay, just as we had done in New York and Australia. One woman we took in was Zulu from South Africa. Her husband had tragically died while performing in a musical in Jerusalem. She stayed with us for a week while we comforted her and helped her sort out the logistical challenges of getting his body back to their homeland. In the apartheid South Africa of our upbringing, a black woman wouldn't be allowed to live under the same roof as a white person.

When Temira was applying to high schools, she had an interview at an egalitarian Orthodox school in Jerusalem. We believed it was the right school for our quirky and fiercely free-thinking daughter, and were hoping she would be accepted. So, during the interview when they asked her which character in the Bible she would choose to be, you can imagine how underwhelming it was to hear her choose the popular matriarch, Sarah.

The rolled eyes and the ho-hum nonverbals from the staff showed they were expecting a more obscure and possibly more feminist-aligned character, such as Deborah or Yael. But when asked to explain, Temira, who was twelve, changed the atmosphere in the room.

"When I grow up, I want to have a home like my parents. Sarah and Abraham were known for hospitality, and my parents have modeled *their* lives after them."

Okay Temira, I sighed with relief. *This was going better than expected.*

"We have an open home and an open Shabbat table," she continued. "For Shabbat, one week we had evangelical Christians, the next week we had East German politicians. Another week we had Chinese businessmen, then intermarried Jewish families, Swedish pastors and then single Orthodox Jews looking to get married. I've met so many different people from around the world and learned so much thanks to my parents' belief in hospitality."

Temira summed up our home life perfectly. Open doors and open minds. When we aren't traveling the world, we are bringing the world to us. We were so proud that this was an active part of Temira's own life now.

While being lauded by the *Times of Israel* for my service to the community, I found that it was the most challenging aspect about my transition from New York to Jerusalem. In Jerusalem, I hit a wall. Israeli life was more chaotic and my normal productivity was suddenly taxed. The same hosting and event planning I did in New York was much harder and more time consuming here.

For example, in New York, I worked full time, but my children took a bus to school and back, having completed all their activities and therapies by dinner time. Planning events and Shabbat dinners, whether hosting at home or at a venue, took a few minutes of online shopping or coordinating with an event planner. Everything was delivered to the appropriate place. The venue was set up and sparkling when I arrived.

By contrast, in Jerusalem, I had to schlep from store to store to complete my shopping list because not everything is sold at one shop. If I wanted to save money at the "cheap" supermarket, I spent at least a half hour in line with the rest of Israel and, in the end, I was not really getting a bargain. And, I had to deliver, set up, break down and clean up myself (I always recruit the rest of the Samuels for help) at the venue hall. To make it worse, all of these activities had to be done by one in the afternoon on weekdays when school would end and the afternoon rush of therapies and activities would begin. I lost *hours* of my day.

Expenses went up as well. Running an event in New York, I could charge a decent price that would cover the costs. But in Israel food and services are disproportionately so expensive that I had to raise money to subsidize tickets. My attendees – usually new immigrants and lone soldiers – were precisely the ones who were financially struggling.

The idealism of making aliyah faded under the weight of hundreds of logistical details. I had always prided myself in staying busy and accomplishing so much before, but in Jerusalem I was overwhelmed and exhausted, and my productivity took a beating.

It's ironic because when I was in New York, I loved Israel. When I was anywhere else in the world I loved Israel. As a teen, my grandfather sent me to a Zionist summer camp in South Africa where I had fun and acquired a good amount of the ideology that shaped my view of Israel. When I was in New York, my business partner and I even successfully launched an aggregate website, BuyIsraelWeek, to support Israeli charities and businesses in the face of the Boycott, Divestment and Sanctions movement.

Here I was now living the dream of generations of Jews in the land of our forefathers. And yet it was a nightmare.

The Jews were slaves in Egypt, yet they wanted to stay there. I could understand where they were coming from. Egypt was their comfort zone. God's call to enter the Promised Land was not packaged with assurances of ease. No, they ended up wandering around the desert for forty years cobbling together manna and quail for meals every single monotonous day. They had to fight armies they encountered along the way. The men even had to undergo circumcision before entering the Promised Land. Egypt seemed astronomically better.

Here I was copping the same attitude as my forefathers after *my* journey to the Promised Land. While idealistically I always understood the importance of aliyah, the princess side of me was still dreaming of Manhattan. I pined for America with all of its ease, convenience and bargains. I missed being known and useful. I was clinging to my packaged life with all the services in the world for Caila, online shopping and customer service.

In addition to all of this, I acquired a stalker while in Jerusalem – a bonafide nutcase who attended one of my events, decided I was the anti-Christ and sent me several death threats. It began after an event I organized in which IDF soldiers of Muslim, Christian and Jewish backgrounds sat together on a panel. The attendee-turned stalker accused me of outlandish ideas that were not even mentioned, such as pushing Arabic as the national language of the Jewish state and, ultimately angling to turn Israel into an Islamic state. He said I was trying to convert Jews to Islam!

The man continued to threaten me until, months later he approached Gavin at synagogue. Not many people know this, but Gavin is a black belt in karate. We all held our breath wondering whether Gavin was going to take him out on the spot. It wouldn't be the first time Gavin had karate-chopped an offender on my behalf. Years prior, a man walked up to Gavin at one of my events.

"You know your wife is a f–ing bitch?"

Without a second thought Gavin struck the man in the neck and had him on his knees.

Remembering this like it was yesterday, I waited to see how this was going to play out. When the stalker told Gavin he wanted to apologize – not for what he had said but the way that he had said it – we all let out a collective breath. Gavin agreed to accept his apology on one condition.

"If you ever threaten anyone in my family, ever again, in any way, I will crush you like an insect," he moved closer. "Deal?"

They shook on it.

In addition to the stalker stress, my anxiety escalated as I faced the reality that I was somebody in New York. Here in Israel, I was back at zero. I had to completely reinvent myself.

And the logistical challenges and woeful inconveniences plagued me. I complained a lot. I cried and stamped my feet like a petulant child who refused to go where her parents told her.

It was my sister-in-law who verbally slapped me into reality. As I was whining to her one day about all the conveniences I had enjoyed in New York and was missing in Israel, she stopped me mid-sentence.

"Jo, your privileged existence in Manhattan was not normal. Do you realize that the rest of the world has to shop at supermarkets and we pick up our own dry cleaning?"

Ouch. When she put the mirror to my face I realized how much I sounded just like one of those ungrateful Israelites that God had delivered from slavery. I was griping…from a place of privilege.

It reminded me of when Caila was five years old. We spent Shabbat with friends who also have a child a few years older with Down syndrome. Near the end of the day we noticed Caila staring at this boy.

"You have a funny face," she told him pointblank.

We all cracked up at the irony of her observation and I wanted to ask Caila, "Have *you* looked in the mirror recently?"

Now, with a mirror to my own face, I saw my challenges for what they were: real First World problems. My forefathers' own grumbling against Moses ignited God's anger. I decided I needed to get over myself. Yes, I had it good – and better than many others. I had to reset my whole perspective and attitude. "All my deeds and speech are for the sake of Heaven," the prayer written by the Chofetz Chaim reminded me.

This marked the beginning of a slow (interminable) turnaround as I began to find routine and my footing in Israel. And you want to know how I did this? I looked at Caila. My daughter with all her challenges became my inspiration. How could I compare my inconveniences to my daughter who was struggling to belong and dealing with rejection? How could I complain about waiting in tedious lines while my youngest child was beginning her day at six in the morning and going full throttle with school, therapies and extra-curricular activities until eight at night?

My troubles were trite by comparison. My daughter speaks, reads and writes Hebrew. She's figured out the Israeli way of using her elbows to stay on line. She even uses Israeli hand gestures, which is slightly mortifying when we are abroad. I do not know how to do any of this. But I had to buck up and try.

If she could do it, so would I.

After some time, Gavin told me I really had improved – I had gone from breaking down in tears and cursing my life in Israel every day to "only" once a week.

Not bad indeed!

Tales of a Modern Jewish Woman

Samuels drama meets Shabbat

Of course, something as simple as a Shabbat dinner is never without drama for us. The same week we moved into our new Jerusalem apartment we were hosting a large group for Shabbat of a Lifetime. From the outset, I should have never agreed to host that week. Renovations were still ongoing. Scaffolding and drop cloths decorated the dining room where we would be hosting our guests. I informed the organization that my place was in shambles and sent pictures as proof. But the group of Chinese businesspeople insisted – their group leader had brought a group to our home before and he insisted on coming to our place again, renovations or not.

Gavin, who had been out of the country, returned from a business trip just an hour before Shabbat and we quickly went into action getting the home ready. We have a pre-Shabbat routine of lighting candles, leaving on strategic lamps and switching the refrigerator to Shabbat mode among other things. But being in a new place, we didn't even yet know where half of the switches were!

Finally, as we went to plug in the hot plate to keep the food warm – pop! – all of our electricity went out. We could not find where the main electric box was and the contractor had already stopped answering his phone because it was so close to Shabbat. This Shabbat, our first one at this new home, would be spent in the dark.

At this point there was no canceling the group. So, our very first Shabbat of a Lifetime in our new place was certainly an unforgettable experience of a lifetime: Forty businessmen and women from China had

Shabbat dinner by candlelight and many of them used the flashlights on their phones when our candles went out. We were able to convey honor and respect for 3,000 years of Jewish history no matter how challenging the present situation. The Chinese guests – coming from a Communist system that has long suppressed religion – were amazed to see such active religious expression.

I have to admit, I was crazy to put myself in this situation of hosting a group before I had even sorted out my own home, but circumstances certainly didn't make it any easier.

CHAPTER 30

All that a man achieves and all that he fails to achieve is the direct result of his own inner thoughts.

James Allen

Nothing makes living in Israel more real than when your oldest child receives his *tzav rishon* (first call-up) for the Israel Defense Forces. The letter instructed him to be present for a full day of medical and psychometric testing – the beginning of the highly competitive process to get into the best possible unit.

One of the rare times the Israeli postal service is efficient is when it comes to delivering the military's call-up papers. Those arrive without fail and precisely on time. That moment we got the letter for Meron was when I realized the depth of the roots we were planting in this country. Actual *human* roots. We were going to share our son with the army. This was rather serious.

Meron was the first to see the letter, since he is the only one who picks up our mail. He knew immediately what the letter contained and came to tell us. Every Israeli child anticipates that letter when they turn sixteen and a half. Many boys, especially those in Meron's Zionistic school, eagerly await this missive with all of the testosterone that comes with that age.

For us, his parents, that moment was ripe with emotion. I recall having two immediate and visceral reactions. The first was, "*Oh s–,* I really do live in Israel!"

My desire to return to New York was diminishing proportionately the more my children became entrenched in Israeli society. This was one of those irrevocable milestones. And once Meron would head to the army – for three years – it wouldn't be long until Temira followed. Clearly there was no going back. I couldn't leave my children here on the frontlines while I moved to the comforts of America.

The second feeling that washed over me was the immense pride I felt that my son would be the first person in our family to serve in a sovereign Jewish army in two thousand years. At Meron's bar mitzvah, Gavin showed a photo of his grandfather's siblings – nine men and women who would not survive the war and not live to see an independent Jewish state. Nor would they ever imagine one of their very own descendants would be defending that state eighty years after they perished in the Holocaust.

When you look around at the anti-Semitism in the world, you realize how important it is that the Jewish people have a state and that Israel has an army. It is only because we have armed forces that we can have hope for our future. Think of pre-war Europe. Anti-Semitic attacks became normal, everyday occurrences. It is happening now around the world, even in New York. The collective conscience of society was seared back then and it seems that history is trying to repeat itself.

While I dread my children going to the army, as any normal mother would, I also fully realize I am more than an armchair Zionist sending a donation or planting a tree. Our family is contributing our children.

One of the best things we did for our children was move to Israel. Their character development skyrocketed. First of all, the schools are different – students are less supervised and must fend for themselves in many ways. In New York, the tendency was for schools to go overboard trying to make sure that no child falls through the cracks. But, as we were coming to understand, less oversight was inadvertently developing responsibility in our children, especially in Caila who had people watching her every second she was at school in New York. I see that in Israel my children have to on their own figure out life, take on challenges, work harder, deal with disappointment and, ultimately, savor success – even Caila. Without the helicopter supervision hovering over her all the time, we've seen our youngest make leaps and bounds in academic and social settings. We even eventually allowed her to walk to her school by herself which was a major achievement and source of pride for her.

When we complained to his teacher that Meron had taken on too many extra-curricular activities and was less focused on his schoolwork, *we* were the ones reprimanded! The teacher advised us to let him develop on his own.

"Your son will be in the army in a few years, so start backing off now," the teacher recommended. "In two years he will be holding a gun and taking orders from someone else. So start getting used to it now."

It was an eye-opening perspective.

Israeli youth are set loose at a much earlier age than their American counterparts. Students take to the streets to collect money for their youth groups. Rather than build their organizations with their grandparents' charity, they recruit the community. It is a powerful message, one that my children would not have learned as well in the U.S. On a daily basis, my children are contributing to their society and community and I love watching them grow like this.

In addition to their freedom and independence, these children engage in meaningful causes. For instance, at fifteen, instead of deciding which movie to go to or stressing out over which college to apply, Meron completed an advanced first aid program and began volunteering for the ambulance service of Magen David Adom. My son was training as a paramedic and was responding to real emergency calls in Jerusalem!

Meron and Temira both became leaders at the local Bnei Akiva youth group. Temira decided to head the group for participants with special needs because she worried no one else would do it.

"I don't want a whole group of kids to miss out on this experience just because no one wants to do the volunteer work," she reasoned. Clearly, having a sister with special needs stirred something in her.

She spent one Shabbat out of every three at a home for children who have severe disabilities.

We expect that Caila will also grow up like this following in her siblings' footsteps. She will be a contributing member of society to the best of her own abilities. She is already a member of Bnei Akiva and we hope to see her in the IDF as well someday.

I realized, in working with young adults from the United States, particularly singles who want to get married, that many of them are entitled, lack depth of character and cannot deal with stress or challenges. I can't help but wonder how they were raised. If we protect children from adversity, they will lack resilience as adults. We should protect our children from danger, but we should allow them to take risks, fail and lead at their age level. This is what living in Israel has done for our children.

Israeli life is anything but superficial. On many levels, life here picked up the parenting slack where we had failed, giving our children real life lessons. It is miraculous to watch resilient Israeli children become emotionally available, capable and entrepreneurial adults who have a lot of chutzpah and a positive sense of self. As the army awaits them on the cusp of adulthood they are forced to grow up faster than the average teen. But you also see the results of that in their character and accomplishments later in life.

While I grew to appreciate this character development for my children, I still had to deal with my own adjustment challenges. If you recall, our social worker was confused that we didn't cry when Caila was diagnosed with Down syndrome. She should have seen me after moving to Israel. I cried on a near daily basis.

I know I needed to work on my own resilience. If I didn't let a diagnosis of Down syndrome divert me from my life's work and mission, then surely I shouldn't let living in Jerusalem stop me.

It was a slow process of coming to terms with my circumstances, but I realized: There was no going back. And that reality was settling in on me. With all that there was to leave behind in Israel, I feared I would end up like Lot's wife if I continued to glance back longingly at America. I was in danger of becoming a pillar of salt.

And as I broke down the analogy even further, Lot's wife was the antithesis to her husband's uncle, Abraham. Abraham and Sarah were the epitomes of hospitality and Lot's last major act in Sodom, ironically, was to welcome two strangers into his home. A Sodomite mob gathered outside his house and demanded Lot deliver the two strangers to them. Lot's wife didn't even want to host these men, according to the commentators. This stood in stark contrast to Abraham's example of taking in strangers and treating them well.

All of our beliefs and passion about having an open home and an open table stem from the example of Abraham and Sarah. When I thought of how Lot's wife looked back at her past, I trembled: I had been longing for my past life as well, while loathing where God called me.

Yet I was still tempted – and may always remain so – by the New York lifestyle with all the ease and entertainment it had to offer. I can only imagine what Lot's wife was thinking when she left her hometown for the unknown. I don't know if she had a life of leisure that she was leaving behind, but she had trouble looking forward. That's exactly where I found myself.

Certainly, I wasn't going back to South Africa where crime remains rampant and utilities are even increasingly harder to come by. But much harder for me to admit was that the chances of going back to America were diminishing. While my convenient Manhattan life was the complete opposite of the South African struggles, I was slowly and subconsciously detaching.

CHAPTER 31

There are no problems, only opportunities for growth.

Rebbetzin Dena Weinberg

People assume when you immigrate that the big-ticket items like a place to live, a school for your children and buying a car are signs that you've "arrived."

For me, it was the subtle things, the small cues that were most compelling and made me realize I had made Jerusalem home. For instance, the first time someone gave me directions using an iconic landmark such as "the monster" in Kiryat Yovel, and I knew where that was. Or when I started tuning into those elusive societal subtleties, and I too would turn up late for an event in Israel – and not miss a second of it because it hadn't started yet. Or when I would attend a party and find myself greeting several people, newfound connections and friends.

Or perhaps it was when the waitress *finally* remembered, after five years of going to the same cafe, that I take Americano with hot milk on the side (she still grimaces when I ask for ice for my water).

These small acts comforted me and made me realize I am no longer a stranger here. I have arrived.

Though I still shy away from confrontation with everyone from supermarket clerks to CEOs, and I loathe bargaining for better prices,

I now appreciate the positive side of Israeli chutzpah. The passion for life that generates chutzpah has resulted in medical and technological breakthroughs, water desalination plants and amazing apps that we all use on a daily basis.

I will probably never get used to bargaining, yelling to get my way and being pushy. I will never come to terms with passive-aggressive waiters and drivers, the little old lady knocking me over for a piece of cake on the buffet line or the shocking bureaucracy involved in just maintaining a bank account.

And, of course, this princess will probably remain tempted to retreat to New York. It would take little for my family to convince me to go back. But knowing they never will, I have adopted a different perspective about my life here.

I appreciate that at the end of any symphony concert at the Jerusalem Theater, world class musicians will invariably end their performance with an emotional rendition of *Hatikva*, Israel's national anthem – The Hope. These professionals could choose to play anywhere in the world, but they choose to stay here.

I appreciate that on any given Shabbat you can see three to four generations of one family enjoying their time on the sultry Mediterranean beach. I love that while attending Jerusalem's Open Restaurants, even at a non-kosher event, the chef waxes poetic about the Torah and extrapolates that Jerusalem's food is, somehow, based on ancient biblical traditions.

I can appreciate that while the city may not compare to New York in the quantity of cultural events and nightlife, nothing in the world can compare to attending a chic invitation-only dinner set in an ancient cave under the Old City where the last king of Judah hid from the Babylonians.

And I marvel that the brilliant Israeli scientists that Gavin works with at biotech and pharmaceutical companies could earn much more money elsewhere, yet they too choose to stay here.

And I also marvel that your son's class travels to see the ghettos and concentration camps of Poland, partly sponsored by the Ministry of Education, because it is important to always remember the past. And I'm swept away by the feeling of national pride at the closing ceremony of his trip, when the families all gathered at the promenade in Jerusalem and looked out over the land that is now ours. Is there any better lesson to connect the ashes of the Holocaust as they materialized in a Jewish state that endures decades after this tragedy?

Living in Israel, no matter what you do, you are always reminded that you are part of a people. You are constantly aware that you are part of something bigger, beyond you personally and even beyond your own family.

These are the feelings that compel me to stay here.

I used to scoff at those surveys that peg Israel near the top in terms of happiest country in the world – especially after my few miserable first years here. But then I realized, Israelis are not thinking of the pressures of war, the inconveniences of life or even the exorbitant cost of living. No, they are probably thinking of their families who live close by, their security in a Jewish state and the constant reminder they have of being part of something bigger than themselves.

Believe it or not, as this realization settled over me that my children would be called up and serving in the IDF, an inner peace began to take over my soul. I was not necessarily conscious of this subtle change as I came to terms with living in Israel.

And if that isn't enough, there is the other remaining factor: Love.

Love is the overriding reason that compels me to stay. It is a decision I make on a daily basis. Seeing how my children are thriving, watching Gavin draw from the idealism of this life, I am here because of love. I love my family, and this is what they want. This is what is good for them and, by default, for us. Even Caila, who doesn't remember just how good she had it in New York with all her services and extra support, believes her life in Jerusalem is better. I suppose all the extras were more for me as her parent.

There is no other explanation for tempering a life of frustration and normalizing it.

I may never really feel truly at home or thoroughly Israeli. I have accepted the fact that I will maintain two seamless lives: one in New York and one in Israel. And I'm okay with that. I have created my own path as a South African-American-Israeli who operates in English and hosts Shabbat dinners and fellowship groups for internationals, new immigrants and people struggling to fit in here.

I am now more adjusted to my crazy life and I have made amazing and diverse friends that have eased the journey of aliyah. It may have been the longest journey I ever took, but I can say I have finally found my way home.

When I think back to Chava Fachler's influence on my life, I see how the kindness that she and her husband showed to this random teenager from South Africa has continued to impact the world. Over the years we have had thousands of guests through our home and at our events. I used to worry that on my own I could not do enough to "move the needle." But now, living in Israel, I see it differently. I may be one person, however, my family and I are small components of a nation and an ancient people.

We are the human building blocks of this country.

-The End-

Epilogue

As I was stretching my multitasking abilities to the max, trying to get this book to press before Passover while at the same time planning Caila's bat mitzvah for the week following Purim, the outbreak of COVID-19 blew all of my Type-A plans and efforts to smithereens.

Worse, I was even forced into quarantine myself having attended an international conference in Washington D.C. before returning to Israel. Suddenly I was left with little to do that could not be accomplished without a phone and email. The wheels of progress were slowly grinding to a halt and we still didn't know to what extent we were going to have to scale back our plans for both my book and the bat mitzvah in light of the coronavirus.

Caila started planning her bat mitzvah celebration since Temira's bat mitzvah, four years prior. She had already decided on a menu, invitations and even wine selections. She repeatedly checked with members of our family overseas if they would be flying in. At some point, Caila was so consumed by her own planning that we told her that she had to wait until her eleventh birthday before she could talk about her bat mitzvah again.

Her plans were finally coming into actuality at the beginning of 2020. And I too was busy planning multiple events for the bat mitzvah with Jodi-style precision and execution. I had my master to-do list which was further broken into sub-lists for packing, shopping, guests, the "Team Caila" Jerusalem marathon list, a list of hosts for my thirty-six friends from overseas and another list of day trips for them as well. At home, we had the furniture cleaned, floors polished, blinds fixed and even had our poodle Zoey groomed so she would also look just perfect on the big day. And of course, the bat mitzvah girl had her pretty dresses lined up and we were working on all of her speeches.

As I was sitting in quarantine, the mayor canceled the Jerusalem marathon and I realized that some parts of our planned celebrations may have to be modified if not delayed. Then, hundreds of flights coming into and leaving Israel were canceled as the government announced more drastic measures. We started downsizing. But like dominos, even our modified plans fell one after the other.

We had no choice but to postpone Caila's bat mitzvah to some unknown date in the future. Even as I go to press with this book, we have no indication of when the country will be back up and running.

But for a girl who had spent years dreaming of her bat mitzvah, this news promised to be devastating. I fretted over how to present this to Caila. Caila, who had been dreaming of this for so long. Caila, who had to overcome so much. Her investment in learning her Torah portion was above and beyond that of a neuro-typical peer. How would she fully understand the situation and put her disappointment in context?

When we told her that we had to downsize our plans for now, disappointment flickered in her eyes. We told her she could have a modified celebration for fifty of our closest friends over Shabbat, but later that had to be reduced to ten people, and, in the end, we were restricted to sheltering at home with only immediate family.

At no point was she devastated. In fact, at our family party, she beamed, proudly wearing a dress and a tiara. She was content and basked in our attention. Afterward she spoke with her grandfather in South Africa and told him about her "V.I.P. party," but reassured him that he could come to her bigger party, whenever that would be.

As her mother I had been especially heartbroken, frustrated and upset by all the changes. But Caila's response reminded me of the passage from Ethics of the Fathers: "Who is rich? One who is satisfied with his lot." Caila is surely wealthy.

And so are we to call her our daughter.

ACKNOWLEDGMENTS

I have to start by thanking my amazing husband, Gavin. Your discretion and logical mind have always been the anchor to my restless spirit. Without your support – and your endless hours of editing – this would not be the book, or story, I wanted it to be.

I also thank my three wonderful children for teaching me how the world works. Specifically, thank you Meron for being the adult in the family, your responsibility is beyond your years. Temira, life would be dull without your witty and ironic insights, which always bring me back down to earth and make me laugh. And Caila, you have been a fresh breath of inspiration since the day you were born. My life's mission and much of my writing is largely thanks to you.

To my parents, Sidney and Esther Newman, you have provided me the platform to dream big and reach my goals. Your lifetime of support has always been invaluable, thank you. And to my in laws, Myrna Samuels and Meyer Samuels, thank you for taking me in as your own daughter and for giving me the best gift in this life, a great husband.

Writing about one's life is an overwhelming process. I am beyond grateful to Nicole Jansezian for her editorial guidance and input in bringing my life to these pages. It was a simultaneously grueling and fun process hashing out the details of my life over coffee and wine with you.

I would like to express my deep gratitude to Rachel Montana for being with me through the entire journey, from the initial idea to the hours spent debating each word; Nechama Levy for processing the prospect of this book with me and encouraging me to do it; and Steven Levy for inspiring me to take the leap.

I have great appreciation for Frances Zelasny, who went above and beyond the call of friendship to line edit my book like nobody's business. David Kramer and Michael Bassin, you provided detailed and constructive comments for which saying "thanks" is barely adequate.

I also want to thank Sim Herring, who after reading a draft, gave some great insight and also got a crash course of the organization he now works for, JICNY.

Steve Eisenberg, a special thanks to you for being a partner in "moving the needle" through Jewish outreach. I'd like to think we made a difference in our world.

You know what they say? You want something done fast, ask a busy person. Thank you so much to these busy people for reading several chapters of my book and providing some valuable feedback: Pamela Chasen, Ronit Nassimi, Philippa Zamir, Tami Newman, and Carol and John Schiavi. I am forever grateful for your feedback and insights.

I could never have taken this journey without the organizations that inspired and then nurtured my interest in Judaism, such as Ohr Somayach, Aish HaTorah and Chabad. Speaking of journey, we have continued abundant gratitude for Chabad, which provides accommodations and nourishing kosher meals on our world travels.

Making aliyah is challenging, and our move to Israel would have been even more difficult if it had not been for several organizations that helped ease our transition, such as Nefesh B'Nefesh and the Jerusalem Olim Center. As parents trying to navigate the special needs world of Israel, we are grateful for the help from so many pioneering parents who are now friends, and organizations such as Beyachad, Bizchut, Friendship Circle and Shutaf.

Last and foremost, I am the person I am today thanks in large part to Chava Fachler. Her example of Jewish values lives on in the people she and her husband Eli affected. I hope I am doing my part to pay it forward as she encouraged me to do.

Index of organizations mentioned in the book

ABOUT THE AUTHOR

Jodi Samuels is always on a mission, even if it means just moving the needle in her corner of the world. She wears many hats as a speaker, non-profit leader, world traveler, community activist, special needs advocate, wife and mom.

Originally from South Africa, Jodi and her husband Gavin have lived in five countries and nine cities, making an impact in each community. They were featured in the New York Post for their successful integration as immigrants. Jodi was named one of the 70 extraordinary female immigrants in Israel in 2018 by *Times of Israel*; received the Nefesh B'Nefesh Initiative for Zionist Innovation prize in 2019; and on Yom HaAliyah in 2019, Jerusalem's Zionist pluralist party, Hitorerut, recognized Jodi for her contribution to Israel, Jerusalem and to other immigrants.

In 2000, Jodi founded Jewish International Connection in order to provide community for foreign Jews in New York. The organization expanded operations to Israel in 2015 and has grown to 15,000 members from more than 40 countries. Jodi still works in a purely volunteer capacity for JIC, running more than 300 events a year in both New York and Israel.

On the for-profit front, Jodi started her first business at age 14 and has been a serial-entrepreneur ever since, starting successful companies in diverse segments from financial training services to online group coupon purchasing.

Jodi is also a passionate speaker, writer and advocate in the special needs world, especially for her own daughter. She writes on her Metroimma blog about special needs, Torah wisdom in a modern world, moving to Israel, traveling to nearly 90 countries and the challenges of being an entrepreneur-mom on Jodi's Voice.

Jodi, Gavin and their three children live in Jerusalem where the family hosts hundreds of people every month for Shabbat meals and events in their home.

For more information see www.jodisvoice.com and jicny.com. Check out Caily's World on Facebook.

Open letter to the rabbi of the school, circulated to school parents and on social media
February 15, 2010

Dear Rabbi,

I am writing to you as a mom who wants you to hear me plead my case. You have heard us plead our case, we have asked friends and supporters to plead our case. And, while I am still saddened and disappointed that you will not even meet Caily and give her an interview, I have also heard (your school's) side of the story.

I want to share a few thoughts.

I recognize that the school is panicked that there will be a surge of Down Syndrome applications at the school. I also think it would be fair for the school to create criteria limiting numbers etc. The school could limit applications to preschool only and to Upper West Side families and to take only x number of students. Also give existing families priority. If you took a read on the parent body there is incredible support to give a two-year-old child of an existing family a space in the toddler class.

I know the school has not done this before but that does not make it right or fair – the world has had to accommodate for many changes. 60,000 children are mainstreamed with DS including in Jewish Day Schools. We are not asking for something so radical. I also want you to appreciate that the success of this rests so much on the parents and their participation in the effort. We are the ones who will have to drive and lead the team. Given who Gavin and I are, if you have ever had parents qualified to lead this process it would have to be us. Again you do not know us well but ask in the community and again I am sure you would hear feedback that if any family can deal with the challenges and make the light shine it's us. We as a team could add so much to your school if you just gave us the chance.

Neither Gavin nor I grew up religious. Along the way we became very close with Rabbi Noah Weinberg from Aish HaTorah. Each day I wake up inspired by his vision, each day I wake up with a vision to change the

277

world. I live what I believe. Just last year we hosted over 1,000 Shabbat guests. That's not including the classes in our home, sheva brachot, brisot, lechayims, *etc. Likewise, with Caily I have fully embraced the mission of changing the world. When Caily was born Gavin said to me that we should have activist branded on our forehead. We see it as our role to fight to give Caily the best opportunities and to make the world she lives in a better place. Rav Weinberg never stopped reaching out and trying to educate. So too is our mission.*

On a personal level, the school's rejection is really painful. When you are baal teshuvah *you have invested so much thought and energy into what community,* hashkafah, *values etc. you want in your world. We did not wake up here…we fought so hard to be here. We moved from Australia to New York to be in a dynamic Jewish community and to find a place where we could educate our kids accordingly. We spent Shabbat with (a friend, name omitted) and he and his wife insisted that the school is the place. Along with (another friend, name omitted) these families encouraged us to choose the school. We love the school and it's very hard to have face the callous way in which this has been handled. Starting from the original meeting when you were so cold to us.*

It is so interesting when we discuss this situation with baal teshuvah *people they all unanimously say, "but isn't it the community's responsibility?" I guess for all of us who came on the journey it was sense of community that attracted us and I guess it's also so surprising for us to see how "lonely" it can be.*

When I started my religious journey the most impressive thing to me was visiting families and seeing how central Jewish education was to their world. Kids giving dvar Torah *at the table, fathers sharing words of wisdom, bookshelves lined with* gemorahs, *people rushing out after a meal to a class etc. This is something we aspire to in our home that ALL our children share in the opportunity to have a yeshiva education.*

Rabbi please hear this if nothing else. Meron is an incredibly sweet and sensitive child with a maturity beyond his years. Last winter when he was just 6 he and Gavin walked past the beggar on our street Diane. Gavin always gives her a dollar. One day he gave her $10. Meron asked why so much and Gavin explained that on freezing days she pays a super *in the neighborhood to let her sleep in the basement. Meron then said, "Abba next time don't give her money – she can come sleep in my bed." Then he was deep in thought and said, "But don't tell Imma." Gavin assumed that he thought I would say she is dirty, etc. He said, "Imma will tell everyone how proud she is of me and Abba its nothing to be proud of its just what Jews should do." How many 6 years old have that type of* neshama? *It's that same sensitive soul that I worry about the most with this challenge. I have heard from so many families with special needs kids that some siblings go off the* derech *as they are angry at the intolerance of the Orthodox world. I never want Meron ever to one day question the values of his school, his rabbi, his community.*

As the menahel *of a school please think about this. You have so much opportunity to influence, change and take a stand. I happened to meet a past student of Bais Yaacov in LA current who saw the YouTube clip about Daniella and she saw her principal speak about accepting Daniella and she said I am so proud that he was my principal.*

When God gives a family like ours a special needs kid that's Gods choice how we treat this child is ours.

Again, we simply ask you to please to open your heart, open your mind and give the school the opportunity to be a light in the community by accepting our daughter.

With respect,
Jodi

My response to an anonymous letter that attacked us for campaigning for Caila's acceptance into the Jewish day school
April 9, 2010

Over Pesach we received an anonymous letter from someone criticizing our stand on Caila and the quest to mainstream her at the school. While I love debating this issue it is challenging when the attacker is too scared to have a debate. I addressed the points of "Mr. Anonymous" in a public forum:

Dear Mr. Anonymous,

Thanks for sharing your thoughts. It is important that we clear up some points in your letter.

1. You claim several universities and schools rejected you and you accepted the fact without resentment. I wonder if the universities would not even accept your application simply because you were "Jewish" how you would feel? While you were given equal opportunity to apply and have your applications decided on your strengths and merits, Caily and the other special needs children that were denied were not given an interview or assessment. This is called discrimination.

2. You also suggest that I put my kid in a special needs school – Mr. Anonymous please read all the details on www.facebook.com/cailysworld. We are not looking for a special needs program we are looking for an opportunity to have Caily fully included in a mainstream class. Yes, with kids just like yours.

> *i. 60,000 children with Down syndrome are mainstreamed in the U.S., in classes just like the classes your kids are in.*

> *ii. Jewish Days Schools in Teaneck, Riverdale, Long Island and Brooklyn all do inclusion – so why is this not possible in Manhattan in the most liberal democratic city, in one of the world's wealthiest zip codes?*

> *iii. Seven non-Jewish schools and JCC on the West Side and Chabad accepted Caily – these school administrators all looked us in the eye and said we would try to make it work. Many of these schools have fewer resources but a commitment to the right of every child to a suitable education. We are determined to give our child a Yeshiva education and to find a school that will accommodate her post nursery.*

> *iv. Not all special needs children are the same. Yes, the special schools are great for some kids, but not for a high functioning Down Syndrome kid – perhaps you should check your facts and you will see many of these schools strongly discourage accepting these kids as this is not the optimal environment for them.*

3. You defend the Yeshiva Katana and the school and say they know their limitations. With due respect Mr. Anonymous we are not asking for anything radical. There is a proven model and its simply not good enough to use that excuse in 2010. *The only capability missing is open minded-ness and open heart.*

4. We are not attacking the school. As we have repeatedly stated in our communications we want to give the school the opportunity to be a light in this area. We would fully partner in the endeavor and as we have previously explained: we will pay for external resources such as integration specialists; many principals of yeshivas from Long Island, Passaic, L.A. and Montreal have offered to help guide the school and we will pay for any additional resources required so that it is cost neutral to the school. So many parents have shared their stories about being denied by the school. For this reason we will continue our campaign of educating the community and providing the facts. "Our lives begin to end the day we become silent about things that matter." ~ Martin Luther King.

As parents it's our goal to help Caily but we want to make the world a better place. We want to give all special needs children the right to a yeshiva education. We believe that many special needs children can succeed and to be integrated into normative society if given the opportunity, environment and instruments to do so. Just imagine what a great opportunity this would be for the school to lead this change.

Mr. Anonymous — you are a parent. What would you want for your child in our situation?

Caily's Story: I deserve a chance as much as any other Jewish child.
April 24, 2010 – Jodi and Gavin Samuels

Hello, my name is Caila Samuels but I like to be called Caily. I'm two years old and I have Down syndrome. Everyone tells me that I'm doing really well – I walk and feed myself and play all the same games as my other two-year-old friends at playgroup. I'm very friendly, full of smiles and sociable, I'm assertive, interactive and intensely curious. Some things are difficult for me to learn but I work really hard and never give up. I have a wonderful family and excellent therapists that help me. I may not be designer perfect but my Imma told me that life doesn't have to be perfect to be wonderful.

My dream is to attend a Jewish Day School in Manhattan – it's the same school that my brother, Meron, and sister, Temira, go to. They are my favorite people in the whole world. Abba and Imma have been trying to get me into the school for five months but the professional and lay leaders of the school just keep saying "No." I don't understand why, especially since they haven't even met me or spoken to me.

How can I show the teachers what I can do if they won't even meet me?

All the other two-year-olds who have applied to the Toddler program at the school get to meet the teachers and be assessed by them. But they told me I couldn't come for an assessment. In fact when Abba and Imma asked, they were specifically told not to bring me. Randi, my special instruction teacher, says that I can do just about anything that any other child my age can do – in some things even more than them. How can I show the teachers what I can do if they won't even meet me? Don't I deserve a chance as much as any other Jewish child?

I have a friend named Avi who is three years old and has Down syndrome too. He goes to a regular Yeshiva in New Jersey and he is doing really well. The school was anxious about including Avi – they had never done this before. The Principal and the teachers now love him so much and tell his Abba every week that they are amazed by what he is capable of and get so much out of having him in the class.

The majority of children with Down syndrome attend regular school. In the US, Israel, UK, South Africa, Australia and many other countries, laws have been passed which make sure that children like me can go to regular schools. They call it LRE – "Least Restrictive Environment" which means special needs children should be allowed to attend school programs that are as close as possible to the other kids. If the authorities in all these counties concluded that inclusion is best for special children like me, why does the school I want to go to think differently than all these people in so many countries? How can they all be wrong and that school be right?

I know of special children who go to Jewish Day Schools all over – Brooklyn, Riverdale, Long Island, Boston, New Jersey, Miami, Montreal, Los Angeles, Jerusalem – everywhere except Manhattan. Why?

Abba and Imma keep asking the school this question – why? They were told that the answer is "No" and nothing that they say or do would make them change their mind or budge one inch. Then the school said that they would not give any reason because my Abba and Imma would not be satisfied with any reason that they gave.

Finally some answers began to surface:

"We're not in that business." What business is that? I thought a Jewish day school was in the business of Jewish education. We have an obligation to give every child a Jewish education. And what about the Special Needs Fund that everyone contributes to – what business is that?

"There is no room for shadows in the classrooms." I know that can't be right because both my brother and sister have had kids with shadows in their classroom.

"The school cannot afford to have a Down syndrome child in the school." What is there to afford? The New York City Board of Education will send a special teacher to be with me in the class. If there are any other costs my Abba and Imma will cover those costs including hiring an integration consultant.

"If Caila is let into the school, she will have to come with two shadows and this will take up the space of three toddlers costing the school thousands of dollars." Why two shadows? One will be more than enough. (In fact my Abba and Imma have friends in Jerusalem whose son with Down syndrome goes to one of the best schools with no shadow at all!) They haven't even met me so how do they know what I will or will not need?

Abba and Imma love me so much and they want the best for me. Every specialist that they have spoken to and who has assessed me agrees that inclusion is the best option for my development.

So they are doing what any other Abba and Imma would do for their child – fight to give him or her the best. They asked all the people who said "No" at the school what they would do if I was their child. Wouldn't they also fight to give me what is best for me?

A few people have even been mean to Abba and Imma. They were very surprised, but they're not discouraged – it makes them even more determined to educate the community about me and my potential. They promised me that they would continue fighting for me no matter how long it takes. Besides, there are so many people who have supported us through this. They have written emails and called the school and over 1,250 people have joined my Facebook page (www.facebook.com/cailysworld).

Abba and Imma are people who want to change the world. They told me that someone should have branded the word activist on their foreheads the day I was born. They will help me not only be the best that I can be, but also change the world to be a better place for me.

Before embarking on their campaign, Abba and Imma spoke to many great rabbis in America and Israel. They wanted to know what Judaism had to say about education and inclusion of special children. They also wanted to know if they could share the campaign publicly with the community or if it would create a chilul Hashem (desecration of God's name).

With the exception of one rabbi in Manhattan, every single rabbi said that I absolutely should have a full Jewish education at a mainstream school. Some of the rabbis called the school. One called the school's position "unconscionable." The rabbis told Abba and Imma that not only could they make this issue public, but that they should for my sake and the sake of other special needs children in the community.

Many kids with Down syndrome don't walk by age two, but our family was determined to try. My Abba did special exercises with me twice a day and my physical therapist came three times a week. It was hard and sometimes it made me cry but we kept trying.

I would get up and fall down 100 times a day but I never got frustrated and I never gave up. And guess what? On the day of my second birthday, I got up and did not fall over – I walked! In my world there is no such thing as "I can't." I am looking to the school to have the same CAN DO attitude.

On Shavuot we will learn how the entire people of Israel stood together at Mount Sinai "like one man with one heart." No one should be excluded. There was no special section for special needs children at Mount Sinai.

With God's help, my family and I will be successful and I will attend a Jewish Day School.

Some parents on the Upper West Side are fighting for Orthodox Jewish day schools to include more children with special needs – Yeshivas Urged to up Special Needs Enrollment
June 7, 2010 – NY1

Jodi and Gavin Samuels moved to New York from Australia so their children could attend Orthodox Jewish schools, and they planned to send their third child to the same Upper West Side yeshiva that their older children attend. But officials at the (the school) told them they wouldn't even interview two-year-old Caily.

Caily has Down syndrome, but her parents say she's not the only special needs child in their Orthodox community whose been rejected from local Jewish schools.

"Why is it that we are in one of the wealthiest communities in the world, yet there is no real option for Jewish children in our community to get a Jewish education?" said Jodi Samuels. "Why is it that Jewish kids are going to Catholic schools on the Upper West Side in one of the most densely populated Jewish cities? Why is it that 97 percent of children with Down syndrome are mainstreamed but my child with Down syndrome has no option to be mainstreamed if we want a Jewish education?"

The Samuels raised those questions, and others, in a recent public forum held at Congregation Shearith Israel and more than 170 people showed up to hear experts on special education and Jewish education speak. The panelists agreed many Orthodox schools need to do a better job of including special needs children.

"Our Jewish community has so much more to do to be more inclusive, to be more tolerant, to be more helpful," said Dr. Jeff Lichtman of the National Jewish Council for Disabilities.

Only a small fraction of the people attending the forum said they have a child with special needs. Most were just interested in learning more about the issue and discussing how the community should handle special education.

But not everyone has been supportive.

"We've received threats. We've been told we'll be squashed. We've had people attack us," Samuels said.

[The school] never returned NY1's calls for comment, but the Samuels say they'll keep fighting for Caily to be considered.

They've also offered to pay for any additional services needed to include her. But even as public schools are reorganizing so almost all special education students will be mainstreamed, the general consensus at the forum was that many Orthodox schools have a long way to go.

New York schools shun special needs kids
August 5, 2010 – The Jewish Chronicle, London

Manhattan offers the Jewish parent everything: gleaming community centres, world-class Jewish day schools, and a synagogue on just about every corner. But when it comes to raising children with special needs, New York's glitziest borough is, apparently, lacking.

One recent Monday evening, about 150 people crowded into the basement of Congregation Shearith Israel, on Central Park West, to discuss "The Jewish Community's Obligation to Special Needs Children."

The imposing synagogue is home to the oldest congregation in America. The previous day, Irish President Mary McAleese had stopped by to thank its members for their predecessors' generosity during the Great Famine of 1845-1852.

However, this particular evening there was little cause for self-congratulation as a six-person panel spoke about the Manhattan Jewish community's lack of support for children with special needs.

The impetus for the event was one family, Gavin and Jodi Samuels, a South African couple whose daughter, Caily, aged two, has Down's Syndrome.

The Samuels - she is an internet marketing consultant, he a pharmaceutical industry executive - already have a son and a daughter who attend the $20,000-a-year (school), a Jewish school on the Upper West Side. But the school will not accept Caily.

The family claim that the school refused even to assess their daughter, arguing she would be better off elsewhere.

But the couple say that the closest Jewish special needs schools are in Brooklyn, Queens and New Jersey, all at least one hour away by bus. Besides, the Samuels maintain that including special needs children in regular classes is better for their daughter, and is standard practice in state schools across the city.

"The only schools that turned us away in Manhattan were the Jewish schools," said Mrs. Samuels.

The school principal [...] declined to comment.

The Samuels appealed against the school's decision. They even offered to pay the additional expenses that Caily's schooling might incur. But to no avail.

Instead, Mrs. Samuels said, families associated with the school "told us they will squash us and we will never be able to show our faces in public. A group of families have pooled together to make sure our daughter never gets in."

The evening's panellists agreed that the community, though moving slowly in the right direction, still had a long way to go.

Richard Bernstein, a disability rights lawyer, who is blind, said other faiths, particularly the Catholic Church, were way ahead on issues of special needs education. And Dr. Jed Luchow, director of special needs at the Board of Jewish Education, said the reason some schools refused to take children with special needs was a fear of being seen as "the nebbuch school."*

For many parents, secular or state schools are not an alternative. Nevertheless, some parents do take that option.

Rabbi Dov Linzer, dean of a Bronx yeshivah, and his wife Devorah Zlochower, a teacher, have two boys with Asperger's syndrome, who attend a secular school for children with special needs in Manhattan. Both parents said that not just Jewish schools, but synagogues, too, were failing families.

Ms. Zlochower said that years of frustration finally boiled over last year when she wrote an article with her husband published in the Jewish Week.

"For our children, inclusion in the prayer services and programming at synagogue is a last chance to be part of the Jewish community," she wrote, "and they are being pushed out with both hands. We want to be a part of the community, desperately. But to do so, our children must be made welcome."

*In Yiddish *nebbuch* means poor or unfortunate and, in urban slang, a "scrub," according to the Jewbiquitous glossary online.

Special-Needs Families Fighting Jewish Day Schools, Painful battles to get their kids placed
June 9, 2010 – Jewish Week

In three years, Jodi and Gavin Samuels may face one of the most difficult decisions of their lives.

Born with Down syndrome, their daughter Caily, now 2, will outgrow the Chabad preschool program she attends on the Upper West Side. That means her parents will have to choose between sending her miles away from home to a Jewish program for children with disabilities, such as one in Teaneck, N.J., or to a public school.

The yeshiva closest to home, (name omitted), where the Samuels' two older children attend, has refused to accept – or even interview – Caily, despite high cognitive test scores that her parents have been told make her an excellent candidate for inclusion.

"Chabad has been very warm and embracing," said Jodi Samuels, a South Africa native who came to America with her husband because they wanted their three children to have a good Jewish education. "They believe in the value that every child deserves a Jewish education. But we have no option after age 5."

The Samuels family is part of a growing movement of special- needs families who are fed up with having to fight the system of Jewish day schools to ensure that their children get a proper Jewish education.

There are several area special-education programs such as Cahal and Kulanu, both in Cedarhurst, L.I., Yeshiva for Special Students in Kew Gardens Hills, Queens; Sinai School in Teaneck, N.J., and Ivdu in Midwood, Brooklyn that provide a specialized Jewish curriculum. Because of the higher staff-to-child ratio required, tuition at these schools tends to be considerably higher than at typical yeshivas.

Those specialized programs have varying degrees of joint activity with mainstream students in other schools, but critics say yeshivas and day schools have been reluctant to expand inclusion or explore creative new ways of integrating special-needs students.

There is currently no Jewish school that provides a full-time inclusion class in which special needs children can learn alongside their peers while receiving assistance from special education teachers, says Jeff Lichtman, national director of Yachad, the Orthodox Union's program for special-needs kids.

Inclusion classes are now available in many public schools.

"Essentially, nobody has it" in Jewish day schools says Lichtman, who estimates that between 5 and 20 percent of children in Jewish day schools have special needs across a wide spectrum.

[The school's] roster of students does include those with learning disabilities, many of whom travel from far away to attend the Modern Orthodox institution on the Upper West Side. But the Samuels family says the school draws the line at children with cognitive disabilities.

[The rabbi], principal of [the school], said in an e-mail message that he could not discuss the specifics of Caily Samuels' case. But he added "[Our school) takes very seriously its responsibility to serve as a community school, and has long been at the forefront of Modern Orthodox Jewish day schools in accepting children with special needs. In fact, given its relative uniqueness, we currently have students enrolled in our Special Ed program from all five boroughs, as well as Westchester and Long Island.

"However, we cannot accept every student, and [we] evaluate each admission request to determine whether [our school] is the appropriate educational setting for that particular child."

But the Samuels say their daughter was never interviewed and they were told that an evaluation of her by an outside agency was not even read. They also say [the rabbi] told them that if Caily is admitted, others with severe disabilities would have to be accepted too.

In a second e-mail to The Jewish Week, [the rabbi] said, "Without discussing the specifics of this case, when the Admissions Committee receives admission requests and accompanying material, all of this is reviewed in order to determine whether [the school] is the appropriate educational setting for a child. If after reviewing the request and all the material the committee concludes that it is not the right setting, then we do not bring the child in for an interview."

Lichtman cautions that discussing inclusion as a general topic overlooks the reality that special-needs kids have a wide range of abilities and deficits. Some may have a high or above average IQ. "You have to provide for the needs of children individually and collectively," he said. For example, he notes that while Yachad has a summer camp that has joint activities with other camps, there is still a need for the Hebrew Academy for Special Children's camp, a self-contained program.

"Not every child, given their own unique needs, can be in an inclusive program," said Lichtman, who speculated that [the school] may be looking further down the road from preschool. "I think they feel they can't respond to the needs of a child with Down syndrome. I may disagree with that, but it is relatively easy to include kids in preschool, but in my opinion educationally when you move beyond that it gets much more complicated."

But parents and advocates are calling for more of a communal effort to think outside the box. There have been two panel discussions held in recent weeks, in Riverdale and on the Upper West Side, to call attention to the problem.

At Congregation Shearith Israel on May 24, about 160 people turned out to hear a panel of experts call for more inclusion. Only a small percentage of audience members said they had children with special needs. Most wanted to know what they could do to help.

Families like the Samuelses worry that they will be forced to give up on a Jewish education. "If my daughter doesn't have a Jewish education, she is not part of the family in the same way," said Jodi Samuels, who works in Internet marketing and has started a Facebook group, Caily's World, to call attention to her battle with [the school]. "She has enough challenges in life. Why should she have social challenges as well? The Upper West Side is one of the wealthiest communities. We're hoping to change the system."

But not much has changed since the 1990s when Shelley Cohen and her husband, Ruvan, battled to have their son, Nathaniel, whose battle with Duchenne muscular dystrophy required him to use a wheelchair, included in a yeshiva program. Unable to enroll him at [the school], their school of choice, the Cohens sent their son from Manhattan on a 90-minute commute to the Kushner Academy in Livingston, N.J. But doctors insisted such a commute was too stressful for Nathaniel and urged them to find a closer school.

"I spent his entire sixth grade year trying to find a day school here in Manhattan that would accept him and went from pluralistic to Reform and not one school was willing to accept Nathaniel," said Cohen. "There

is learning disability that is associated with Duchenne, but he is not at all a behavior issue. He was one of the most eager-to-learn children you'd meet in a lifetime."

And the challenges weren't only at school. "I had to fight to get him into a Jewish camp and to have a ramp at the bima [at Lincoln Square Synagogue] so he can have an aliyah. There are issues always."

[The school] ultimately admitted Nathaniel for seventh and eighth grade, and the Cohens were told by a rabbi that he not only had a positive effect on other classmates but on the administration.

"He ended up being a total asset," said Cohen. "It is usually the case that a special-needs kid raises the level of the school. Most schools find that it adds to the culture and doesn't detract and doesn't make the best and brightest any less best or less bright."

When Nathaniel, whose condition gradually paralyzed him, died at age 21 in 2007, the Cohens became activists to ensure that other parents wouldn't have to share their experience. In his memory, they have sponsored a workshop program every year at Yeshiva Chovevei Torah, the Modern Orthodox rabbinical seminary in Riverdale that focuses, on a rotating basis, on the needs of the physically disabled and those of the developmentally disabled.

"I'm hoping there will be a trickle-down effect, that if [rabbis] are sensitive to what is essentially the weakest link in society, people who have trouble speaking for themselves, we will have a more sensitive Jewish community as a whole," said Shelley Cohen.

Lichtman of Yachad says the "majority of [special-needs] kids across the country are included in some way, while virtually none were in the past," but he says kids with serious developmental disabilities like Down syndrome and autism are "typically not included" outside specific programs, some of which are located in mainstream schools.

He stressed that education programs that include shared mainstream activities, such as assemblies, gym, lunch and recess, are as important as shared learning time.

"Inclusion is inclusion," he said. "Kids are interacting with each other much more at recess and lunch than in the classroom."

"The Jewish community, in my opinion, should have a broad spectrum of education services developed over time to meet the needs of all Jewish

children," said Lichtman. "But that doesn't mean every single child should have a fully inclusive education."

Rabbi Dov Linzer, who with his wife, Devorah Zlochower, has also become an activist for special-needs families, believes that the first step toward inclusion must be to place it more prominently on the communal agenda.

As rosh yeshiva of Chovevei Torah, he wants to ensure that the future rabbis in his charge understand the issues involved.

"The goal is to sensitize all the students and make them aware of the problems, especially with invisible disabilities," said Rabbi Linzer, who, with his wife, has two children with special needs. "It's so easy not to be aware that this exists in the community." The workshop offered a chance to provide early insights that will shape their approaches to the problem once they assume a pulpit or communal leadership position.

Special Girl, Special Mother
January 18, 2011 – By Elicia Brown, Special To The Jewish Week

As an adolescent, Jodi Samuels didn't whine when her parents explained that the trip to Israel was out of the question, beyond the family's budget. Determined to tour the Holy Land with a youth group, Jodi, then 14, found herself a job at a supermarket in her native Johannesburg and worked there every day for at least two hours after school, all morning on weekends, earning the money for her trip.

Now, more than two decades later, Jodi – a mother of three and an entrepreneur overseeing three ventures she helped found – finds herself at odds with the establishment. And once again, she declines to accept "no" as the only answer.

The other morning, she pulled her two older children onto her bed and delivered the news: For the second year in a row, the family would be requesting that the children's yeshiva, ["The School"], consider admitting their youngest, Caila – a smiley 2 ½- year-old who recites the Shema before bedtime; who diapers her dolls; who was diagnosed shortly after birth with Down Syndrome.

It's been a year since the first time the Samuels submitted an application for Caila, known as Caily, to [the school], where her two siblings, Temira, 6, and Meron, 8, have been attending since preschool. It's been seven months since The Jewish Week wrote up the tale of how the school rejected the application without even meeting Caila, declining to consider the Samuels' request to place Caila in the classroom on a three-month trial basis, during which period she would be accompanied by a special-needs instructor paid for by New York City, with the Samuels covering any additional costs.

Of course, it's not certain that Caila would thrive at [the school] (although many Down Syndrome children do flourish in mainstream settings around the world). Of course, there are other schools, even Jewish ones, which would welcome Caila (albeit none with a Modern Orthodox orientation and none located in Manhattan). Of course, [the school], which has offered a special education program for 30 years to children with language-based impairments, addresses the needs of a diverse array of students.

When asked about Caila, [the principal] sent excerpts from his June e-mails to The Jewish Week, which explain that after the admissions committee reviews an application, if it "concludes that it is not the right setting, then we do not bring the child in for an interview."

Still, one can't help but wonder why the school can't spare a few minutes to meet with Caila. Still, one can't help but be horrified by Jodi's reports of the insults and threats proffered by community leaders. After all, this is a story of a mother's wish that someday her little girl can participate in a Passover seder like her older siblings, and perhaps even stand on a chair and offer a few words of Torah at the family's weekly Shabbat table like her big brother.

"This is about all of our children," says Jodi on a recent weekday morning, when we meet at Whole Foods Market on West 99th Street. She counts five Modern Orthodox families with special-needs children under the age of 5 who live on her block alone.

Jodi doesn't drink coffee at our meeting; she's already wired. She only slept three hours the night before – not because of a child's nightmare or her own, but because she's juggling so many balls and determined to keep them all aloft.

A passionate traveler, Jodi continues to run her nonprofit outreach program, Jewish International Connection. She recently launched J-Deal, a sort of Jewish version of Groupon, offering a daily bargain to its community of "shoppers." And in 2008, after Caila was born, Jodi founded metroimma, an online community for Jewish mothers.

As Jodi recalls it, she didn't sink into depression upon hearing of Caila's diagnosis. She sat bolt upright in bed, digested the news, and then understood: This baby would be their blessing; their gift; their princess.

In a recent metroimma blog, Jodi pondered the meaning of "special." She recounted how Caila spotted Angie, a little girl who is physically challenged, all alone in the playground. "Caily sat down next to her and said, 'Hi' in a gentle voice. She then took Angie's hand and held it for a few moments before gently stroking her cheek, giving her a kiss and a big hug, and began coaxing her to come join in with the other kids."

Wherever she ends up as a student, Caila has something to teach us all.

How One Family is changing the Way we see Down syndrome
Posted by Jodi on October 20, 2014 – Living the Treaty Life.

Imagine for a moment, selecting a preschool for your child. You go through all the options, make enquiries and schedule appointments to see which fit is best for you and your child.

Now imagine after all that, the school you selected not only rejected you but refused to so much as meet your child.

Imagine hearing these words.

"You brought this problem into the world, don't make it our problem"

For Jodi and Gavin Samuels, no imagination is required. Rather, this scenario and these words were the exact words uttered to them by a board member of a school they had wanted to enroll their daughter Caily into.

Their daughter Caily was born February 25, 2008 with Down syndrome, a genetic disorder caused by the presence of all or part of a third copy of Chromosome 21. Caily was diagnosed when she was three days old and the effects of the diagnosis were shocking to the Samuel family.

"So many people disappeared from our lives but we also had the rare opportunity of seeing who our real friends are. We also met many amazing people in the special needs world."

Down syndrome, the largest single cause of intellectual disabilities in South Africa, affects one in every 500 children born each year.

Today, October 20, is National Down syndrome Day in South Africa – a day which aims to create awareness and promote the abilities of those with Down syndrome.

The campaign this year is "It's all in the genes" and in light of a day created to bring awareness, Jodi shared with us her family's lessons, struggles and triumphs as they navigate the world with Down syndrome.

Fast forward to 2014, Caily is now a vibrant and thriving six-year-old girl and has been able to become one because of her parents.

Over the past six years Jodi and Gavin have fought for inclusion, raised awareness and broken down the stereotypes and perceptions of Down syndrome with the help of Jodi's blog Metro Imma, the Caily's World Facebook page and speaking to parent groups, university's students, high school kids, rabbinic students and even medical students.

"People take your cue for how to behave and interact with your child. We always treated Caily as our princess and gift. We have changed a whole community's knee jerk reaction to Down syndrome"

A top priority for Jodi and Gavin was including Caily in every aspect of life. Passionate about inclusion, Jody believes that there is a place for every person to be in this world.

"All our teachings from Torah (Bible) teach us that people with special needs can be included and have a role in society. Some of the great biblical leaders had challenges. Moses had a stutter, Isaac was blind. The world has changed and is more accepting - we have a black president of the US, women have rights in Western Countries, it's only fitting in this environment people with special needs also be included."

Finding a mainstream school willing to enroll Caily was a difficult task.

"The biggest challenge is getting people to judge Caily by her abilities and not by her diagnosis. Professionals see Down syndrome and they have a knee jerk reaction that she has mental retardation. Caily has repeatedly scored in the normal range on IQ tests but it is so hard to break

the stereotype. I recall once a therapist coming with us in the car to an appointment and Caily was singing all the Chanukah songs and after 5 months of working with her she expressed surprise that she knew the songs. She was only limited by her own prejudice."

Once enrolled, they enlisted the help of an inclusion consultant who could help guide team meetings and advise on challenging issues. There was also a need to educate the parents of Caily's classmates about her and what they should say to their own kids about having a special needs class mate.

For Jodi and Gavin the answer was, "Say nothing" and definitely don't label Caily. Explain that different children have different strengths and challenges and that Caily needs help learning to do certain things."

While inclusion worked for Caily, Jodi admits it is not for all children in all circumstances. However she does believe that more people can be included than are currently in an inclusion setting.

"As a parent you need to fight to have your child included not because it's easy but because it's the right thing to do. Too often our children are excluded not because they cannot be included but because organizations and institutions are afraid of including people with special needs or unwilling to put in the effort. Parents have to both advocate and educate why inclusion is important and can work."

But Jodi warns that it is not easy. "Inclusion is hard work; it's easier to put your child in a safe special needs environment. It requires a huge amount of effort but the rewards are worth it"

For the Samuels, looking at their daughter who is happy and extremely confident, they know inclusion was the right choice. As Caily grows older and becomes self-aware of her challenges they make sure she is not stressed or pushed beyond her ability to cope with inclusion. "We always joke that Caily does not see herself as different just better than anyone else. The day I see she is struggling emotionally in her environment is when I will reconsider inclusion."

One of the reasons why Caily has thrived in an inclusion setting can be attributed to their approach of active acceptance:

"The fundamental principle of the Feuerstein Center [an international education, treatment and research center for special needs] is cognitive modifiability and that intelligence is not fixed.

Professor Feuerstein published a book that is a must read "If You Love Me Don't Accept Me As I Am." This approach is about active acceptance, you love your child no matter what and you believe they can change"

This concept has helped them from the beginning to treat Caily as someone with potential. "We never treated her differently to our other kids, we never made excuses for her and had typical expectations. The only difference is that we would not be disappointed if she did not achieve or was slow to achieve her goals"

Jodi says that the same approach can be applied to your regular kids, a job situation or marriage. "With the right support people have a profound ability to change."

Jodi's two older children Meron and Temira adore Caily and like all siblings argue and have sibling squabbles. Their amazing connection is visible to anyone who sees them and Jodi puts it down to Caily's ability to charm "She is charming, loving, forgiving and uncomplicated so it's in a way very easy for them."

Having a sibling with Down syndrome has also made them extra sensitive and, Jodi believes, better people too. For instance, Meron a sixth grader recently came to Jodi with the news that he was no longer friends with the "in" boys who he had been close with because they were bullying a new kid. "This new kid had been to our place a few times and I had no idea. It takes a strong person at age 11 to leave the "in" crowd for what is right"

It is not only her siblings Caily has changed. Jodi a self-confessed A-type personality has had to slow down and appreciate that success comes in various ways. "I am also very judgmental and she has often made me stop in my tracks and allowed me to reconsider things. I used to be scared of people with disabilities and she has made me realize how important advocacy and education are to change the world."

Ensuring that each child receives attention and knows how important they are as individuals is tricky, says Jodi. "There is no question that Caily demands more of our time. We try many things and we hope that one day our other kids will not feel that they were less important."

To ensure this Jodi and her husband have established two rules:

"My husband and I make special alone time with the kids. It could be me taking my daughter with me for a manicure or my husband

taking my son to a game. It does not matter what, just as long as we do it regularly.

The second rule is if it is important to them it's important to us. So we will move mountains to be at a ballet recital or we will make sure they have the best birthday party."

Travelling is a favourite pastime of the Samuels family which has exposed them to environments and cultures. With travelling being normal and a family that asks questions, discusses topics and reads a lot, Caily has become an avid learner who is exposed to so many stimuli that keeps her engaged.

Caily, like many people with Down syndrome is often stubborn and fixed in her ways, but travel and change have forced her to be flexible and that, Jodi says, has been amazing.

The biggest misconception about Down syndrome according to Jodi is that it is widely assumed that people with Down syndrome cannot learn or be independent adults.

"It's only in the last 20 years that families stopped institutionalizing people with Down syndrome. By hiding them away and giving limited intervention, people with Down syndrome were not given the opportunity to grow or achieve. This is no different to typical children in abusive environments or in extreme poverty where they fail to thrive."

To the Samuels Caily is simply a child who happens to have some challenges. These challenges are being approached with early intervention and a strong therapeutic approach which is still relatively new. But the amazing success stories of people now in their twenties give encouragement and hope at the opportunities that await Caily.

As for advice to parents facing these challenges, Jodi says the most important thing is belief. "Believe that your child is capable of growth and change."

Parent support groups are invaluable and Jodi says she learnt more from other parents than anyone else. She suggests also following parents with inspirational blogs which gives you hope and shows you what is possible.

As Jodi reflects on the past six years, she realises that she has redefined perfection to mean appreciating the good in every situation and she now lives by the mantra is "life does not have to be perfect to be good"

Manufactured by Amazon.ca
Bolton, ON

17799070R00180